An Introduction to Economics for West African Students

R. Olufemi Ekundare

Routledge
Taylor & Francis Group

First published in 1980
by George Allen & Unwin Ltd

This edition first published in 2026 by Routledge
4 Park Square, Milton Park, Abingdon, Oxon, OX14 4RN

and by Routledge
605 Third Avenue, New York, NY 10017

Routledge is an imprint of the Taylor & Francis Group, an informa business

A Library of Congress record exists under ISBN: 0043303013

ISBN: 978-1-041-29833-5 (hbk)
ISBN: 978-1-003-77182-1 (ebk)
ISBN: 978-1-041-29892-2 (pbk)

Book DOI 10.4324/9781003771821

An Introduction to Economics for West African Students

R. OLUFEMI EKUNDARE
Professor of Economic History
University of Ife

London
GEORGE ALLEN & UNWIN
Boston Sydney

First published in 1980

GEORGE ALLEN & UNWIN LTD
40 Museum Street, London WC1A 1LU

British Library Cataloguing in Publication Data

Ekundare, Richard Olufemi
An introduction to economics for West African students
1. Africa, West – Economic conditions
I. Title
330.9'66 HC517.W5 79–42642

ISBN 0–04–330301–3

Typeset in 10 on 11 point Times by Inforum, Portsmouth

Printed by A. Wheaton & Co. Ltd., Exeter

Contents

Preface

With each succeeding generation of West Africans, there has been an increasing awareness of the need to understand the economic world in which they live. Indeed, the study of economics has ceased to be the exclusive privilege of university undergraduates and their teachers. The subject is now being taught in secondary schools, trade centres, teacher training colleges, technical colleges and the polytechnics.

A number of economics textbooks already exist, most of which were written with little or no regard to the ordinary way of life in West Africa. Moreover, some texts have introduced mathematical models even at the very first stage of learning. Although the use of mathematical concepts cannot be avoided, students have to realise that the subject deals essentially with human behaviour, which is often difficult to quantify.

The main object of this book is to present economics in simple language, using familiar West African examples. Before a student moves into the modern sophisticated techniques of economics, he should be able to understand the basic common sense of economics, which will help him to understand the subject himself and communicate with the larger group of people who have not undertaken a formal study of it.

A few multiple choice questions and essay questions relating to each chapter are given as an appendix to enable the student to assess how much he understands and to prepare him for his examinations. I hope that students preparing for the West African School Certificate, the General Certificate of Education (GCE), the Joint Admissions and Matriculation Board examinations (in Nigeria) and for other professional examinations will find this book particularly useful. Students in colleges, polytechnics and universities may also find the book helpful as preliminary reading.

I wish to thank my colleagues in the Department of Economics of the University of Ife, particularly Mr G. A. Ogunpola, Dr O. Ojo, Dr O. Fajana and Dr G. P. Uwujaren, who gave me useful advice on some of the topics covered in this book. I take responsibility for any errors it may contain.

R. OLUFEMI EKUNDARE

Department of Economics
University of Ife
Ile-Ife

Chapter 1

Introduction

It is important to start the study of economics by carefully explaining, if only briefly, the main economic systems which exist in the modern world. In recent years, a number of professional economists and the ordinary man, the layman in the field of economic science, have been taking a critical look at the performances of the accepted economic systems which can be broadly classified as free enterprise economic systems, popularly called capitalism and controlled economies, such as those called socialism. Indeed, there has been an increasing attempt to relate the performance of an economic system to the economic welfare of the people. An economic system is no longer seen as just a mechanism for enlarging the wealth of the nation, but also as a mechanism for creating a socioeconomic climate which makes life worth living for all its citizens. The question being asked nowadays is: which economic system provides the best and most equitable distribition of wealth among the citizens? It is difficult to provide any one non-controversial answer to this question. However, we shall attempt to explain some of the basic issues surrounding the two main economic systems.

THE FREE ENTERPRISE ECONOMY

The traditional and basic economic philosophy of a free enterprise economy is best expressed by Adam Smith who said in his book *The Wealth of Nations* (first published in London, 1776):

> Every individual is continually exerting himself to find out the most advantageous employment for whatever capital he can command . . . every individual . . . endeavours so [to employ his capital] . . . that its produce may be of the greatest possible value

> . . . He generally, indeed, neither intends to promote the public interest, nor knows how much he is promoting it . . . By pursuing his own interest he frequently promotes that of the society more effectually than when he really intends to promote it.

The fundamentals of a free enterprise economy can, therefore, be summarised to include:

(1) the right of an individual to own factors of production, land and capital
(2) the right to organise and employ such factors for the profit motive, and
(3) the exercise of these rights within the constraints on economic activity, such as public monopoly legislation, imposed by law.

It means that an individual in a free enterprise economy can own factors of production and can accumulate private property; he can set himself up in business or join others in partnership or in a joint-stock company; he can then sell his produce or his property with the intention of making profit without any intervention from the government, provided that he observes the laws of the state. A free enterprise economy accepts and operates 'competitive capitalism'.

It is important to emphasise that the individual, as a production unit, is the foundation of the free enterprise economic system. The unfettered economic self-interest of the individual, the realisation of differences of natural talents in men, coupled with the varied exposures to custom, habit and education – not necessarily formal modern education – lead to the division of labour, which helps to generate the mechanism for the creation of the economic wealth of the state. The individual economic pursuit of self-interest leads ultimately to the overal economic development of the community concerned.

There are two conditions which need to be explained as regards the operation of a free enterprise economy. First, a free enterprise economic system assumes free competition among the factors of production. That is to say, for example, that various categories of capital or various types of labour can compete freely amongst themselves, and also that one factor (labour) can compete with another factor (capital) or vice versa by way of one becoming a substitute for the other without any restrictions whatsoever. The competition among factors is regulated solely by the free operation of the market price mechanism. Secondly, mobility of factors of production within the economy is assumed to exist. Mobility means that any factor of production can move freely within one industry or sector; and from one industry or sector to another; and within geographical or political boundaries. Again it is important to emphasise that the mobility of factors is ensured by the market price mechanism. Anything at all which prevents the fulfilment of these two basic conditions negates the fundamental principles on which a free enterprise economic system is based.

Since Adam Smith clearly formulated the basic principles of a free enterprise economic system, it has been claimed that the merit of the system derives from the free operation of the market price mechanism which helps to allocate scarce economic resources among competing production units; that it rations the consumers to what is available and enables them to spread their incomes judiciously over their wants; and that it rewards the producers by making it possible for them to earn profits for organising production.

However, the merits of the free enterprise economy, or capitalism, have also provided the basis for its criticism. The free market price mechanism on which the merits are largely based has not been universally accepted as a perfect system of operating an economy. It has been argued, for example, that the allocation of scarce economic resources among the various competing production units often leads to economic waste because of the unhealthy competition that may be generated. This may happen if a production unit or organisation enjoying a stronger financial position obtains a particular scarce economic resource at an advantage over less financially strong production units. It has also been argued that the free market price mechanism limits consumption to those people who can afford to pay the price for goods and services available at a given period, whilst others who cannot pay the ruling prices are denied the enjoyment of such goods and services. This also applies to production units or organisations. Another argument against the free enterprise economy is that the free market price mechanism helps to establish prices which ensure profits that are often too high and unrelated to the efforts of the entrepreneurs and therefore constitute an element of exploitation of the other factors which have contributed to production.

THE SOCIALIST ECONOMIC SYSTEM

Apart from the basic economic philosophy, some sociological, ethical and political principles are embodied in the socialist economic system, a typical example of which exists in Russia. First, the ruling or governing political party, the Communist Party, is claimed to represent the whole working class. Since the Communist Party is synonymous with the government, it is correct to say that the

Communist Party determines all economic strategy, although implementation of plans, and sometimes formulation also, is the responsibility of the bureaucracy. Secondly, the socialist economic system is based upon social ownership of all the factors of production. That is to say, all factors of production are owned collectively by the people – the working class. Thirdly, the economic system is centrally planned. The emphasis of the socialist economic system is not on the individual as a production unit, but on the working class as a whole. All production units are brought under the control of the state which decides on what to produce, when to produce and at what volume, how to produce and for whom to produce; all this is centrally fixed.

Those who advocate the socialist economic system believe that it has greater merits than the capitalist system. First, it is claimed that the mainspring of economic activity is determined by the national economic plan and not on a whimsical market price mechanism; it eliminates all the ills of a market price mechanism which were mentioned above. Indeed the socialist economic system is said to appeal to higher social instincts, and profit is regarded merely as a means rather than an end. Secondly, and following from the points made above, the socialist economic system eliminates monopolistic control of economic resources by a few people or groups of people. Thirdly, the fundamental cleavage under capitalism between the employer and the employee is avoided. Fourthly, the social ownership of the means of production and central economic planning help in the maintenance of continuous full employment. Every effort is made to eliminate overproduction and cyclical fluctuations by adopting appropriate planned adjustments to the economic system as the occasion demands. Lastly, the socialist economic system can ensure that what is produced is distributed among the people according to their needs, so achieving a more equitable distribution of income. Since there is virtually no private ownership of the means of production, wages (including salaries) remain the only source of income. There are no special classes of people receiving rent from land, interest on capital or profit from entrepreneurship, as is the case under the free enterprise economic system. It must be added, however, that wage differentials do exist under the socialist economic system, although the lower wages are supplemented by generous government subsidies or benefits out of the national social consumption fund.

The socialist economic system is not beyond criticism. It is regarded by some as inefficient in that factors of production are often deliberately diverted to less efficient uses, resulting in a kind of economic waste. It is also claimed that a centrally planned economy leaves little room for individual initiative on the part of the citizen to pursue economic advantages. In addition, it has been argued that a centrally planned economy is more vulnerable to fluctuations than a free enterprise economy because of the likelihood of miscalculations of the performances of the factors of production and of errors in organising them for productive purposes. Also, it has been argued that the economic and political policies of the state may not in many cases serve the best interest of the people. For example, excessive expenditure on military weapons may lead to shortages of ordinary consumer goods and services, thus leading to a loss in the economic welfare of the people.

CAN THE TWO SYSTEMS CONVERGE?

It has been observed that in more recent years both the capitalist and the socialist systems are departing from the basic principles on which they were founded. For example, the socialist economic system is said to be moving away from strict centralised economic planning, while the capitalist system is departing from the free enterprise principle. It is claimed that both economic systems now adopt methods and practices of economics which are increasingly similar.

In capitalist countries increasing attention has been given to the problems of social welfare. The economics of growth has also attracted much attention. It is now fashionable in capitalist countries to study the pattern and problems of economic growth as they affect the general economic welfare of the entire people of a country. This has not only led to sectoral economic planning but also to greater centralised planning, particularly in the public sector. Indeed, the private sector has had to face an increasing number of restrictions and controls, such as customs duties, exchange controls and profits taxes, in an attempt to introduce social justice into the economy. A number of the traditional capitalist countries have now established economic planning ministries, commissions or institutions. In addition, the nationalisation of some businesses and property previously privately owned has been on the increase, thus emphasising the importance of collective ownership of some factors or institutions of production. Interference with the free market price mechanism by various methods, including indirect taxes, subsidies, price stabilisation schemes and direct price controls, is now common. It must also be added that the capitalist countries have increased their trade and economic relations with the socialist countries.

In the socialist countries, on the other hand, there has been increasing attention paid to the role of the individual as a production unit. Strict centralised economic planning is gradually giving way to planning from below. In terms of the administration of the economy, central authorities are gradually loosening their controls, allowing greater scope and independence to the lower administrative authorities. Banks in socialist countries now actively participate in selecting and financing economically sound investment projects and commercial ventures. Thus some economic and financial discretion is now being allowed within the financial infrastructure of the economy. Also, profit as a source of income has now been accepted in the socialist economy. That is to say that profit is now accepted as the main criterion of enterprise performance and it is shared by the workers and management. The distribution of income within the socialist economic system has been undergoing some changes. The ideal of the equalisation of incomes has been discarded. Wage differentials are not only recognised but are being encouraged as incentives to produce specific manpower needs in the economy. Recently, perhaps one of the most important developments in the socialist economic system is the relaxation of the rigid price fixing system. There is a growing tendency in advanced socialist countries to allow free markets to operate to determine prices although it is still a limited acceptance of the free market price mechanism as a regulator of the economic system. The socialist countries have also increased their economic ties with the capitalist countries and the trend is likely to continue.

One can conclude by saying that both economic systems have been learning from each other, by adopting those policies which tend to eliminate the defects which have been noticed and criticised in each economic system even though the basic principles of a purely free enterprise economic system remain essentially different from those of the socialist system.

THE AFRICAN ECONOMIC SYSTEM

What can be regarded as the typical 'modern' African economic system is a product of history. The subsistence economy of old has been yielding ground to the modern exchange economy which was introduced during the colonial period and which has been further developed since political independence in most African countries. Different African countries are, however, at various stages of economic development and the economic systems being adopted in one country may also differ slightly from those in another. In any country where the processes of division of labour and exchange have not been fully introduced into the economic system some reliance on subsistence production is inevitable. Subsistence production does not, however, preclude exchange. The limited exchange that occurs reflects the stage which division of labour has reached in the everyday economic life of the people. It may be added that the subsistence economy is not necessarily a cause of underdevelopment and can be a consequence of it.

The economics of the extended family system, which is typically African, can be related to the subsistence economy. In the extended family system, not only has an individual to depend on the earnings from his own work, he must be well disposed at all times and as far as possible to helping the less fortunate member of the family, so that the latter can at least support himself, by training him or setting him up in a trade or business. What is often overemphasised is the dependence, sometimes of a large number of people, within the extended family on the income of one well-to-do member: an income which by European and American standards might in itself be below the subsistence level even if it remained the disposable income of the earner. One should add, however, that what constitutes income in an African context differs to some extent from that of a modern technologically advanced and monetised country. (This will be explained in some detail in a later chapter.) The extended family system, therefore, has as one of its functions the promotion of development which is unique to Africa.

During the colonial period, the traditional subsistence economy gradually gave way to the modern exchange economy. The old media of exchange, barter and commodity currencies were replaced with modern coins and currencies. The production of some agricultural export crops was stimulated and Africans were encouraged to develop a taste for certain European manufactured goods. As a result, the African economy began to develop on modern lines but with great dependence on the colonial powers. Foreign private commercial companies set the pattern for modern economic activities in Africa.

Since the advent of political independence, African countries have been taking a critical look at the inherited economic system so as to evolve a system which shall on the one hand meet the challenges of modern developments and which shall on the other hand be socially acceptable to the people. Attempts have been made to socialise the economic system because it is believed that the inherited capitalist system, if allowed to operate without modification, will continue to exploit the ordinary man. This belief may be a by-product of the colonial era. However, the present economic system in West Africa is basically a free enterprise system but with some major modifications. First, the African economic man does not exactly answer Adam Smith's description, because his everyday economic pursuits are often influenced or determined by his social and cultural background which is essentially different from that of the man living in a typical capitalist or socialist country. Secondly, African society is beginning to question the economic goals of a free enterprise economy as it affects the distribution of the national income both between sectors and between the individuals who help to produce it. It is no longer readily accepted that the spontaneous economic interests of individuals, if allowed to operate in a reasonably free and unrestricted atmosphere, will automatically produce the greatest contribution to economic development or welfare.

The society, rather than the individual, has become the focal point of economic motives and achievements. A private enterprise can exist and make profits so long as its economic activity is not inimical to the economic and social well-being of the people. It is not pure capitalism; neither is it identical with socialism.

THE MEANING OF ECONOMICS

Several attempts have been made in the past to give a precise definition of economics. A student has a choice of any one of the various definitions that have been offered. A definition which has been widely adopted was that given by Lord Robbins. He defined economics as 'the science which studies human behaviour as a relationship between ends and scarce means which have alternative uses'. However, with the increasing emphasis on the economic performance of a society as a measure of economic progress and welfare, and on the effects of such performances on the individual, one can define economics as *that aspect of human behaviour which deals with production, exchange and consumption of wealth in the process of accomplishing the socioeconomic goals of a society*.

Economics is a science because it consists of a collection of related facts about the economic activity of man, and such facts can be arranged in such a way as to make it possible to draw from them certain conclusions which are known as economic laws. It is perhaps more appropriate to regard economics as an aspect of the social sciences because it concerns itself primarily with the study of human behaviour in efforts to satisfy wants, such as food, clothing and housing.

Every individual finds some difficulty in satisfying his wants because the resources available to him are limited in quantity and rarely enable him to satisfy all his desires; such resources are scarce and can be put to alternative uses, but if one use is chosen another has to be sacrificed. Cassava, for example, is limited in supply at any given time and may be offered fresh to provide food for animals, boiled to provide food for man, or made into gari, or some other cassava product. Again, any available piece of land may be used for building purposes or for farming. Or, if one takes an example of an industrial product such as steel, it may be used amongst other things to manufacture guns or machinery. But even if the resources available are adequate to meet all wants, the time at the disposal of an individual to utilise such resources is limited and this particular scarcity creates a need to economise. In each day there are only twenty-four hours during which to conduct all activities, including economic activity.

Scarcity of resources and time are fundamental aspects of the study of economics. It must be appreciated that scarcity is relative to demand. If nobody demands a product or service at any given time one cannot talk about its scarcity. Again, if everyone is able to satisfy his demand for a particular product at a given time and there is a surplus, there is no scarcity and one can talk in terms of excess supply. However, as soon as demand increases to more than the available supply the element of scarcity occurs.

The next problem is which of his wants an individual will satisfy with the limited resources available to him at a given period. Even if an individual stretches his resources or income as much as he can, he may still only be able to satisfy a few of his many wants. Almost everybody is faced with this problem of choice, that is, the choice between those wants that he wishes to satisfy most urgently and those that he can postpone for a future time or must give up altogether. It is important to realise that there is no particular or recognised set pattern of choice to which individuals must conform. A man may decide to spend the last naira in his pocket on cigarettes and beer rather than spend it on having an adequate meal of fufu or rice, or he may decide to buy cigarettes and a small meal, and forgo his beer. Each individual, then, has a scale of preference. The wants which an individual wishes to satisfy are arranged in their order of importance to him, and it is in this order that he endeavours to satisfy those wants. While an individual may rank palm-wine or cigarettes very highly in his scale of preferences, another man may not include either of them in his list of wants.

Choice implies that whenever an individual satisfies a particular want, there are a number of other wants left unsatisfied. What then is the *real cost* of satisfying a want? The answer is that the real cost of satisfying any want is the most attractive alternative want that has to be forgone in order to do so. For example, if an individual has 50 kobe to spend, and there are two items which he would have liked to consume, costing 50 kobe each, he has to choose between the two. Let us say that the two items are a book and a bottle of palm-wine. If he decides to buy the book, then the opportunity cost of the book is the bottle of palm-wine. The same principle is applicable to the expenditure of time. If a student misses his lecture because he wants to watch a traditional masquerade show, the real cost of watching the show is the lecture he has missed. The real cost of satisfying any want, in the sense of the alternative that has to be forgone, is known as its 'opportunity cost'. It is not just the equivalent money cost of two wants that is involved in this concept. Indeed, the concept of 'opportunity cost' is meaningful and most useful in the context of economic welfare. The loss of the satisfaction from the alternative want is a loss of economic welfare which is the real cost – the opportunity cost – of the other want which has been satisfied.

THE AVERAGE MAN IN ECONOMICS

The study of various aspects of human behaviour, which is the primary concern of the social sciences, presents a number of difficulties arising from the number of people living in this world and the heterogeneity of human nature. We recognise many differences in the ways of life of different communities in our world and even within a given community there exist some obvious differences in culture, language, religion, customs and tastes.

The purpose of a community varies with the different stages of civilisation and the social and economic needs associated with them. It is also evident that the smaller a community is, the less diverse are its social values; and conversely the larger the community, the less agreement there will be upon social values, whether they be ideological, religious, political, economic or, for that matter, musical. However, through time one has come to recognise that, in the aggregate, human beings react in certain ways and have social values common to most individuals. These common patterns of behaviour have led the social scientist to invent the concept of 'the average man' in his attempt to analyse and examine the various aspects of human behaviour and the social values inherent in them. The concept of 'the average man' is a theoretical tool which is useful to social scientists.

In economics, the concept of the average man is much the same as the concept or notion of 'economic man'. Economic man is assumed to be primarily concerned with utilising his scarce means or resources to secure the maximum satisfaction of his wants. The concept of 'economic man' has been devised to aid analytical economic problems. The task of an economist can be simplified by the use of generalised standards of human behaviour expected from 'the average man', or 'economic man'.

In illustrating the concept of economic man, Adam Smith holds the view that the division of labour binds society together, but that this 'is not originally the effect of any human wisdom which foresees and intends that general opulence to which it gives occasion. It is the necessary, though very slow and gradual, consequence of a certain propensity in human nature which has in view no such extensive utility, the propensity to truck, barter, and exchange one thing for another.'[1] Adam Smith assumes, therefore, that an 'average man' naturally thinks of production, exchange and consumption, in the process of pursuing his self-interest. The spontaneity of the economic actions of an 'economic man' is the outcome of personal interest. The concept of 'an economic man' as explained by Adam Smith was modified by David Ricardo in his work *The Principles of Political Economy and Taxation*.[2] Ricardo retains the concept of economic man, but shows clearly that the working of the 'invisible hand' (mentioned by Adam Smith) gradually loses its providential basis and comes to depend on the social fact of competition. The economic man of Ricardo has to struggle in order to exist. He has to struggle with nature in order to exploit economic resources, and he has to compete with other 'economic men' in order to retain and enjoy what he has gained.

Lord Robbins takes this a stage further and suggests that the basic assumption implied is that economic man's behaviour is rational behaviour. He writes:

> Whether economic institutions are founded on the spontaneous natural love for self-interest of Adam Smith or on the social fact of competition of Ricardo, there remains the primary question, whether the generalisations of economics do not also depend upon a more general psychological assumption – upon the assumption of completely rational conduct.[3]

It has also been said: 'The study of human decisions involves a study of human psychology, but the background of psychology which economics require is a purely behaviourist psychology.'[4] But most economists are content to assume that the rational behaviour of economic man may be taken to mean 'consistent' behaviour.

Economics assumes that the average man or economic man wishes to satisfy many wants. He is fully aware of the fact that he

[1]Adam Smith, *The Wealth of Nations*, Vol. 1 (London: Everyman's Library, 1910), p. 12.

[2]David Ricardo, *The Principles of Political Economy and Taxation* (London: Everyman's Library, 1973).

[3]Lionel Robbins, *An Essay on the Nature and Significance of Economic Science* (London: Macmillan, 1935), p. 90.

[4]Joan Robinson, *The Economics of Imperfect Competition* (London: Macmillan, 1954), p. 16.

needs to work in order to earn a living. He has accepted the primary fact that he has to struggle with nature in order to exist. Competition with other people has become a regular feature of his life. If he decides to earn a living by stealing, he is still an economic man, that is, a man pursuing his self-interest (according to Adam Smith); even though he ceases to be 'an average man' in law, ethics and politics, he is still considered to be behaving rationally.

The average man wants to satisfy his wants with the limited means or resources at his disposal. It is commonly asserted that wants are limited. This is quite true. The wants that readily come to mind are those which the economic system in which a man lives normally provides. The various stages of economic development, however, dictate what an 'average man' would want to consume, and the more developed the economic system is, the more the horizon of wants expands, so much so that it is sometimes said that man's wants are 'unlimited'. This can only mean that they are far beyond his capacity to satisfy them.

ECONOMIC LAWS

One may ask whether the human behaviour with which economics is concerned can be subjected to any scientific study. Indeed it has been argued that natural sciences deal with inanimate matter that is subject to definite and rigid laws, while economics deals with man who is free to react to any condition in any way he chooses. Despite occasional inconsistencies in human behaviour, it can be observed that people tend to react in a fairly consistent manner to various circumstances of life. For example, during the Moslem or Christian festive seasons one can observe many people shopping and buying new clothes, decorations and additional food items. One may not be able to know by mere observation exactly how much is spent but the increase in human traffic and economic activity is noticeable. The use of modern statistical methods has been of great help to the economist in observing and quantifying various aspects of human behaviour, and this adds greatly to the accuracy of the generalisations which economists make.

As an example of such a generalisation, it has been established that the lower the price of a commodity, the greater is the amount bought, and that the higher the price, the less is the amount bought. The consistency of the behaviour of economic man has made it possible for economists to formulate economic laws, which are generalisations based on uniformity of behaviour which the economist discovers in his examination of all economic activity.

Most economic laws are statements of tendencies, and assume that matters not being considered, matters extraneous to the issue at hand but which would influence the result, are eliminated. The economist in formulating economic laws has adopted a device to eliminate extraneous matters or variables. He expects certain results from the study of a specific human activity, other things being equal. This is the assumption of *ceteris paribus*. The statement 'other things being equal' eliminates extraneous variables which might invalidate the economic generalisation. We can illustrate this by the aid of simple algebra.

Let us take the equation $a + b + c = x$, where a, b and c are variables. To start with, if we assume that $a = 2$, $b = 3$ and $c = 5$, then $x = 10$. It is clear that the value of x will depend on the changes in the values of a, b and c. For example, if we say that the value of c has changed to 7, we cannot jump to the conclusion that the value of x is now 12, because we need to know with certainty what has happened to the values of a and b. If we assume that the values of a and b remain constant, then we shall be correct to say that the new value of x is 12.

In economics, we can put it this way. If the value of c changes from 5 to 7, 'all other things being equal', the value of x will be 12. We cannot afford to be silent over a and/or b if we are to avoid any ambiguity. This in a simple way is what the statement 'other things being equal' (*ceteris paribus*) seeks to achieve.

THE METHODS OF ECONOMICS

In general, science proceeds by two methods. The scientist may start from some proposition known to be true and work out all its implications. Or he may build up records of a large number of events, and look for patterns in them which may indicate the existence of new scientific 'laws'. These two methods are the deductive, or theoretical, and the inductive, or empirical, methods respectively. Like all scientists, the economist aims at discovering generalisations and shaping them into a system of knowledge. Such generalisations are the result of the widest possible observations and critical examination and they can be varified empirically. Further observations are also made in order to check the validity of any generalisation. At one time, it was argued that the bulk of scientific work is based upon the deductive method. It has been appreciated, however, that in adopting the deductive method, the scientist must start from some kind of hypothesis and does not start looking at facts at random. In this respect, the statistical data and the collection of facts by various government departments and institutions provide the economist with an important field of study. Modern economists have come to recognise that the inductive and deductive methods are complementary and the system they follow combines both methods. An economist adopts the inductive method in order to accumulate and arrange facts from which to seek a tentative generalisation and if the generalisation is confirmable, he adopts the deductive method to see whether other generalisations can be logically deduced from the first.

ECONOMICS AND OTHER SOCIAL SCIENCES

The studies of the various branches of the social sciences are all complementary, in the sense that one cannot study any one of these disciplines without at least recognising the existence and the influence of the others. It is important to appreciate the extent to which one branch of the social sciences influences the study of the other branches so we shall examine some examples of the influence of culture, ethics and politics on economics.

Culture

The culture of a nation is the accepted way of life of the people, based on its social values. These include, amongst other things, the extended family system, traditional religions (for example, the worship of Ogun, the god of iron, or of Sango, the god of thunder), hospitality, styles of living, and the day-to-day pattern of a person's behaviour in relation to the other people in the community as it affects social harmony or equilibrium. Only a few of these can be discussed.

Africans attach great importance to hospitality; to be hospitable is regarded as a natural way of life. Most Africans, therefore, keep in their homes extra food and money over and above the immediate needs of the family in order to meet this important social obligation. It means that a family unit or the individual in the family must expend his income in such a way as to make some provision for minor demands from other people, such as friends and relations. As there is no rigid regularity as to when the occasion for hospitality may arise, it means that each family unit must hoard some food and money for this contingency. Moreover, hospitality extends to presenting gifts in money or in kind to friends and relations on such occasions as funeral ceremonies, child-naming ceremonies and house-warming ceremonies.

Also, in an effort to maintain social harmony or equilibrium, goods and services are often provided free or at reduced prices to friends, neighbours and relations. A result of this practice is the reduction in the income of the family but there is increased social harmony. Although social harmony cannot be measured in money terms, yet the enhanced goodwill helps to ensure the cordial atmosphere which promotes greater overall economic activity in the society. These and some other aspects of the African culture, although found in other cultures, are not usually such a significant part of everyday life as they are in Africa. The difference in degree is such as to create a major difference between the African economic system and those of the other parts of the world, particularly Europe and America.

Ethics

Attitudes towards the smoking of cigarettes and the consumption of alcohol may be taken to illustrate typical African ethics. Apart from the fact that smoking has now been linked with the disease of lung cancer, the African moralist has always regarded smoking as an indication of moral degradation. A number of people have accepted the moralist idea on smoking. Some have refrained from smoking, and those who could influence others, such as parents and pastors, have also exerted their influence to prevent others from smoking. On the other hand a good many people have remained indifferent to the moralist view and have continued to smoke. The same argument has been applied to the consumption of alcohol. The African moralist, basing his judgement on the behaviour of a few alcoholics, tends to regard the habit of taking alcohol as a sign of wretchedness. The moralist holds the view that anybody who forms the habit of consuming alcohol will never do well in life. While this may be true in respect of a few people in the society, the fear of the moralist has not been justified. However, the economist is primarily interested in the habit of smoking or the consumption of alcohol in so far as they give satisfaction to smokers and drinkers and so generate supply of and demand for tobacco and alcohol. The economist is interested to know how many packets of cigarettes are consumed and to what extent an increase or fall in consumption will affect production, that it, supply. Similarly, the economist is interested in how many bottles of bear are consumed and how the supply of beer will adjust to the demand for it. He examines the habits and the pressures which can lead to the readjustment of wants and the reallocation of resources to cover the wants.

Some moral principles associated with religion tend to lead on to economic problems. A devout Moslem is expected not to consume pork, neither is he expected to take alcohol or smoke tobacco. A devout Christian on the other hand can eat pork but members of some Christian sects are expected to abstain from alcohol and smoking. Among Moslems and Christians in West Africa, the strict observance of these moral rules, tied up with religion, could cripple the breweries and the cigarette factories or businesses. However, both Moslems and Christians now preach moderation and not total abstention except from pork for the Moslems. The economist notes the new liberal approach of the church and the mosque to social habits and examines its effect on the supply and demand for the products which such habits require.

Politics

Political developments in West Africa since the early 1950s bring out clearly the influence of politics on economics. The introduction of representative government had one immediate economic effect; people had to be paid to run the government. This is recognition of the fact that parliamentarians are productive but, more important, that legislators make laws which profoundly affect the economic life of the people.

Since the advent of military rule in most West African countries from the mid-1960s, the military governing councils in each country have assumed the role of the legislator. Decrees are issued to replace Acts of Parliament and these decrees control the political, social and economic activities of the nation, A good example is the imposition of a tax law or decree. The imposition of an income tax results in a reduction in the purchasing power of the taxpayers. The taxpayers are bound to readjust their wants in the light of the compulsory reduction in personal income. Similarly, a tax on beer or cigarettes will call for a readjustment of the spending patterns of drinkers and smokers. Many other laws and decrees have direct and indirect economic effects. For example, the laws on pioneer industries encourage the growth of new industries which create more employment, provide new products and possibly reduce imports of manufactures and increase imports of raw materials. All these are important economic changes.

One can see, therefore, that politics influence economics through the political structure, through the enactment of laws or decrees, and through the administration of such laws or decrees.

THE SCOPE OF ECONOMICS

Economics is regarded by many students as a difficult subject. They may be right. The main problems encountered by a student are probably in his study of economic theory. His theoretical reasoning tends to be confused by his awareness of the complexity of day-to-day economic activities which contribute to the creation and distribution of incomes. But Maynard Keynes, the distinguished British economist, rightly pointed out, 'the theory of economics does not furnish a body of settled conclusions immediately applicable to policy. It is a method rather than a doctrine, an apparatus of the mind, a technique of thinking, which helps its possessor to draw correct conclusions.'

Microeconomic theory is primarily concerned with the individual economic unit. In examining the structure and pattern of the individual economic unit, economic theory tends to establish the ideal economic pattern which then serves as a tool for the economist in his effort to analyse and interpret the unit which actually exists. Macroeconomics, on the other hand, is primarily concerned with national aggregates such as income and employment in the entire society, and with institutions such as money which penetrate the whole economy.

The economist is concerned with means rather than ends. It is not for the economist but for the statesman to interpret the will and evaluate the interest of the community, making a synthesis of all the moral, economic and other values involved in policy decisions. But it is for the economist to advise the statesman what a proposed course of action will involve in terms of economic costs and benefits, as embodied in the current demand and preferences of the people, or what it may involve in terms of general economic development, and he will also draw the statesman's attention to the costs and benefits of any alternative action which may be open to him. This does not mean that the economist is limited to the study of the way in which scarce means are distributed between ends; his responsibility goes beyond the logic of choice, because he is also concerned with the level of economic activity, and with the maximisation of economic welfare. Even so, in the last analysis, the function of the economist is to predict and to advise, not to define the good life.

For the purpose of convenient study, economics can be divided somewhat arbitrarily into five branches; production, exchange, distribution, consumption and governmental activites. Production is concerned with an examination of the ways and means of producing economic goods and services. Exchange is concerned with men's endeavours to exchange economic goods and services for those of other people both in their own country and in foreign countries. Distribution deals with the sharing out of what has been produced by the community among the various factors of production. Consumption deals with the satisfying of human wants by the goods and services produced. Lastly, governmental economic activities concern the various ways and means by which governments produce and consume goods and services and influence any or all of the other four branches mentioned above.

After what has been said by way of introduction, students will realise that economics is not merely memory work. Economics is essentially a method of reasoning, a way of handling an economic problem, breaking it down into its component parts and working systematically towards a sound and reasonable solution. In mastering this method of reasoning a student will find it extremely helpful to cultivate the habit of using economic terms in his analysis and being clear about their meanings. If the language of economics is studied, understood and used, clarity of thinking will be improved and an instrument to communicate with others will be at hand at all times.

Chapter 2

The Production of Goods and Services

THE MEANING OF PRODUCTION

Production of goods and services is a most important aspect of economics; it is the process of creating utilities or satisfaction. Most manufacturing processes consist of taking raw materials and transforming them into goods which possess utility; for example, palm-leaves into brooms, a tree into tables, and iron ore into a machine. Such activity is said to create *utility of form*. If one changes the place of materials from that in which they are of little or no use to where they are of greater use one is said to have created *utility of place*; for example, by moving coal, gold, diamonds or crude oil from deep in the earth to the surface. Similarly, cocoa-beans or palm-kernels in the bush are of little value until they are brought to the marketing centres for manufacture or export. These are examples of services. Utility of place emphasises the extra utility added to goods by the transport system, which is an economic service. The efficiency of the transport system has a direct effect on the utility of place. Again, *utility of time* is created by making materials or goods available at times when they are more useful, for example, by the canning of fruits or fish, and the storage of maize, yams, cassava, rice and other stocks so as to be available for consumption at times other than the harvest season.

In economics, we are concerned with any human effort or the product of human effort which is scarce and for which people are prepared to give something in exchange. Production is meaningful in so far as its object is the satisfying of those wants for which there is effective demand. Effective demand may be defined as the desire for a commodity coupled with the willingness and ability to pay for the satisfaction of the desire or want.

It has been the convention in economics to conclude that if no exchange value is attached to an activity or effort, it is not a productive activity or effort. However, this convention is now being challenged on the ground that it distorts the valuation of human efforts in trying to satisfy human wants. Any human activity which satisfies a human want, even if it has no money value in exchange, such as providing services free to one's friends or relations, should be recognised by the economist as having value. The issue is discussed when the subject of the national income is considered.

Values in economics are rates of exchange. They express the rate at which one commodity exchanges for others. Thus, if one head of cattle exchanges for three goats, the value of one head of cattle in terms of goats is three goats, and the value of a goat in terms of cattle is one-third of one head of cattle. To say that any commodity or service has value is therefore to say that it has exchange-power, and the value is expressed in terms of the things for which it will exchange.

In economic analysis, values have nothing to do with whether the ends served by the goods or services are good or bad or whether they are regarded by most people as useful or not. Paradoxically, some things with great significance to mankind have a low exchange-value or no exchange-value at all. Thus air has great significance; it sustains life itself; but no one has to give, and no one in normal circumstances is prepared to give, anything in exchange for air and, therefore, it has no exchange-value.

The explanation of this paradox is that the significance, and therefore the value, of a commodity varies with the degree of its *scarcity*. The value-in-use (that is the usefulness) of a commodity must be differentiated from the value-in-exchange. A commodity which is judged to be harmful to life, for example, Indian hemp, may be very scarce and so command a high value-in-exchange from people who are addicted to smoking it.

FACTORS OF PRODUCTION

A factor of production can be defined as anything that is used up, at any stage, in producing a commodity or service.

Goods or services may themselves be factors of production in one circumstance and consumers' goods in another: thus to the farmer, palm-oil is not a factor of production but itself a final product, whereas to the housewife it is a consumers' product because she uses it for cooking, and to the soap manufacturer it is a factor of production.

A factor having only one use is said to be completely specific to that use. Such a factor can only be used for one specific purpose, otherwise it is useless. However, many factors are capable of alternative uses, that is to say, they are mobile.

Traditionally, the factors of production are classified into *land*, *labour* and *capital*. It has been argued that most human wants cannot be satisfied without the existence of some natural objects and the application of human energy to these. This suggests two factors of production, namely, land and labour. However, in the course of time, men invented and developed a number of tools, implements, machinery and other devices to assist them in production. To these was given the name *capital*. The money with which to buy such means to assist production is regarded as 'money' capital.

In the last century, great changes took place in the size and organisation of production. The growth of large-scale enterprises led some economists to include *organisation* or *enterprise* as a separate factor of production. It became clear that modern production required some kind of intelligent direction, control and, most important of all, the ability to take risks.

It has been argued that much of the value of land is simply the result of improvements made by capital and labour. It is true that agricultural lands in developed countries such as those of Europe and North America owe little nowadays to their original qualities but much to the labour and capital which have been used to cultivate them over the centuries. The same is not true of the West African countries. In West Africa, agricultural land owes most of the productivity to its original and natural qualities, and this is preserved by the practice of shifting cultivation which predominates. There is no doubt, however, that the gradual improvement in the systems and techniques of agricultural production necessarily involves the use of more highly skilled labour and greater amounts of capital.

Whatever classification is adopted, be it fourfold, threefold or twofold (human and non-human factors), production is nevertheless only achieved by using land, labour, capital and organisation, combined in some way or used separately. It is convenient to examine these factors of production in turn.

LAND

The term land has a very wide meaning. It includes the following: the earth's surface, which is the source of all animal and vegetable life; minerals, such as tin, gold, diamonds, petroleum, gas, manganese and bauxite beneath the earth's surface; advantages of climate which one part of the earth may possess over other parts, such as the hot, wet climate of the tropics which favours the production of such crops as rubber, cocoa, palm produce and rice; advantageous physical features of land such as natural harbours; and natural phenomena on the earth's surface, such as rivers, tides, gravity and magnetism.

Because of the wide meaning of the term land, some economists prefer to use instead the term 'natural resources' or 'gifts of nature'. Provided that the exact meaning is kept clearly in mind, the term land is probably still the simplest and most convenient. The economic function of land, as a factor of production is to provide man with natural resources upon which to exert his energies and to which to apply his tools in order to satisfy his wants.

Characteristics of land

Land has certain distinctive characteristics. First, it is a primary factor of production. The majority of the world's population depends directly on land for a living, particularly in West Africa where agriculture in one form or another is still the predominant occupation. Land forms the basis of the subsistance economy even though this is rapidly disappearing in West Africa. Secondly, land is spatially an immovable factor of production. Land can only be used where it is found since it cannot be physically moved from one site to another in any significant amount. Thirdly, the natural resources in their raw forms have no cost of production. These resources are gifts of nature available to man which can be improved and adapted to be of greater use to man by applying capital and labour to them. Fourthly, the physical quantity of land is fixed; its supply cannot be increased by a process of growth or manufacture in response to any increased demand for further land. The effects of mineral extraction, erosion by sea or river, and reclamation and drainage of land may be to increase or reduce the physical surface of the earth but such changes in the supply of land are infinitesimal in relation to the whole of the earth's surface. Lastly, the fertility of land, unless scientifically selected systems of crop rotation are adopted or fertilisers regularly added, is lessened with every crop the land is made to bear. The tendency is for nature to respond less rapidly to man's efforts, and the yield obtained in return for a given expenditure of human effort on a given tract of land tends to decrease. The tendency on the part of a specific area of land to give a diminishing product has been recognised from earliest times and has led to the shifting system of agriculture which is still widely adopted in West Africa. In developed countries with modern systems and techniques of agricultural production, crop rotation, the use of fertilisers and other devices are adopted to combat the tendency to diminishing returns. Diminishing returns are experienced in all forms of extractive industry, and also under certain circumstances in manufacturing industry. The law of diminishing returns is discussed below.

It is the productivity of land with which the economist is concerned. This depends on a number of factors. First, the physical and climatic conditions influence it. The amount of rain, sunshine and wind to which land is exposed varies from place to place. Deposits of natural resources cannot be altered by man, but the fertility of the land can to some extent be controlled by the methods of cultivation adopted and by artificially supplying more or less water or heat or by adding or subtracting chemical constituents. This takes us to the second factor, that of human effort. The fertility of the soil can be improved by using fertiliser, by the adoption of systematic ploughing and by crop rotation, each crop preparing and improving the soil to some extent for its successor. The skilful drainage of the delta areas in West Africa could turn such areas into rich agricultural lands. The irrigation of some areas in the northern territories of West Africa has improved agricultural production substantially. The planting of trees to replace those cut out for timber will act as wind-breaks and also help to keep the forest evergreen.

Human interference can also have adverse effects. For instance, indiscriminate cutting of trees for timber can lead to the modification of climatic conditions, and eventually to the spread of deserts. This failure to adopt a system of crop rotation may result in land becoming totally unproductive. Irrigation can result in chemicals being washed out of the soil leaving it less fertile, and excessive cultivation can lead to soil erosion which leaves no soil to cultivate.

Lastly, the geographical location of land affects its productivity. Fertile areas which are situated at great distances from the markets for their potential products are of little utility unless adequate transport facilities are available.

With increasing human effort on land, it is practically impossible to say what part of agricultural produce is due to the 'original and indestructible powers of the soil' (a phrase first used by David Ricardo, a famous economist of the nineteenth century), and what part is due to improvements made by man. With non-agricultural land it is quite impossible to distinguish the productivity due to improvements by man. Social conditions are a constantly changing factor in determining the productivity of settled land. The growth of new towns and villages, movements of people particularly from the rural areas to urban areas, the development of transport and communications, all help to make social conditions more important than natural conditions in deciding the value of non-agricultural land for productive purposes.

LABOUR

Labour can be defined as all forms of human effort, physical or mental or both, which satisfy wants. Usually, the economist is concerned with the kind of labour which is undertaken in expectation of a reward, effort expended to provide something of exchange value, for example, wages, salaries and fees and goods or services which can be sold. Labour which is voluntary or which is not undertaken primarily for payment undoubtedly has its economic aspects. Sometimes referred to as 'unproductive' labour, it nevertheless satisfies wants; it often calls forth a demand for other goods and services; and being devoted to one purpose it is not available for another, so it has an opportunity cost. A good example of such labour is community development work.

Various classifications of labour are encountered; for example, labour can be classified into manual or mental. The effort of a labourer is regarded as manual work, while the effort of a school teacher or a university lecturer is regarded as mental work. Or we have the classification into skilled and unskilled labour. The job of a machine fitter, which is technical, is regarded as skilled, while the effort of a head-porter is regarded as unskilled labour. Some jobs have been classified as responsible, a company director, a doctor or surgeon, while the job of, say, a typist is classified as routine because it carries no appreciable responsibility. It is important to realise, however, that any classification of labour is somewhat arbitrary, for the various kinds of labour often overlap each other. The work of a labourer carrying a bag of cocoa or groundnuts involves the employment of some skill and of some mental exercise; typing does involve a degree of skill and responsibility; and the most mental of jobs involves some element of physical endurance. A teacher has to speak loudly enough for his pupils to hear – this is particularly difficult with a big class and for long periods. Similarly, the surgeon has to stand the physical as well as the mental strain of performing operations.

The working population

The entire population of a country forms the basis of its available human resources. In general terms, the greater the population of a country, the greater would be its available human resources or labour force. Population is discussed below. However, we are concerned with the working population; that is, those men, women and children of working age.

The proportion of the population that constitutes the labour force depends on social, economic and sometimes political factors. In

West Africa, the social system demands that a child provides certain services for his parents whenever called upon to do so. Children of, say, 7 years of age and upwards who are not attending school are expected to work on their father's farm or help in hawking articles, and they are also expected to do some domestic chores. Even some children who attend school are expected to perform any or all of these services after school hours. There is no compulsory education in West Africa and neither is there a statutory age for leaving school and starting to work. At the other end of the age range, the age of retirement from work in the public services is between 45 and 55. Except for some professional classes such as university lecturers and judges, who are normally employed until the age of 60, most workers in the government and quasi-government institutions have the choice to retire voluntarily after the age of 45 or to be compulsorily retired on attaining the age of 55. With a compulsory retirement from public service at an age when many workers are still physically and mentally fit to continue to work, it is usual for public servants to take up employment in the private sector, to go into business or to turn to farming after they retire. As there is no compulsory retiring age from private employment or from self-employment, many people go on being productively employed to the age of 65 or even later.

A significant feature of the supply of labour in West Africa in recent years has been the increasing proportion of women in the working population. This has been the result of the growth of the education system in many areas, and the increasing number of educated women. The society has gradually been modifying its attitude to allowing women, particularly housewives, to work. Indeed, the changing economic conditions and the rising cost of living have together induced many people to accept the idea of allowing women to take up paid jobs. It is no longer considered degrading for women, unmarried or married, to go out to work.

The census of Nigeria taken in November 1963 gives some figures for the labour force at that time. It enumerated 18,305,810 persons who were economically active, of whom 13,886,756 were males and 4,419,054 were females. This was out of a total population of 55,670,055. The United Nations' statisticians regard these figures as possibly unreliable and think that a more accurate estimate of the total population in 1963 is 46,300,000, but no one disputes that at the time approximately one Nigerian in three was economically active, the rest being either too young to work or too old or housewives who are, for international statistical purposes, not included in the labour force even though they are probably the most hard-working persons in the community.

Table 2.1 shows the Nigerian labour force classified into its three major economic activities, for the years 1960 and 1970 as estimated by the International Labour Office. It will be seen that the numbers have been growing rapidly and are no doubt much larger today, since the total population had grown by 1976, it is estimated, to 64,790,000. It will be noticed that the figures in the table are not compatible with the enumerations of the Official Census of 1963, but the latter are regarded as unreliable.

Table 2.1 *Labour Force of Nigeria*

	1960			*1970*		
	Males	*Females*	*Total*	*Males*	*Females*	*Total*
Agriculture, etc.	7,647,000	5,528,000	13,175,000	8,506,000	5,319,000	13,825,000
Industry	1,475,000	461,000	1,936,000	2,124,000	958,000	3,082,000
Services	1,803,000	1,689,000	3,492,000	2,611,000	2,760,000	5,371,000
TOTAL	10,925,000	7,678,000	18,603,000	13,241,000	9,037,000	22,278,000

Source: ILO, *Labour Force Estimates and Projections, 1950–2000.*

The productivity of labour

The productivity of labour is dependent upon the skill, physical capacity and efficiency of the individual, upon the organisation of the labour force and upon the other factors of production with which it works. The efficiency of a worker is determined by climate, intelligence, physical ability, education, willingness, and by the working conditions. In a tropical climate, such as that in West Africa, hard, sustained labour is more difficult than in the temperate zones. The increasing use of air-conditioners and the building of air-conditioned offices and factories in the tropics have reduced the strain of hard work, at least on some workers. The efficiency of a worker is influenced by his intellectual fitness and mental alertness which are in part dependent on the stock from which the worker springs and in part from his general and specialised education. The physical ability of a worker also affects his efficiency. A worker who takes good food, wears good clothing and lives in a good house is likely to be more efficient than his counterpart who enjoys none of these conditions. Better health conditions, the willingness to work, perseverance and ambition can all be considerably improved by an appropriate system of education and training. The overall conditions of work affect the productivity of a worker. A factory which is inadequately lit and badly ventilated is likely to reduce the efficiency of the workers. A factory with a modern canteen for the workers will almost certainly increase the productivity of the workers. Shorter hours of work and the shift system of work, if carefully introduced, may be beneficial to the employer and the employee alike. The efficiency of the labourer also depends on the wages he receives. The greater the amount of money income at the disposal of a worker, the more he can spend on good food and other essentials of life. There is no doubt that the efficiency of the worker also varies according to the manner in which money income is spent. If a wage is spend judiciously, the reaction upon the efficiency is far better than if the wage is carelessly squandered. To sum up one can say that the factors affecting the efficiency of labour stem from nature but can be considerably modified and controlled by effective management.

CAPITAL

Capital can be defined as that part of wealth, or goods, which is used in the production of further wealth. It is the use that is made of wealth which determines whether it is capital or not. If wealth is directly consumed in satisfying wants, it is not being used as capital. A farmer usually holds back part of his seasonal harvests for seed in order to maintain future output; these stocks represent part of his capital. Sometimes capital is regarded as wealth which is expected to yield an income. This is particularly true of money capital or loanable funds. However, in both forms, material capital and money capital, the fundamental notion is the same, namely, the ability to provide for the satisfaction of future wants. The owner of the capital who lends it out for a productive purpose regards it as a source of income, but to the producer who borrows it, this same capital acts as an aid in the production of wealth.

The function of capital is to assist labour in its task of transforming raw material in order to produce goods that will satisfy human wants. Capital assists production by providing goods to be used as raw materials for producing something else; by supplying equipment and appliances with which materials are turned into articles that will then satisfy human wants; and by sustaining labour while production is in progress. Because modern production is somewhat lengthy and indirect, food, clothing and shelter are consumed by the worker to keep himself alive and healthy while he is engaged in producing wealth. In establishing a cocoa farm for example, a farmer needs capital to purchase farm land if he is unable to obtain a portion of the family land, to buy cocoa-seedlings, to pay wages to the labourers who maintain the cocoa farm for about five years until the cocoa-trees start yielding a crop, and in providing food and shelter for himself. He then needs to spend money in processing his cocoa before it can be successfully and profitably marketed.

It should be observed that all capital disappears ultimately in the process of production, and it must therefore be replaced out of revenue or income. The productivity of capital must not only yield enough revenue or income to replace the original capital consumed in the process of production, but must also create surplus income from which additional capital can be obtained through the process of saving and investment. The capital available to a businessman, a company or a country must increase progressively through time if increased production is to be achieved to meet the pressure of a larger population and the demand for higher standards of living. Capital can only be increased by saving and investment. Saving provides the liquid capital which is used to buy the material goods and services needed for the productive process. Savings depend upon the ability and the willingness to save. The strength of the various motives which favour the withholding of a part of income from consumption, thus creating savings,

> will vary enormously according to the institutions and organizations of the economic society which we presume, according to habits formed by race, education, convention, religion and current moral according to present hopes and past experience, according to the prevailing distribution of wealth and the established standards of life.[1]

The low level of incomes and the high propensity to consume, that is, the relatively high proportion of the income being spent on consumption, keep savings low in West Africa. More will be said on this when we come to consider the interest rate in Chapter 6. In the meantime, it should be noted that the social structure in West Africa based primarily on the extended family system tends to maintain a high propensity to consume, thus limiting the capacity to save. Also, there are very few institutions, such as insurance and business companies, which could generate institutional savings and investment.

Many classifications of capital have been suggested, each intended to emphasise a particular aspect of capital. A common classification is that of fixed capital and circulating capital. Machinery, cocoa-stores, blacksmiths' sheds, factories, airports and shipyards are all examples of fixed capital.

Fixed capital does not change its physical form; it is never trans-

[1] J.M. Keynes, *The General Theory of Employment Interest and Money* (London: Macmillan, 1954, first published 1936), p. 109.

formed into something else; and can be used repeatedly over a relatively long period without completely exhausting its utility while engaged in the production of wealth, although such capital is likely to need to be repaired from time to time. It should be noted that the supply of fixed capital is not readily responsive to changes in price; it usually takes some time before the supply of an item of fixed capital can be increased if there is a sudden increase in demand for it.

Circulating capital is capital which is completely consumed in the process of production and its value gets absorbed in the new product. The most important form of circulating capital is money. Money can be used to buy any goods or services. A businessman requires enough ready money to pay wages, buy raw materials and meet the cost of fuel, transport and other services. All these items are used up in producing the goods he makes and when he sells them at a profit all that he has spent and more comes back to him. His money is then ready to circulate again in the next round of production. This is why it is called 'circulating' capital. Thus, circulating capital is used to keep the producer and his business going during the period between the initiation of production and the selling of the final product, which may be a matter of days, months or years. Unlike fixed capital, the supply of circulating capital is readily responsive to the price offered for its use. A bank, for example, will be more willing to lend more money to a borrower if it knows that he is a businessman who intends to use it as circulating capital and so will be getting it back again as soon as he has sold the goods he uses it to produce.

ORGANISATION

It is the task of the organiser or the entrepreneur to bring together the other three factors of production, land, labour and capital, in the required proportions and to combine them in a productive form whose output is wanted. In West Africa, where one-man businesses predominate, it is not difficult to identify the organiser. Often he is a man easily recognised by his sign-board or signpost bearing his name and the form of his business. All the main streets in West Africa have these signposts. In large businesses the entrepreneural function is usually undertaken by a group of people, 'the management'.

The organiser undertakes risks incidental to the initiation and conduct of the business. In any modern free enterprise economy production is complex, lengthy, indirect and based on anticipations of demand which involve great risks. Nowadays, production starts long in advance of the demand for the finished product and prices may change for the worse or for the better in between. The cost of raw materials, the bill for wages and interest on capital may also vary, so that the organiser must cleverly judge all these circumstances in order to be able to secure a surplus of receipts over cost. He must also bear the great risks of possible competition from new producers or substitutes for his product which may involve him in a loss.

With the development of large-scale enterprises, usually in the form of joint-stock companies, the twofold function of co-ordination of the enterprise and risk-bearing has come to be divided between the board of directors, which delegates power to a managing director or general manager, for the day-to-day running of the business, on the one hand, and the rest of the shareholders who also join in bearing the business risks, on the other hand. The essential aspect of a joint-stock company being emphasised here is that the bulk of the shareholders do not participate in the day-to-day administration of the business of the company although they do share the risk and the profits if any. Chairmen and members of state or government corporations perform the same function as the directors of joint-stock companies, while the taxpayers bear the risks of operating such corporations.

The organiser or entrepreneur is the pivot of the process of production because production receives its impulse from him; all the other factors are engaged and paid by him; and he is ultimately responsible for all the decisions which have to be made. The reward for organisation or entrepreneurship is profit, that is, the excess of revenue from sales over the costs of production.

CHARACTERISTICS OF MODERN PRODUCTION

In West Africa today, two types of production can be identified. First, there are some remote areas where subsistence production is still dominant. Each family relies on agricultural production for the subsistence of its members. In such a local subsistence economy no direct attempt is made to produce any surplus for possible exchange. Indeed, money is of little use in such local areas. Even though this type of production is fast disappearing, yet it can still be found in some remote areas of West Africa. Secondly, there is production for the market. This may be for a local market or for the national and international market.

Production for a purely local market is usually on a small scale. A number of villages and towns may comprise the local market and quite a lot of cash changes hands. The commodities which are bought and sold are mainly agricultural products with food crops taking the greater proportion. Some local industrial products such as mats, pots and cloth are also brought to the market. Market days are usually arranged at regular intervals of three, five or seven days. Some of the villages in each district act in rotation as host villages on market days. In addition to these, permanent markets are found each day in the big towns.

Modern market production is large scale and is no longer exclusively for the local market. Most commodities that are produced nowadays are sold in distant markets within and outside the country. The local markets often serve as the centres where products are first collected before being finally exported. There is no doubt that subsistence production which dominated the economics of West Africa about a century ago is rapidly giving way to a growing money economy and production for the market.

The farmers and the few industrialists in West Africa now produce mainly in anticipation of demand; and so production involves an element of risk. The cocoa farmer, for example, spends money and time in improving his cocoa farm with the hope that the price which the Marketing Board or the appropriate government agency will be prepared to pay at the beginning of the cocoa season will bring adequate revenue to cover costs of production and allow him some margin of profit. Similarly, the cotton manufacturer who buys raw cotton in order to manufacture cotton piece goods will anticipate a demand sufficiently high to justify the effort of production.

Modern production depends on the efficient and smooth running of every aspect of the economic system. A good transport and communication system is indispensable. There must be regular contacts between the producers and the consumers at all stages of production. The raw materials needed must be easily accessible to the producers. The sources of power to industries, too, must not only be regular, but also available at reasonable prices. Coal, gas, electricity and oil must be available where they are needed. Probably the most important element of modern production is the availability of credit. In West Africa, where the volume of private capital is low, the importance of an efficient and reliable credit system cannot be overemphasised. The farmer needs credit in order to maintain his farm and himself before the harvesting period. Similarly, the businessman needs credit in order to pay wages, buy raw materials and hold stock in anticipation of demand. (The credit system is discussed in Chapter 7.) In recent years the co-operative movement and governments have helped to provide credit for the farmers, while the commercial banks are of increasing help to businessmen in granting short-term credits.

THE LAWS OF PRODUCTION

It has already been mentioned that the task of the producer or entrepreneur is to combine land, labour and capital in the best possible arrangement of the factors for efficient production. In reducing costs, a producer may decide to employ more labour and less capital or vice versa. Usually, the most important consideration is the relative costs of the factors of production which the producer needs to engage and the degree to which they can be technically substituted. In fact, the producer is in constant search for the most efficient combination of the factors, substituting one for the other so as to achieve the least cost.

The entrepreneur will find he has to engage certain fixed factors of production. These are factors of which, once he has decided to use them, the amount cannot be altered until he has completed one or more cycles of production. To these fixed factors he will add some other factors whose amount can be varied. Typical fixed factors are the factory and the machinery installed in it. Typical variable factors are labour and raw materials, the amounts of which will depend on how much of the product the entrepreneur decides to produce using the existing factory and machinery. If the entrepreneur discovers that the return in output he obtains on additional expenditure on variable factors, say, raw materials and labour, increases more than in proportion to his additional expenditure, then he will recognise that he is operating with increasing returns. But if, with a still larger expansion of his output, the producer discovers that additional costs of raw materials and labour give only a proportionate return to the additional costs, then over this range of output he will be experiencing constant returns. Finally, if with an even larger expansion of output the producer finds that additional expenditure on raw materials and labour produces a return which is less than in proportion to his additional costs, he will be experiencing diminishing returns. The returns in each case refer to the quantity of output and not to the price at which the product is sold or to the realised profit.

Increasing returns are the same in theory as diminishing costs, and diminishing returns are increasing costs.

Additional applications of a varying factor applied to a fixed factor in the process of production can result in a more than proportionate increase in the amount of the product. This phenomenon comes into operation because the increased product may be the result of a more efficient combination of the factors of production or improvements in the methods of production which can only be used when production is on a larger scale.

Increasing returns are experienced in many productive enterprises but they are not inevitably a part of the structure of the productive process. On the other hand, diminishing returns are inevitable if production is taken to a large enough amount with a productive enterprise which has some fixed factors: so much so that economists early on formulated the law of diminishing returns which says that beyond a certain output, as more and more of a variable factor is used with a fixed factor, the return in the form of increased product will be less and less. The total output does not diminish but the increase in output is less and less for each additional unit of the variable factor.

In formulating the law of diminishing returns some assumptions are made. It is assumed that all units of a factor of production are equally efficient. Also, it is assumed that technological conditions remain constant. It may be correct to say that the law operates in the short run, when economic and technological conditions have not changed so as to affect the proportion and the efficiency of the factors to be engaged in the process of production.

The law of diminishing returns has its foundation in scarcity; scarcity of the fixed factor. Experience has shown that nature is generous up to a point only; beyond that point yields can be increased only by a more than proportionate increase in expenditure of labour and capital. For example, the constant cultivation of the same piece of land will eventually yield smaller crops and this tendency can only be checked by increasing applications of labour and capital, so that to obtain the same volume of output more labourers must be employed and more fertilisers applied to the land. Only if new land can be found and cultivated can the original returns to labour or capital be achieved. Similarly, each thousand kilogrammes of gold, coal, or any other mineral taken from a mine means that the next thousand kilogrammes requires greater effort in terms of capital and labour. Eventually the mine will be exhausted and the return to additional capital and labour will be zero.

The law of diminishing returns operates because of the inability to expand one of the factors of production as one would have liked. In the short run, the capacity of a fixed factor is limited and there is a limit to which one factor can be substituted for another factor. In agricultural production, for example, capital and labour cannot be substituted for land. Whatever improved forms of labour and capital are available, land will still be needed. It does not matter which factor of production is fixed, for this is a physical law the proof of which can be seen in everyday life. We can see that up to a point each additional labourer on the farm will increase the crop produced, but then the increase in production from each additional labourer will fall gradually, until eventually still further men would be a nuisance and even a menace, as they would get in each other's way, and make cultivation impossible.

The law of diminishing returns was first thought to apply to agriculture alone; but it has now been realised that the law operates in all production. However, the law is more noticeable in those industries which depend largely on natural resources: agriculture, mining and the extractive industries. The law is less pronounced in those industries in which man is the more active agent than in manufacturing and constructive industries which use large amounts of the manmade factor, capital, and relatively less of natural resources. The law of diminishing returns cannot be totally evaded; but its operation can be postponed by means of improvements which may be the result of economic and technical progress such as improved transport and communication, inventions, and more productive combinations of other factors of production.

THE ECONOMICS OF POPULATION

Economists have devoted some attention to the study of population, because its size affects the working population and, therefore, production on the one hand, and the demand for goods and services on the other hand.

The population of a country consists of the total number of human beings in that country and the size and structure are ascertained by means of a periodic census. In the developed countries of Europe and America, population censuses are held at regular intervals. In Great Britain, for example, a population census is taken every ten years. The West African countries have not yet developed any reliable and regular system of taking censuses. In Nigeria, the first countrywide population census was taken in 1931 and the second census followed twenty-two years later, in 1953. In 1963, the third population census of Nigeria was taken. In fact, the 1963 population census was conducted twice because of alleged irregularities. There was a fourth population census in 1973, but the population figures which were arrived at on that occasion were considered unsatisfactory. It was alleged that the figures were grossly inflated for political reasons and the results were officially repudiated.

It was believed that the number of parliamentary seats to be allocated to each state in the country would be on a population basis. Besides the possible interference of politicians in the conduct of the enumeration, there were other factors which prevented an accurate census being taken. Many of the enumerators had no statistical training and hence were unable to appreciate the necessity of obtaining accurate figures. Further, most uneducated people and even a good number of literate people believed that the population census had something to do with tax assessment and so avoided being counted or claimed to have non-existent dependants.

THE MALTHUSIAN THEORY OF POPULATION

Thomas Malthus was the first economist to direct the attention of the world to the relationship between population and the means of subsistence. Towards the end of the eighteenth century, Britain experienced a series of bad harvests. Britain was also engaged in a long and exhausting war against the French. In addition to these basic problems, the changes in the system of agriculture and the advent of the industrial revolution resulted in a food supply insufficient to cope with the rapidly increasing population. The poverty and misery in Britain led Malthus to inquire into the nature and causes of poverty, and to compare increases in annual production of food with increases of population. He published his *Essay on Population* in 1798. Malthus maintained that population grows faster than the means of subsistence and that population if not controlled will always tend to exceed the available food resources. In order to avert the misery for mankind involved in the elimination of the surplus population by natural processes, Malthus maintained that certain voluntary checks on population growth were essential. These checks on population growth were classified into two types – positive checks and preventive checks. The 'positive' checks or those of nature, according to Malthus, were infant mortality, starvation, disease, wars and natural catastrophes such as floods and earthquakes. The 'preventive' checks were those that man himself could bring about by means of a low birth-rate achieved by abstaining from marriage, by abstaining from having children if already married and by deferring the age of marriage.

Modern economic developments have already falsified some of the practical aspects of Malthusian theory. Food supplies have increased considerably more than Malthus ever envisaged. Scientific agriculture has led to increased production of foodstuffs, and improvements in communications have opened up new areas to such an extent that individual countries are no longer dependent upon their own resources for food, but can draw upon food supplies from different parts of the world through the process of international trade. The 'positive' checks of Malthus are lessening in the modern world. Improvements in medical services are helping to reduce the death-rate in all classes. The improved services being provided by an increasing number of maternity homes, dispensaries and hospitals have reduced infant mortality and checked the incidence of diseases.

Despite all that has been said about the limitations of Malthus's theory of population, it should be noted that there are some areas of the world where the production of foodstuffs is not keeping pace with population growth. There are also isolated, but abnormal, instances of the operation of Malthus's theory; for example in the former secessionist region of Nigeria, 'Biafra', the civil war provided the positive checks to population growth both by the military action and by the blockade limiting the supply of food to the area. The serious drought which produced famine in the Sahel is another example.

MODERN POPULATION THEORY

Modern population theories are now concentrated on two main problems. First, there is an increasing study of the factors producing changes in the size of any population. Such changes can be traced to migration, fertility or rates of birth and mortality. Here the level of wages and income is also relevant, because there is a significant relationship between fertility and economic conditions, the birth-rate in poorer families being higher than that in richer families. It costs less to maintain a child in a poor family than it does in a rich family. The standard of living, therefore, is inversely related to differences in the birth-rate. Secondly, modern economists devote much attention to the relation between the size of any population and its productive efficiency. It is maintained that it is not so much the size of the population that matters as the relation between the population and the available productive resources. For any given area or country, there is a given population which will achieve maximum production per head: this population is called the optimum population. It can be implied, therefore, that a country with a population which is not of the optimum size is either overpopulated or underpopulated. An area or a country may be said to be overpopulated if, given its other resources and their qualities, the standard of life or production per head would be higher, were the population smaller. Underpopulation may be said to exist in an area or a country if, given its other resources and their qualities, the standard of life or production per head would be higher were the population larger. According to Lord Robbins, it is

> theoretically possible to imagine a country, all of whose members enjoyed the standard of life of millionaires, which was yet over-

populated in the economic sense. If the elimination of one millionaire would increase the returns per head to the efforts of others, over-population would be present.

Similarly, one can imagine a community all of whose members live on a bare subsistence level and yet which is underpopulated if the advent of more people would lead to an increased standard of life or production per head. This could well happen as greater opportunities for division of labour could lead to increased production per head. It is important to realise that the changes in the volume and qualities of the resources of a country could cause it to be either overpopulated or underpopulated.

It could be argued that the West African countries are, at the present time, underpopulated, in the sense that the standard of life or production per head is being steadily increased and at the same time the total population is rising. The discoveries and exploitation of more natural resources and the improved qualities of capital and labour are largely responsible for this. The better people are trained, all other things being equal, the greater their productive efficiency. The increase in the population of West Africa has been at the rate of 2 to 2.5 per cent per annum in recent years but has not led to any fall in the standard of life or per capita income because the overall economic growth has been at a much higher rate. (The problems of economic growth in West Africa are discussed in Chapter 10.)

Chapter 3

The Structure and Organisation of Modern Industry

DIVISION OF LABOUR

The subsistence economy which dominated West Africa until the end of the nineteenth century is fast disappearing and giving way to a rapidly growing exchange economy. Each family no longer attempts to produce all its own needs. The main characteristic of modern agricultural and industrial organisation is the analysis of production into its component parts, and the concentration of the workers on each separate operation in the production of a crop or an article. This characteristic is easier to identify in industrial production than in agriculture.

In modern production, each man is rather a specialist providing one kind of service, often not for himself alone but for the general public, to whom he sells his service for money with which he buys the products of other specialists. One man may spend all his working life shovelling cocoa or groundnuts or rice into sacks, another in sewing up bags that are full and passing them to another labourer who does no other work than stack the bags in a lorry, waiting to take a full load to the export centre. Each specialist receives a reward, a wage or salary, for his work, and subsists by exchanging his reward for the products or services of other specialists.

Division of labour makes it possible to achieve greater speed in the rate of production. The volume and variety of goods are increased, usually at lower costs, thus leading to a much fuller satisfaction of wants. The hours of work can be considerably reduced because no time is lost in passing from one process to another. Division of labour which results in the simplification of processes has increased the scope for inventions. The extensive use of machinery and power, with all the attendant advantages of speed and accuracy, has consequently eased the task of the worker. In addition to these, division of labour leads to the acceleration of technical progress through the development of machines. A modern worker is now free to develop his talent and follow his own bent. It is easier to utilise the differences in natural aptitudes, age and sex, by fitting tasks to the individual capacities of the workers. The physical effort which attended most jobs in the past, and remains even now in some cases, is gradually being reduced, with the worker tending to work less with his body and more with his hands and brain. Less time is now being taken in learning special processes in most trades and professions. Without the division of labour, it would have been impossible to achieve the great improvement in the material conditions of life, in the shape of cheaper and better consumer goods, more leisure and greater income. Plenty depends mainly on division of labour; without it, our community could not support the increasing standard of life, nor would we enjoy the amenities of modern civilisation.

After all that has been said about the advantages of division of labour, attention must be drawn to some of its disadvantages. First, the repetitive nature of the worker's task leads to monotony, which in turn may lead to carelessness and lack of interest. This disadvantage is not as serious as it seems, for there are the offsetting advantages of greater leisure, greater amenities for the enjoyment of leisure and the varied opportunities of finding an outlet for initiative outside one's job. Secondly, the worker is more liable to unemployment. If a man specialises only in one activity, he may find it very difficult to get new employment if the demand for his 'special' labour has fallen off. This disadvantage is easily identified in the developed countries of Europe and America, where the highly specialised labourer or worker tends to be at the mercy of the market demand for his particular kind of skill. A fall in the demand for coal, for example, leads to unemployment among the coal-miners. Similarly a fall in the demand for motor-cars leads to unemployment among the workers in the motor industry.

In the developing countries of West Africa, where division of labour has not been pursued to its fullest extent, some unemployment and immobility of labour are caused partly by political divisions which restrict the spontaneous willingness to move to different areas in search of jobs, and partly by some social factors, such as ethnic and religious differences, which also make movement to other areas unattractive. Lastly, division of labour tends to lead to the concentration of labour in large business organisations. The individual worker is, therefore, less important to the entrepreneur, and his welfare depends in the main on the effectiveness of collective bargaining. The old personal bond between the employer and the employee is lacking. The worker has to depend on the trade union, if there is one, to which he belongs in order to improve his conditions of work.

'Division of labour' is often taken as synonymous with 'specialisation'. While this can be accepted in the broad sense, a further clarification is necessary. The most important point is that the term specialisation can be applied to any factor of production. Land, labour, capital and indeed enterprise are all capable of being broken down into several specialised functions. 'Division of labour', therefore, means the division of the work force into different groups each of which has its own specialisation. The railway system of a country is a specialised form of capital. Similarly, the shopping centre of a city is an area of land specialising in retail trade. 'Specialisation', therefore, can be found in each class of factors of production, while the term division of labour applies specifically to labour as a factor of production. Instead of speaking of the division of labour or capital or land or enterprise, we use the general term 'specialisation'.

LIMITS TO SPECIALISATION

Adam Smith pointed out as long ago as 1766: 'as it is the power of exchanging that gives occasion to the division of labour, so the extent of this division must also be limited by the extent of that power, or in other words, by the extent of the market'.[1] Particular attention has to be given to the interpretation of the word 'market'. In this context, the word market means effective demand. The effective demand for a product must be sufficiently large for the process of production to be advantageously split up into several simple processes, each one of which requires the whole time of at least one worker. If demand for a product is limited to a small village, then specialisation cannot be introduced because one man working alone can meet the whole amount required. However, if the demand is countrywide, many men can be employed and each can specialise in one relatively simple process rather than having to master the whole productive process. But anything which fragments the large market is bound to reduce the opportunities for specialisation. The transport and communication systems of any country are of vital importance in this respect. Even if there is a large total demand for a commodity in a particular area but there are no good roads to transport the commodity concerned to the buyers, the market will be broken up into a number of small markets and

[1]Adam Smith, *op. cit.*, Vol. 1, p. 15.

production will be on a small scale for each. We must remember that production is not complete until the commodity or service has reached the final consumer. Indeed, the international specialisation of labour, which is the basis of international trade, depends largely on effective transport and communications. By the use of ocean shipping, international and intercontinental roads, railways and airlines, the extent of the market has become worldwide for many commodities. In consequence, specialisation all over the world has increased greatly in recent years even though a number of factors still exist which limit the extent of the world market. Examples are tariffs, exchange control and international politics.

LARGE-SCALE PRODUCTION

Mass production may develop from small-scale as a result of two possible courses. The first is by an increase in the size of the individual business: this is growth by an extention of each unit of business and is called large-scale production. The second is by an increase in the number of businesses or establishments making up the industry.

It is relevant here to explain the terms a plant, a firm and an industry. An industry is the term given to all businesses or firms producing the same commodity or group of technically similar commodities. For example, the motor industry embraces the production of all cars and lorries of different makes and styles. Each producer of a particular kind of car is a firm, which may operate several plants. The makers of the Volkswagen or the Peugeot cars are motor-producing firms within the motor industry. The branch bank of the Standard Bank at Accra or Freetown or Lagos is a plant of the firm, the Standard Bank, which is part of the 'industry' whose product is banking.

As we have already noted, an entrepreneur is always striving to combine factors of production in such a way as to ensure the greatest profit. In trying to do this he explores any possibility of economies in the use of the factors through large-scale production. One of his primary objectives is to achieve a reduction in the costs of production and this might enable him to reduce his price, so enlarging his market to absorb the large-scale output. The economies of large-scale production which the entrepreneur seeks may be either 'internal' to his firm or 'external' or both. Internal economies are those which are open to a single factory or a single firm independently of the action of other firms. External economies are those which are available to all the firms in an industry or industries in consequence of changes external to the individual firm.

Internal economies may be achieved in a number of ways. In order to engage in large-scale production, a firm may acquire a machine which is too large for a one-man business to use intensively so as to achieve lower costs of production. For example, the use of a plough on the typical indigenous farm, which is usually small, may not be economical, but when used on a co-operative or collective farm it may lead to greater production and a reduction in costs. In modern industrial production the doubling of the size of a factory may not double the operating costs, but may lead to more than double the volume of production. A firm may also enjoy internal economies by centralising the research efforts of the separate plants or establishments under its control. Also, internal economies can be achieved by utilising what would otherwise be waste products through the establishment of subsidiary industries.

External economies are of different types. For example, the concentration at a single point of a number of firms enables them to derive advantages from the attraction this offers to workers and other enterprises. Such firms will be able to draw on a larger supply of skilled labour, enjoy better transport arrangements and facilities, and will benefit from competition which eventually stimulates overall productive efficiency both of other firms and themselves. The various industrial estates which now exist in some big cities of West Africa provide fitting examples of external economies. Arrangements among firms for the bulk purchase of raw materials will reduce the costs of raw materials per firm. Similarly, the selling of finished products, the transportation and advertising of such products in bulk, all lead to economies.

By producing a diversity of products and by the possibility of selling in many markets the entrepreneur is able to spread business risks. Large-scale production also enables the entrepreneur to obtain capital more easily and often on preferential terms by being able to borrow large sums. He is able to spread his overhead charges over the greater volume of production, thus reducing his unit costs of production.

In spite of the advantages of large-scale production mentioned above, there are a number of disadvantages too. Personal involvement of the worker in production is diminished if his job becomes only a small part of a complex production process. Since large-scale production leads inevitably to standardisation, it is no longer possible to take into consideration the personal tastes of consumers. Indeed, personal contact with the consumer is no longer possible. Usually, there is concentration of control in large-scale production which means concentration of risks and as a result any wrong decision of the management may plunge the whole business into difficulty. Lastly, economic waste may appear in the process of production due primarily to the inability of the manager to supervise effectively every part of the productive process.

FACTORS INFLUENCING THE SIZE OF A BUSINESS UNIT

There are a number of factors which determine the size of a business unit. The nature of an industry usually indicates whether it is capable of being handled on a large scale or not. The extractive industries in West Africa provide examples of both large- and small-unit production. The fishing industry in West Africa is handled largely by numerous fishermen operating as individual boat crews. Attempts are now being made to introduce large-scale fishing into West Africa by big companies making use of fishing trawlers and thus the industry is becoming one embracing both small-scale and large-scale producers. In the mining of alluvial diamonds in Ghana and Sierra Leone many individual prospectors operate side by side with a large international company. In contrast, one finds that exploration and production of petroleum in Nigeria is only undertaken by very large organisations. The main point is that in industries where the costs of apparatus and equipment are great it will be impossible even to start business except on a large scale.

Since large-scale production can only be operated profitably when goods or services are standardised, there is little scope for successful expansion where much attention to individual customer's requirements is necessary and the business unit will tend to be small. This accounts for the great number of bicycle repairers, shoemakers (and repairers), tailors, hairdressers, goldsmiths and others operating in the streets of West African villages, towns and cities.

Even if production is capable of being handled on a large scale, the difficulty of obtaining capital to finance further development may limit the size of the operation. Individual producers and small companies are usually not well known and therefore command insufficient reputation to be able to obtain credit from financial institutions, particularly from commercial and industrial banks. Such small businesses have to finance any expansion out of their profits or by borrowing money from friends, relatives and, in the last resort, from money-lenders. This is one of the factors limiting the size of businesses in West Africa.

The nature of the goods being produced may also limit the scale of operation. If the product is perishable as with agricultural foodstuffs, with no refrigeration, the unit of operation is usually small. Also, if the materials are scattered over a wide geographical area and are difficult to collect, the units of operation will tend to be small. Timber-felling in West Africa is an example of such an industry.

LOCALISATION OF INDUSTRY

The tendency for producing units of any industry to gravitate towards, or concentrate in, particular districts is known as the localisation of industry. Localisation of industry is an extension of the principle of division of labour or specialisation and is sometimes called territorial division of labour. An area or district specialises in the production of the commodities for which conditions afford it special advantages.

Localisation of industry is different from the planned location of industry. Planned location of industry goes hand in hand with the government efforts to plan and regulate general economic activity. In the developed countries of Europe and America, experience has shown that areas where one localised industry is established are more vulnerable to severe unemployment than areas with diversified industries. One reason is that in such areas labour becomes immobile, because of the nature of specialised production. Therefore, anything which causes the demand for the products of the industry to fall, all other things being equal, will lead to contraction in production and hence to unemployment. (Planned location of industry is discussed further below.)

Generally, localisation is the result of being able to operate an industry more profitably or at lower costs in one locality than in another. However, some industries are localised primarily because of historical or even accidental circumstances. It can no longer be convincingly argued that most of the old but traditional industries in West Africa, such as pottery and weaving of cloth, were localised on the minimum cost principle. Modern technology, however, provides new sources of power, equipment and transport, without altering the basis on which some old industries were localised.

There are a number of principle factors influencing the location of industry. First, and probably the most uncontrollable, are the natural factors. These include climatic conditions, the composition of the soil and the mineral deposits.

Secondly, economic factors which can be controlled enter into the consideration of industrial location. Indeed, apart from the natural factors mentioned above, an entrepreneur wanting to establish a business or industry will be most concerned about economic factors which he can control, and which determine his costs of production upon which his profits depend. He must consider the source of his raw materials. He is likely to establish his industry near the source of the raw materials if they are heavy or bulky, but at or near his market if the raw materials are light and the finished product fragile. Such a decision minimises the joint cost of transporting raw materials and the final product. Closely related to this problem is that of good transport. In fact, transport considerations nowadays tend to be of greater importance than nearness to markets; for even industries close to markets may not prosper if transport facilities are unreliable or unsuitable or totally absent. Another economic factor which is of importance is the proximity to sources of cheap power. In the old industrial countries, industrial centres in the nineteenth century grew up near coalfields. However, the ease of conveying electric power has made this factor one of much less importance. In West Africa, the successful completion of the Volta and Kainji hydro-electric schemes in Ghana and Nigeria respectively has made possible increased use of electricity as a source of cheap power. Also, in Nigeria, the substantial production of petroleum encourages the use of oil as a source of power. One should add that subsidiary and feeder industries are usually located around the main industry which they serve.

Thirdly, there are some political factors which influence decisions about the location of industries. Many countries now impose tariffs in order to restrict the import of foreign goods and encourage the growth of a corresponding domestic industry. A government may also introduce subsidies and tax remissions to assist the establishment of new industries or to help distressed ones.

PLANNED LOCATION OF INDUSTRIES

Though the principles which underlie the planned location of industry are the same in developed and developing countries, yet there are some differences in their application. In developed countries where most industries have been localised historically there is usually the risk of structural unemployment as a result of a change in demand. The unemployment situation thus arising may influence the government to look into the possibilities of creating new industries to absorb the jobless. During the depression of the late 1920s and the early 1930s in England, some manufacturing industries, for instance the motor-car industry, continued to prosper, while some industries, such as the cotton textile industry, which were highly localised, declined. The British government declared some areas 'distressed areas' which needed more employment opportunities and were helped by locating new industries in them. The aim of planned location of industry in such circumstances was to establish a greater variety of industry to the distressed areas.

However, in developing countries such as those of West Africa, planned location of industry was adopted as part of overall economic planning. Since the end of the Second World War, the need for rapid economic growth has been realised. Economic development plans have been devised which give emphasis to industrial development, and some industrial estates have been established. In Nigeria, for example, industrial estates now exist at Ikeja, Ilupeju, Enugu, Port Harcourt, Zaria, Kano and Kaduna; and in Ghana, Accra has an industrial estate. The governments of West Africa have created a number of statutory bodies to promote the establishment of manufacturing industries either fully owned by such statutory bodies or owned in partnership with foreign firms. In addition, legislation has been passed granting income tax and customs concessions to industrial and agricultural enterprises which are needed for the development of these countries.

Apart from national economic development, the objects of planned industrial location in West Africa are to diversify the economy, to create employment in many areas which were hitherto regarded as rural areas thus arresting the influx of people from the rural areas into the big towns and cities, and to take avantage of international specialisation of industries.

An important aspect of the planned location of industry in West Africa is the deliberate policy of some governments to ignore the purely economic reasons for planning specific locations for modern industries. For example, the Nigerian government in its Second National Development Plan 1970–4, indicated that one of the objectives of the new industrial policy was to 'promote even development and fair distribution of industries in all parts of the country'. This seemed to suggest that economic considerations would be secondary to equity or politics when deciding where to locate new industries, but one must recognise that the governments in West Africa are concerned with balancing the economic and social amenities among the various ethnic and regional or state groups which comprise the nation. In maintaining political and social equilibria, it might be difficult to adhere very strictly to purely economic considerations.

TYPES OF INDUSTRIAL OR BUSINESS ORGANISATIONS

The types of business firms or units that can be identified in West Africa are: the sole trader, the private partnership, the joint stock company, the co-operative enterprise and the public corporation.

The sole trader

The individual trader or producer, the one-man business, which is the simplest form of business organisation, exists where the whole enterprise is owned and controlled by one person. It is the most common form of business unit in West Africa, and it predominates in retail trade where the amount of capital and the number of employees required is small. A number of one-man businesses also exist in other trades, such as those of tailors, mechanics, bakers, goldsmiths and blacksmiths. Usually a small one-man business can be established with ease because the capital required for its establishment is not very great and the capital invested can be increased at will. However, in recent years, there are a few exceptions, where the initial capital requirements of a one-man business are high. Examples are engineering, medicine, legal advocacy and wholesale trading.

One of the reasons why one-man businesses predominate in West Africa is the lack of the large amounts of capital required to establish large businesses. The level of income in West Africa is low, and the propensity to consume is relatively high; consequently, the saving that can be done is low, and so investment is low too. In addition to this, there is the general feeling of mistrust among partners, which, unfortunately, prevents pooling of capital funds for investment. One advantage, however, is that small one-man businesses can cater effectively for the personal tastes and requests of customers. They are able to satisfy personal demands that cannot be standardised and supplied on a large scale. They also secure a combination of ownership and control which helps the sole businessman to show greater initiative and avoid routine and waste.

Even though there are a number of very successful one-man businesses in West Africa, many of them suffer from some weakness. To start with, the activities of the business are limited by the capital available. Then the business may be unable to expand sufficiently to enjoy all the economies of scale. Also, the liability of the business is unlimited and this tends to curtail its scope and growth. The small businessman tries to avoid large business risks which may bring about considerable losses. Often, the businessman overworks himself to the point of endangering his life. Indeed, the business often ends with the death of the owner; or alternatively, the death of the owner results in a collapse of the business because ability cannot be passed on to children or relatives who might take it over.

The private partnership

The major disadvantages of the one-man business led to the appearance of the private partnership as a device to reduce the problem of an insufficient supply of capital, and to improve management. The private partnership is the oldest method of enlarging a business unit. A partnership is created when two or more people join together to carry on a business with a view to making profit. An association of two or more people which has no profit motive is not regarded strictly as a partnership in the economic sense. In West Africa, only a few partnerships exist. As already mentioned, there is a general feeling of mistrust, and distrust of business partners, largely arising from the urge to get rich quick which has resulted in some dishonest practices.

The private partnership has some advantages. The partners, two or more, are able to pool their capital resources thus enabling the business to operate on a larger scale and thereby enjoy more economies of scale. Though the liability of a partner remains unlimited as in a one-man business, yet partnership facilitates the spreading of business risks between a number of partners, although the unlimited liability of the partners for the business acts as a deterrent to rash business speculations and decisions. Under normal circumstances, partnerships usually survive longer than one-man businesses because their existence is not dependent on the life of one man. In fact, their life can be prolonged and revitalised by admitting new energetic and progressive partners. The private partnership affords some degree of division of labour, as each partner tends to be responsible for the one aspect of the management task for which he is most capable.

Even though partnership is a larger form of business than sole proprietorship, yet its capital resources remain small compared with a joint-stock company, thus limiting the scope of its economic activities. In some cases partners are capable of building up strong goodwill, which apart from the success of their business is necessary for establishing credit-worthiness. But as with one-man businesses, partnerships sometimes also suffer lack of continuity, as the death, withdrawal or retirement of one partner may bring the partnership to an end. In West Africa, the common problems of intestate succession, that is, the administration of the estate of a deceased person without a will, coupled with that of the extended family system, tend to break up partnerships. The liability being unlimited, each partner is normally liable to the full extent of his property for paying the debts which the partnership might incur, but it is possible to have a 'limited' partnership, in which a partner's liability may be limited to the amount he has invested in the business; such a partner is not allowed to participate in the management of the firm and there must still be at least one partner whose liability remains unlimited.

The joint-stock company

The joint-stock company is an extension of the basic principle of partnership with the primary object of securing a more effective method of mobilising financial resources and manpower for producing goods and services. Such a company is formed when at least seven people join together to invest money or other resources in a common enterprise with the view to making profit. The company law of each country regulates the formation, the powers and the dissolution of companies. Since the form of organisation and the law governing it make it possible for the number of shareholders or investors to be increased almost without limit, the administration of the business is normally delegated to paid directors and managers.

In the event of the failure of a company, the liability of each shareholder for the debts of the company is limited to the amount of the original purchase price of his shares. The existing law provides for two types of joint-stock company – public and private. While the public joint-stock companies are open to the public without any numerical limitation on the number of shareholders, private joint-stock companies have at the most fifty shareholders. The latter cannot raise share capital from the public but have to rely upon the founders, their successors, lenders of loan capital and upon undistributed profits.

The joint-stock company has some important economic characteristics. By the very nature of this important type of business unit, large-scale enterprise is facilitated. It appeals easily to a large number of 'dormant' shareholders who are willing and able to invest in an enterprise in which their liability is limited to their total investment with their shares transferable by sale when they wish. It also gives wide scope to different types of investment, particularly in the form of ordinary shares, preference shares and debentures. Ordinary shares have no fixed rate of dividend which are paid out of profit after all expenses have been met. When there are no profits, the ordinary shares carry no dividends. Preference shares, on the other hand, carry a fixed rate of dividend and are paid fully before any share of profits is alloted to the ordinary shares. Debentures are not shares but loans to the company. Interest paid on debentures forms part of the expenses of the company which must be met before any preference or ordinary dividends are paid. Joint-stock companies enable investors, if they so choose, to reduce their risks by spreading their investments over several different enterprises.

A joint-stock company is a 'legal person' and has a life of its own which is not terminated by the death of a shareholder. The company has a longer life than that of any individual shareholder, and is therefore able to embark on long-term policies of capital accumulation and business expansion. On occasion, combination and monopoly are facilitated as one joint-stock company may be financially strong enough to purchase controlling interests in a number of other companies. The tendency for combination and monopoly is more noticeable in the developed countries of Western Europe than in West Africa.

In most joint-stock companies, if not all, ownership and control of the business are separated, the control being with a comparatively small number of paid directors and managers who accept the obligation to make profits and to pay dividends to the shareholders who own the business.

Co-operative societies

A co-operative society is a combination of a number of people for the common end of together either producing goods for sale or for their own use, or for buying goods at the lowest price they can secure and then distributing or re-selling them to the members. The basic idea of co-operative enterprise is not foreign to West Africa. Co-operative societies in West Africa first appeared in the field of agriculture. In the days when the subsistence economy predominated, farm labour was provided by the farmers in each locality in rotation. With the advent of a money economy, it became more convenient to employ labour and other factors of production for payment and consequently money costs entered into the process of even co-operative production and distribution.

The modern West African co-operative society was first seen in the marketing rather than the production of agricultural crops, particularly in cocoa-marketing. The rapid growth of the 'cash crops' in West Africa induced farmers to give greater consideration to the pecuniary aspect of farming. Among the co-operative marketing societies, produce is handled and marketed centrally in order to reduce the average costs of marketing. Any surplus which accrues from the marketing operations is usually divided among members according to their sales. Other producers' co-operative societies in West Africa include crafts and group farming.

The other type of co-operative, the consumers' co-operative, takes the form of retail or distributive co-operation, in which a number of persons combine to engage in retail trade. The co-operative consumers' society buys goods collectively at wholesale prices and sells to its members at retail prices a little above cost price, so as to make some surplus. This surplus is usually divided among the members of the society in proportion to their purchases, after meeting the costs of administration.

There exist a number of other forms of co-operative society in

West Africa. These include the thrift and loan or credit societies. These co-operative societies do not engage in direct production or sales, but encourage their members to cultivate the habit of saving, and to employ their savings productively.

The capital of a co-operative society is usually subscribed by its members. This capital, together with other sums which the society is able to borrow, particularly from the commercial banks or the co-operative banks, and from some government financial institutions, is then employed in production, in the marketing operations, or in buying goods for re-sale, as the case may be. The co-operative society avoids the incurring of middlemen's costs. A large society also enjoys some of the economies of large-scale organisation.

One of the major problems facing co-operative societies in West Africa is that of securing the services of trained, competent and honest personnel to handle the affairs of such societies. On many occasions, the finances are mismanaged by incompetent secretaries and treasurers. In recent years, however, governments have embarked on training schemes for co-operative secretaries, treasurers and auditors to try to improve their professional competence.

Public corporations

The various types of business organisations which we have discussed so far are all different forms of private enterprise. The governments of West Africa, drawing on the experience of the United Kingdom, realised that to allow private companies to engage in the supply of some public utilities, such as electricity and water, would lead either to wasteful competition or undesirable monopolies. In order to avoid the duplication of plants or supplies, as for instance two water mains in the same street, which is an unnecessary expense, the government decided to introduce some form of monopoly in the organisation of public utilities. Public utilities are now being provided by such bodies as the electricity, water, broadcasting and railway corporations or authorities. Other public corporations include printing, housing, agricultural credit and finance. Further, local councils are encouraged to embark on municipal schemes to provide other public utilities. The only important municipal public utilities in West Africa so far established are the municipal bus transport services which are found in a few cities such as in Lagos, Freetown, Accra and Ibadan.

Since 1946, the West African governments have been extending the public corporation, owned and controlled by the government, to another vital economic activity. This new type is the development corporation which is primarily concerned with the implementation of government economic development policies: financial, industrial and agricultural.

The capital of each corporation is provided by the government or by the municipality, as the case may be. The corporations are usually organised upon normal business lines and they are expected to make a surplus, equivalent to profits in the private sector. The taxpayers are in effect the shareholders who bear the risk. Surpluses accruing from the operations of public corporations are employed in various ways by the government or the municipality to benefit the public. It is important to add that, apart from the development projects which some corporations operate, some of them enter into partnership with foreign business interests in the establishment of manufacturing industries.

The corporations which are primarily concerned with public utilities do not aim to make large surpluses. In fact, they concentrate on providing an efficient public service. The other corporations which are established for development purposes are expected to be efficient enough to make surpluses equivalent to normal profits in the private sector. All the corporations have the obligation of public accountability, because by the statutes which established them, they must present annual reports and accounts to Parliament, under civilian rule, or to the supreme military council under a military regime. Such reports are usually debated and the public always has the chance to criticise the operations of such corporations. Some of the corporations, particularly those engaged in industrial production, not only secure the economies of large scale operations, but their statutory powers enable them to take advantage of monopolistic control of the market. They have the further advantage that the government, with the support of the central bank, provides them with strong financial backing.

One of the major problems of public corporations in West Africa as in many other countries where such institutions exist is the general feeling that such corporations are not expected to make any surplus. The result has been, at least until now, that they are not worried by inefficiency and the government often has to subsidise them by meeting losses. To avoid this some of the corporations merely use their monopoly powers to increase prices to the consumer rather than by striving to achieve greater efficiency in order to meet their costs.

In fact, it has rarely been adequately explained to the public how such corporations fix the prices they charge for the services they render. If one then considers the substandard performance of some corporations, one may feel that the public is being cheated as it is not getting value for money. The efficiency of the corporations, particularly those providing public utilities, is a matter of vital importance to the welfare of the whole community, because errors and mistaken policies on their part may have wide and serious effects. The irregularity of electricity supply, for example, affects adversely the operation of businesses and causes serious inconveniences and distress to the consuming public.

Chapter 4

Production for the Market

PRODUCTION AND MARKETS

Production is not complete until goods and services produced have finally reached the consumers. The channel through which goods and services normally reach the consumers is the market. The question that then follows is: what is a market? A market that readily comes to one's mind is a place or location where buyers and sellers meet to transact business. In West Africa, such markets,[1] are innumerable, ranging from the local village markets to the street markets and the town or city markets. Some of these function daily, while some are held periodically, perhaps once in three days or once a week or fortnightly. These are markets which exist in particular locations where buyers and sellers are physically present. However, in recent years, the development of transport and communications, and the increasing use of facilities provided by the commercial banks and other financial institutions, have made it possible for buyers and sellers to get in touch with one another, even though they may be many miles apart. The important point is that whenever there is a buyer in touch with a supplier of any commodity a market exists. One can state, therefore, that a market exists if there is a mechanism by which buyers and sellers are brought in touch with one another to effect exchange.

There are markets for various kinds of goods and services; for example, export crops, foodstuffs, manufactured goods, raw materials, minerals and stocks and shares. Indeed, there may be as many markets as there are different brands of the same commodity.

In any kind of market, demand and supply must coexist before

[1]See Hodder and Ukwu, *Markets in West Africa* (Ibadan University Press, 1969).

any exchange can take place. It is appropriate, therefore, to begin this study by explaining in some detail the various components of demand and supply, which provide the background to the theory of prices and then to the theory of the firm and the industry. We shall then be able to examine the theory of the markets in which the firms and industries purchase their factors of production.

DEMAND

Demand should be distinguished from desire or want. A mere want or desire for a commodity will not in itself cause that commodity to be produced and neither will it in itself lead to any exchange. Before a want or desire can have any economic aspect it must be translated into effective demand. Effective demand is the desire for a commodity or service coupled with the willingness and ability to pay for it at the ruling price. Demand is of no significance in economics unless it is effective.

Why should there be demand for a commodity or service at a given price? There is a demand for a good or service because of the satisfaction or utility it provides. The next question is, what determines the quantity of a commodity to be bought at a given price? In order to answer this question we must look briefly into some fundamental principles of consumption.

It is a universal experience of human nature to derive diminishing satisfaction or utility from additional units of consumption of any commodity or service. Thus, to a very hungry man, one slice of bread will give him immense satisfaction – assuming, of course, that the slice is of normal size. Two slices will give him more satisfaction but the second slice will give him less satisfaction than the first, though still considerable. The third will give less additional satisfaction than the second, just moderate satisfaction. For the fourth he might even have a distaste. In order to simplify this analysis, we will assume that 'immense satisfaction' can be measured as four units, 'considerable satisfaction' as two units and 'moderate satisfaction' as one unit, while distaste has none. This illustration shows clearly that the total satisfaction or utility to the hungry man increases with successive slices of the bread; but that the total utility increases at a diminishing rate for each slice of bread. Clearly, each additional slice gives less utility than the preceding one. This tendency for successive amounts of the same commodity or service to give diminishing satisfaction is called the law of diminishing marginal utility. From the bread illustration, if we assume that the hungry man stopped after acquiring the third slice of bread, then the margin of his consumption is drawn after the third slice of bread, which is the marginal unit consumed; and the satisfaction derived therefrom is the marginal utility.

The law of diminishing marginal utility or significance will only operate if, first, units of a commodity or service are homogeneous, for any differences between the units of the commodity or service will invalidate the comparison of their utilities and, secondly, if the commodity or service is consumed in successive instalments, this is done at very short intervals between the consumption of each instalment: otherwise the operation of the law will commence with each instalment at a significantly different time and the consumer's tastes may have changed meanwhile.

It has been argued by some people that there are exceptions to the law of diminishing marginal utility. For example, the desire of a drink or drug addict increases with additional consumption; but this is something which results from changing desires as time elapses, whereas our analysis assumes that tastes remain constant during the period of consumption.

As the consumption of additional units of a commodity or service brings less and less extra satisfaction, it follows that if a commodity or service has to be purchased, the price which the consumer is prepared to pay for additional instalments becomes less and less also. In the example of the slices of bread given above, the hungry man may be prepared to pay 4 kobo for the first slice; and nothing for a fourth slice. However, in practice, he has to pay a fixed price; that is, the price ruling in the market at the time of purchase. The effect of this is that the market price determines the amount the consumer will purchase. If the price is 1 kobo per slice, for example, he will buy three slices for 3 kobo, a further slice being just not worth the money (1 kobo) that he has to pay for it.

From the illustration of the hungry man, it is interesting to note that although he would only have to pay 1 kobo each for the three slices of bread, he is prepared to pay something more for the first two slices rather than go without them. If what is available is only one slice of bread, he is prepared to pay 4 kobo for it. Also, he is prepared to pay 2 kobo for the second slice. It means that while the satisfaction he derives from the third slice of bread just balances the price he pays, he gains some extra satisfaction on the purchase of the first two slices. Those units of a commodity or service consumed within the margin, that is, prior to the last unit consumed, produce surpluses of satisfaction. The excess is called consumer's surplus. In a more simplified way, one can say that consumer's surplus is the difference between what the consumer is prepared to pay and what he actually pays.

From the law of diminishing marginal utility, it follows that demand tends to vary with price. A fall in the price of any normal commodity increases its demand because (a) existing purchasers will be willing to buy more, since units of the commodity that were previously sub-marginal (below the margin) become intra-marginal (on the margin and above); and (b) new consumers, who previously refrained from buying because all units were sub-marginal for them can now afford to buy – sub-marginal purchasers now become intra-marginal purchasers. Similarly, a rise in the price of any normal commodity decreases the demand because (a) existing purchasers are unwilling to buy as much since some intra-marginal units for them now become sub-marginal; and (b) marginal purchasers will now refrain from buying since for marginal purchasers all units become sub-marginal. This means that the utility at the margin will decide what quantity the purchasers are prepared to pay. If the price is low, the utility at the margin will be low and the quantity bought will be relatively large; and if the price is high then utility at the margin will be high and the quantity bought relatively small. In other words, marginal utility governs demand at a given price.

The relationship between demand and price can be illustrated mathematically with a demand schedule (see Table 4.1). For our demand schedule we shall consider the local demand for palm-oil in a typical small West African town where the standard measure for selling palm-oil is a glass bottle containing two pints. From the demand schedule in the table it can be seen that each successive fall in price results in more palm-oil being wanted. No doubt the extra quantity is wanted partly by existing buyers wanting more and partly by new buyers entering the market. The demand schedule is illustrated graphically in Figure 4.1. A student should note that it is conventional in economics to measure demand horizontally and price vertically in graphical illustrations.

The demand curve DD in Figure 4.1 slopes downward from left to right. This is due to the operation of the law of diminishing marginal utility. The illustration reveals clearly that demand cannot

Table 4.1 *Demand Schedule for Palm-Oil*

bottles bought	*if the price per bottle is*
100	20 kobo
125	17 kobo
150	15 kobo
200	12 kobo
250	10 kobo
350	7 kobo

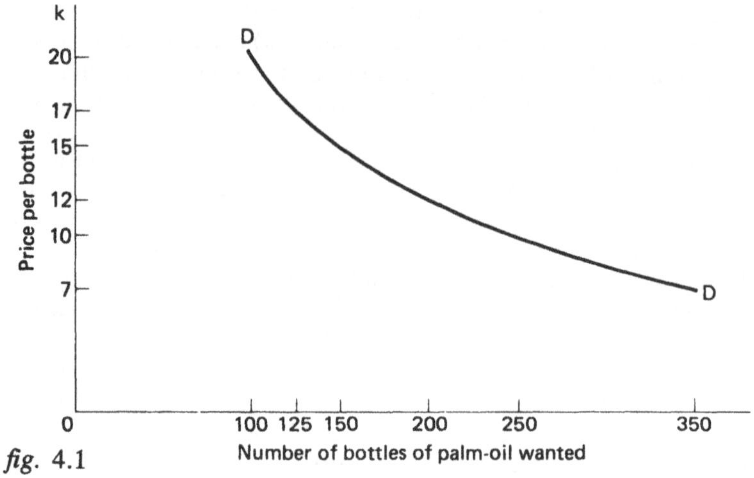

fig. 4.1

be separated from the amount of goods or services bought and the price paid for that amount. We can only talk of demand as the quantity which a purchaser is willing to buy at a given price and at a given time.

We can now formalise relationship between demand and price: all other things being equal, a rise in price brings about a decrease in the quantity demanded; and a fall in price brings about an increase in the quantity demanded. This is the law of demand which says that the quantity demanded increases when the price falls, and decreases when the price rises, all other things being equal. It is sometimes put in the following form: changes in the quantity demanded are inversely related to changes in price.

ELASTICITY OF DEMAND

Elasticity of demand is the responsiveness or sensitivity of demand to changes in price or income. Price-elasticity of demand is the responsiveness of demand to changes in price, while income elasticity of demand indicates the responsiveness of demand to changes in income without any change in prices.

Price-elasticity of demand is said to be unitary if a change (rise or fall) in price results in an equal proportionate change (fall or rise) in the amount demanded. Demand is said to be elastic; when a change in price produces a greater proportionate change in the amount demanded, it is then greater than unitary. Demand is said to be inelastic; when a change in price results in a less than proportionate change in the amount demanded, it is then less than unitary. The mathematical method of computing price-elasticity is to divide the proportionate change in quantity demanded by the proportionate change in the price causing the change in quantity. For instance, in the example above, at the price of 20 k per bottle 100 bottles of palm-oil would be demanded, and if the price fell to 17 k per bottle, 125 bottles would be demanded. The proportionate change in price is $^3/_{20}$ while the proportionate change in the amount demanded is $\frac{1}{4}$. Therefore, the price-elasticity of demand for this change in price is $\frac{1}{4} \div {}^3/_{20} = 1^2/_3$ which is elastic.

A warning is, however, necessary here. Such calculations of elasticity are accurate only if the changes in price and quantity are proportionately small. In this example they are 15 per cent and 25 per cent both very large. A correction which gives good results can be made by taking the average of the two prices and the average of the two quantities. In this case the calculation will then be:

proportionate change in quantity ÷ proportionate change in price

$$= \frac{25}{112 \cdot 5} \div \frac{3}{18 \cdot 5} = 1 \cdot 37$$

This is considerably less than $1^2/_3$ which is the result of the less accurate calculation.

To take another example from Table 4.1, if the price of a bottle of palm-oil falls from 10 k to 7 k, the quantity demanded increases from 250 to 350 bottles. So the price-elasticity of demand for this price change is

$$\frac{100}{300} \div \frac{3}{8 \cdot 5} = \frac{8 \cdot 5}{9} = 0 \cdot 94$$

This is slightly inelastic but very close indeed to being unitary.

Graphically, the range of price-elasticity is illustrated in Figure 4.2. The elasticity of any selected point on a straight-line demand curve can be measured by extending the line to meet the two axes. By the simple process of dividing the distance from the point to the X axis by the distance from the point to the Y axis, one can obtain the price-elasticity at the selected point. Thus the elasticity at point R = RQ/AR. The elasticity of point T = TQ/AT = 1. It can be seen that the elasticity at points on AT is greater than 1 and at points on TQ is less than 1. The same method can be applied to demand curves which are not straight lines if a tangent is drawn at the

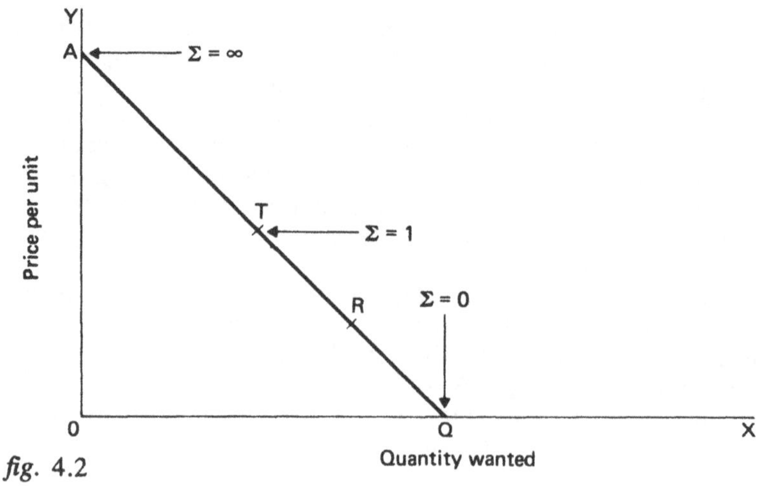

fig. 4.2

selected point on the demand curve to cut both axes. This is shown on Figure 4.3. A student will realise that the mere appearance of a demand curve does not in all cases indicate whether it shows elasticity greater or less than 1. Care must be taken to ensure that the scales of the axes are accurate and that equal distances represent equal quantities or prices before calculating elasticity.

Another way of estimating price-elasticity is to measure the changes in total expenditure due to changes in prices. When a demand curve is elastic over a certain range, a fall in price will result in an increase in total expenditure by consumers and a rise in price will result in a decrease in total expenditure. This can be illustrated from the examples already taken from Table 4.1.

At a price of 20 k per bottle of palm-oil, 100 bottles will be bought, so the total expenditure by consumers will be 2,000 k. If the price falls to 17 k per bottle, the quantity bought will be 125 bottles requiring an expenditure of 2,125 k. Thus the price-elasticity is greater than 1; demand is elastic at these prices.

At the lower price of 10 k per bottle, 250 bottles would be bought at a total expenditure of 2,500 k. If the price fell still further to 7 k per bottle, 350 bottles would be bought and these would cost a total of 2,450 k. This is less than 2,500 k so the demand at these prices is inelastic; it is less than 1. This elasticity is very close to being unitary; if $357^1/_7$ bottles were to be bought at 7 k per bottle, the total expenditure would be 2,500 k and the elasticity of demand would be unitary exactly because the same total expenditure would be incurred at a price of 10 k and at 7 k per bottle. This can be confirmed by applying the formula:

$$\text{price elasticity of demand} = \frac{\text{proportionate change in quantity}}{\text{proportionate change in price}}$$
$$= \frac{107^{1}/_{7}}{303^{3}/_{7}} \div \frac{3}{8\frac{1}{2}}$$
$$= 1$$

A simple diagrammatic method of distinguishing elasticity of demand by reference to total expenditure is shown in Figure 4.4. If the area OPRQ is greater than the area $OP_1\ SQ_1$ the demand curve is inelastic between R and S; if $OP_1\ SQ_1$ is greater the curve is elastic; and if OPRQ equals $OP_1\ SQ_1$ in area, the curve has unitary elasticity between R and S.

Elasticity of demand depends on a number of factors. The most important is the availability of substitutes. If close substitutes for any particular commodity can be bought in the same market, this is likely to create an elastic demand for the given commodity. This happens because a slight rise in the price of a commodity may lead to the substitution of alternative commodities. Similarly, a slight fall in price may transfer demand from the available substitutes to the given commodity. The tendency, therefore, is for the prices of substitute commodities to rise or fall together. This is sometimes

fig. 4.3

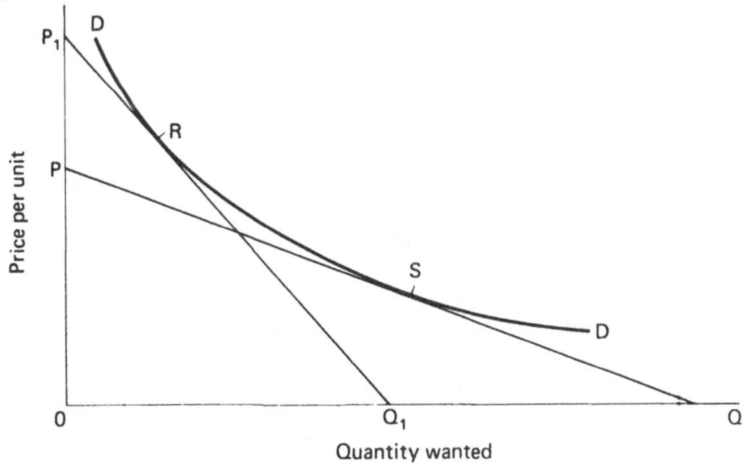

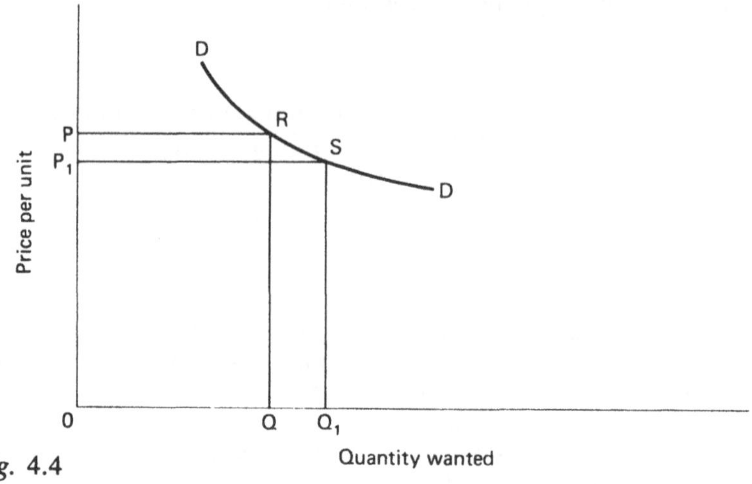

fig. 4.4

referred to as prices changing in sympathy.

If a commodity is used for a variety of purposes this is another factor likely to result in the demand for it being elastic.

It is sometimes suggested that the demand for a necessity or essential commodity will be inelastic, because a certain minimum will be bought whatever the price; and that the demand for a luxury will be elastic because one can conveniently do without the commodity. This line of argument cannot be easily justified. What is a necessity or luxury in a particular situation and at a particular time may not constitute a necessity or luxury, as the case may be, at a different situation and at another time. As already explained above, the most important consideration is whether a commodity has close substitutes or not.

Another important factor is the proportion of income which is spent on a product. If a large proportion of income is spent on a commodity, the effect of a change in price will alter the consumer's spending patterns greatly. For example, a rise in the price of fufu (where this is a staple food item) will cause many people to look for alternative foods (perhaps gari or rice) whereas a higher price for salt causes no substitution.

Again, one has to consider the element of time as it affects elasticity. A sudden change overnight in the price of a commodity will not drastically change the demand the following morning, as it will take some time for consumers to find acceptable alternatives or substitutes.

Lastly, and as already mentioned above, income-elasticity of

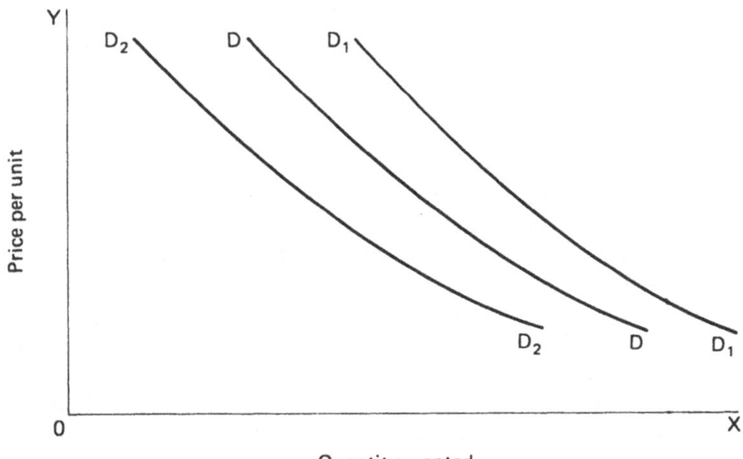

fig. 4.5

demand for a commodity measures the responsiveness of the quantity demanded to a change in income when there is no change in the price of that commodity. This concept is of particular interest in West African countries where the pace of economic growth and economic development is increasing the average level of incomes rapidly. The concept indicates how consumption patterns change with changes in the level of income.

It must be realised, however, that changes in demand may occur independently of price changes, but in response to changes in other things. For example, a change of fashion or taste may dry up or increase the demand for an article, even if the price remains unaltered.

An increase or decrease in demand indicates a shift in the demand curve at all prices. This is shown graphically in Figure 4.5. If there is an increase in demand it means that more of a commodity will be demanded at the same price, thus leading to a shift to the right of the demand curve (from DD to D_1D_1). Similarly, a decrease in demand means that less of a commodity will be demanded at the same price, thus resulting in a shift to the left of the demand curve (from DD to D_2D_2).

Generally, a number of factors influence demand conditions. An increase or decrease in demand may occur as a result of changes in income. High incomes tend to correspond with great demand and low incomes with less demand for normal commodities. In recent years advertisements – newspaper, radio and television – have played a significant role in stimulating greater demand for various commodities through the dissemination of information and by persuasion. Also, credit sales and the hire-purchase system now being increasingly adopted in West Africa tend to increase the level of demand for certain commodities. Further, the size and the composition of the population of a country have important effects on demand. For instance, a country with a high percentage of teenage population is likely to have a high demand for goods and services which are currently fashionable among teenagers.

A student may now realise that the effects of a change in the price of one commodity are rarely confined to that commodity. It often happens that commodities are in joint demand or complementary demand. When a want is satisfied not by one commodity but by a combination of commodities, for example, tea and sugar, motor-cars and petrol, clay oil-lamps and palm-oil, any increase in the demand for one article will result in an increase in the demand for the complementary articles, or vice versa.

Composite demand exists when a single article is demanded for a number of different uses, as for instance the demand for rubber for shoes, tyres and balls. An increase in the demand for one use will result in an increased scarcity of the commodity for other uses, thus raising the prices of all the commodities. Lastly, derived demand is demand for factors of production derived from the demand for the goods they produce. For example, the demand for labour in house-building is derived from the demand for houses. In fact, the demand for a product will necessarily lead to the demand for the factors that produce it. In other words, once an entrepreneur embarks on producing a commodity or service, he will set in motion the demand for the factors which he needs to produce the commodity or service.

SUPPLY

The supply of any commodity is the amount that is placed for sale on the market. Effective supply is the ability and the willingness on the part of the supplier to place on the market a certain amount of his stock of a commodity at a given price. One must clearly distinguish between the stock and the supply of a commodity. In the case of perishable commodities, the stock and the supply tend to coincide, because quantities of such goods cannot be withheld from the market for any length of time. However, in the case of durable goods, supply is usually a part – it may be small or big – of the stock, as the flow of these goods to the market, under normal conditions, will be accelerated or slackened by rises or falls in prices.

It is generally assumed that the main motive of the producer or supplier is to make profit. He must engage some factors in the process of production, and he has to pay for their services. The costs of production are the amount of money which the producer pays to reward all the efforts, risks and sacrifices of land, labour and capital plus the imputed cost of the factors he owns himself. Imputed cost is the term used for the value of his own factors which for him are an opportunity cost, since he would have them available for other purposes if he did not use them for production in the way being considered. The costs of production are classified broadly as prime costs and supplementary costs.

Prime costs are also called variable costs. They include the cost of raw materials, the cost of some kinds of labour, and any other items which have to be used in larger quantities if more is produced. Whenever there is an increase in the volume of production there must necessarily be an increase in the quantity of raw materials used so more labour is likely to be employed, probably more circulating capital is needed and there may be other items such as power, lighting or transport. These prime or variable costs vary with the volume of production.

Supplementary costs are also called overhead or fixed costs. They are the charges which have to be incurred if anything at all is to be produced. Any modern production involves the employment of managers to undertake the initial organisation and supervision; the purchase and maintenance of plant and equipment; the services of the basic administrative staff and the selling organisation; possibly other costs which are fixed in the sense that they do not vary with output; and interest has to be paid on borrowed capital as does rent for the site of the factory or other buildings. All these are examples of supplementary or fixed costs which do not change with an increase or decrease in the volume of production and have to be met whatever the quantity of the product.

It is only in the short term that a distinction can be made between fixed costs and variable costs. In the long term all costs of production can be varied. In fact, economists define the long term, or long run, as the time between a production decision being made and the goods reaching the market such that the producer can vary all his costs if necessary. He can hire a larger or smaller factory and so change his rent: he can dismiss any managers or employ more and he can reduce or enlarge his administration and selling organisation. In the long run only costs limit the expansion of output, but in the short run the fixed costs of production impose an upper limit to the volume of output they can assist to produce. For example, an electric generating plant cannot produce more electricity than it was designed to produce, and a warehouse cannot take more goods than its space allows. The administration, particularly supervisory staff, takes some time to enlarge or be reduced and so is fixed in the short run with a maximum capacity which cannot be exceeded. It means that if output were to be increased beyond this limit, it could only endure if sufficient time were allowed for the 'original' fixed costs to be changed; but this is in the long run when all costs are variable.

One main significance of the distinction between prime and supplementary costs, at least for the present purpose of our study, is found in the fact that it explains why, for certain periods and in the short run only, producers are prepared to continue to produce and sell at prices which do not cover all the costs of production. For example, during a depression, when prices are low and do not cover full costs, producers may be prepared to sell at a price which covers prime cost and part of the supplementary cost if they expect that eventually their business is going to be profitable again. This might be a better business decision than to keep their machines and equipment idle or to liquidate the business. It must be emphasised, however, that the decision to produce and sell at a price lower than the full cost of production can only be taken as a short-term measure. In the long run it is expected that business and market conditions will change for the better for prices to rise enough to be able to cover full costs and allow for some profit as well.

The proportion of supplementary cost and prime cost in total costs play a significant part in producers' decisions whether or not to continue to produce. If the supplementary cost is too large a proportion of the total costs, the producer might find it difficult to wait for recovery before deciding to stop production altogether or transfer to another line of production.

We can define average cost as the total cost divided by the units produced, while the marginal cost is the addition to total cost brought about by the production of an additional unit.

Table 4.2 shows the pattern of costs in relation to production; and Figure 4.6 shows the graphical representation of marginal cost (MC), average cost (AC) and average variable cost (AVC). By using Table 4.2 the student can plot these curves as an arithmetical example. Some characteristics of the cost curves can be observed from Table 4.2. The average cost curve (AC) slopes downward to the right as the units produced increase until it reaches its lowest point if eight or nine units are produced. At that output, the average cost is ₦20 each. After the ninth unit, the average cost increases and the average cost curve slopes upwards to the right. The average variable cost curve (AVC) behaves in the same manner as the average cost curve (AC) except that it reaches its lowest point if the output is seven. Similarly, the marginal cost curve (MC) slopes downward from the left to the right reaching its lowest point with

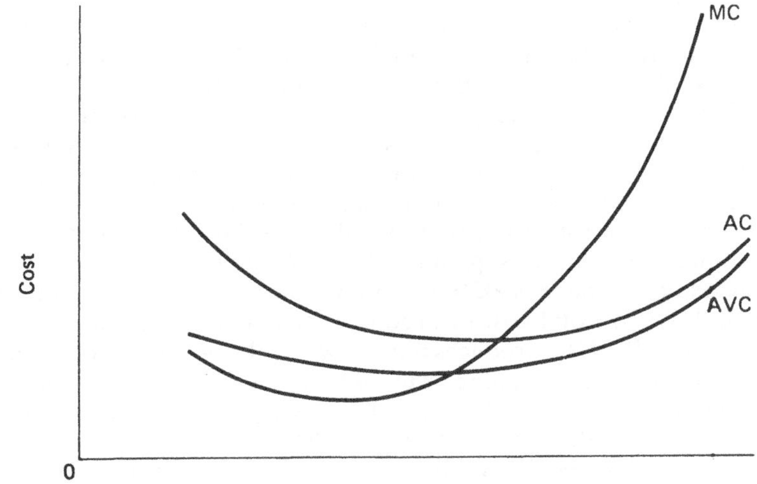

fig. 4.6

the production of the fourth unit. It rises for any larger output, cutting the average cost curve at its lowest point, that is, at the ninth unit for which the marginal cost is ₦20 and this is equal to the average cost of producing nine units, ₦20 each. The output at which

Table 4.2

Unit of 'X' Commodity	*Total Fixed Cost*	*Total Variable Cost*	*Total Cost*	*Average Fixed Cost*	*Average Variable Cost*	*Average Cost*	*Marginal Cost*
	FC	VC	TC	AFC	AVC	AC	MC
	(₦)	(₦)	(₦)	(₦)	(₦)	(₦)	(₦)
1	60	30	90	60·00	30·00	90	—
2	60	50	110	30·00	25·00	55	20
3	60	60	120	20·00	20·00	40	10
4	60	64	124	15·00	16·00	31	4
5	60	70	130	12·00	14·00	26	6
6	60	78	138	10·00	13·00	23	8
7	60	87	147	8·57	12·43	21	9
8	60	100	160	7·50	12·50	20	13
9	60	120	180	6·67	13·33	20	20
10	60	150	210	6·00	15·00	21	30
11	60	204	264	5·45	18·55	24	54
12	60	288	348	5·00	24·00	29	84
13	60	408	468	4·62	31·38	36	120
14	60	570	630	4·29	40·71	45	162
15	60	765	825	4·00	51·00	55	195

the marginal cost (MC) equals the average cost (AC) is significant for our production and price analysis as we shall see presently; it is always the minimum of the average cost (AC).

The producer or supplier under conditions of pure or perfect competition is influenced by his marginal cost in relation to price. He will decide to produce the quantity for which the price he gets in the market will be equal to his marginal cost.

The reason for this is that he will make his largest profit if he produces and sells this quantity. Thus, if the price in the market in the example above is ₦30, he will produce ten. These will sell for ₦300. As his total cost of producing ten is ₦210 he will make a profit of ₦90. If he produces nine he will make no more profit and if he produces less than nine or more than ten he will make a smaller profit. On eight, for instance, his total receipts will be ₦240 and his total cost ₦160, so his profit is only ₦80; and on eleven his total receipts will be ₦330 and his total cost ₦264, so his profit will be only ₦76.

Another important conclusion to be drawn from this analysis is that supply tends to vary with price. In our example, if the price rises to ₦54 each this producer would increase his output by 10 per cent, that is, to eleven units, and at price of ₦84 he would increase his output to twelve.

Supply will be influenced by market price for another reason. A fall in price will tend to contract supply, because the least efficient firms (marginal firms) who were just paying their way at the old price, when it was equal to their marginal cost (MC), will find that the new price is lower than their lowest possible average cost. They will then either restrict or cease production. The other, more efficient firms (intra-marginal firms), like the one in our example, will no longer produce that part of their output which is unprofitable at the new price, i.e. output having its marginal cost higher than the price. In the same manner, a rise in price will tend to increase supply, because firms with their minimum average cost below the old price will now find it profitable to produce if the price is now higher than their minimum average cost; and the production of existing producers (intra-marginal producers) such as the one in our example will increase output until their marginal cost equals the new higher price.

If we consider again a market for palm-oil, Table 4.3 and Figure 4.7 could be a supply schedule and the supply curve for this commodity. (The appropriate demand schedule could be that given in Table 4.1.) The supply curve rises from left to right because, as the price rises, so the quantity of the commodity offered for sale would be increased.

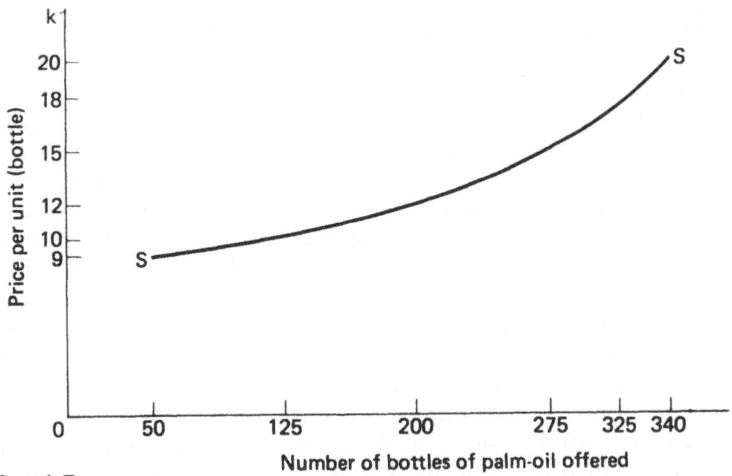

fig. 4.7

The figures illustrate that the supply of any commodity is the amount which will be offered for sale at a certain price, and that the supply price is the price required to induce the sellers to bring a given quantity of any commodity to market.

The relationship between supply and price indicates two tendencies. First, a rise in price increases the supply; and secondly, a fall in price decreases the supply. A combination of these two tendencies gives us the law of supply in a perfectly competitive market; that a rising price tends to increase the supply, and a falling price tends to decrease the supply of any commodity, all other things being equal.

ELASTICITY OF SUPPLY

Price changes cause supply to vary. They may produce great or small changes in the supply of any commodity; and through time, they may produce a quick or a slow response in supply. Elasticity of

Table 4.3 *Supply Schedule for Palm-Oil*

bottles supplied	*if the price per bottle is*
50	9 kobe
125	10 kobe
200	12 kobe
275	15 kobe
325	18 kobe
340	20 kobe

supply is the response of supply to price changes. If the supply of any commodity can readily be adjusted in time or amount to rising or falling prices, the supply of that commodity is likely to be elastic. For example, the supply of most manufactured goods, which can be quickly increased or reduced in volume to meet price changes, is *elastic* if the proportionate adjustment in quantity is greater than the proportionate change in price which brings it about. On the other hand, if the supply cannot be readily adjusted in time or amount to rising or falling prices and changes in price are greater than the proportionate changes in quantity, the supply of that commodity is *inelastic*. Commodities normally in inelastic supply include a number of agricultural products, particularly those which can be harvested only after lengthy periods of time, such as cocoa, rubber and palm products. There are also some manufactured goods in inelastic supply; for example, ships and heavy machinery, which take a considerable time to produce and so are slow to adjust supply to changes in price. The mathematical method of calculating an arithmetical measure of elasticity of supply is to divide the proportionate change in quantity supplied by the proportionate change in the price causing the change in the quantity.

Elasticity of supply depends on a number of factors. First, if a producer is able to sell in a number of different markets, allowing for transport costs, his goods will tend to be elastic in supply in each market, because a rise or fall in the price in any one of his markets will induce him to bring more goods to that market or take them to other markets in case of a fall in price. Secondly, the ease with which a manufacturer or producer can change from the production of one article to another affects elasticity of supply; the more easily he can change from one commodity to another the more elastic will be the supply of any items he decides to produce. Similarly, if a producer can turn over his specialised equipment readily to other uses, the supply of this product will tend to be relatively elastic. Thirdly, if supply depends on a long period of production, supply tends to be inelastic. The supply of cocoa or oranges, for example, tends to be inelastic, at least in the short period, since cocoa- and orange-trees cannot bear fruit overnight. Fourthly, if in the short term it will cause any business a great loss to cease production altogether, the supply of the article it produces will tend to be relatively inelastic. For example, at a period of industrial depression, a heavy steel firm which has a certain minimum output if it operates at all will try to remain in business by continuing in production and selling some of its output even at prices below the cost of production until higher prices can be obtained on the market to make it profitable once more.

Just as in the case of demand, changes may also take place in supply independently of price changes, but in response to changes in other things. Such changes in supply conditions result in a rise or fall in supply. This will cause the supply curve to shift either to the right, to S_1S_1, in the case of a rise, or to the left, to S_2S_2 in the case of a fall, as shown in Figure 4.8.

Economies of large-scale production may bring about a fall in costs of production, thus lowering the marginal cost if the supply of the commodity is increased. On the other hand, any measure which increases costs, for example, taxation, will tend to reduce supply at any given price. Further, an increase in the number of suppliers will tend to increase the total supply of the commodity concerned, all other things being equal, and the total supply will fall if the number of suppliers decreases.

Mention must be made of two popular notions associated with supply, namely, joint supply and composite supply. Commodities are in joint supply if they can only be produced together. If one commodity is a by-product of the other, it will be impossible to increase the supply of one without simultaneously increasing the supply of the other; for example cotton and cotton-seed or mutton and wool. In the case of the latter example, it may be noted that wool can be obtained without necessarily producing mutton; but mutton cannot be increased without necessarily causing an increase in the supply of wool. A student must be careful, therefore, in his choice of examples. Commodities are in composite supply when they are substitutes for one another. For example, butter can be

fig. 4.8

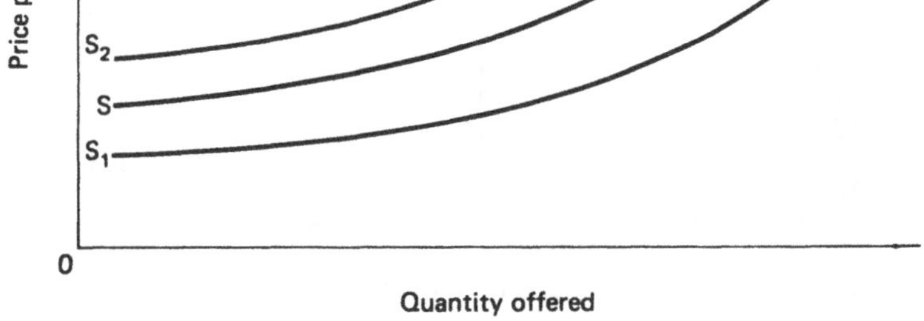

substituted for margarine as a cooking fat; and cocoa for tea or coffee as a beverage. In the case of composite supply, prices of substitutes tend to move in sympathy. If the price of one or two commodities in composite supply falls, the demand for the other commodity is likely also to fall and its price will also fall.

THE PRICE MECHANISM

The price mechanism reconciles the conflicting interests of the buyer and the seller. It is the mechanism by which prices adjust themselves to the pressure of demand and supply and in their turn operate to keep demand and supply in balance. The mechanism fosters the free association of buyers and sellers in a market, each side concluding such bargains as it finds satisfactory at the ruling price. The buyers want to buy at the lowest price possible for a given quantity while the sellers want to sell at the highest price they can get for a given supply. In other words, the buyer will favour the downward movement of the price, while the seller will favour the upward movement. It follows, therefore, that there must normally be a price at which the interests of both parties meet.

The market equilibrium is achieved when the supply intentions of all the sellers together in the market match the demand intentions of the buyers in the market. It is the meeting point of effective supply on the one hand, and effective demand on the other. The market price when the market is in equilibrium with no pressure for the price to rise or fall is called the equilibrium price. If we combine our demand schedule in Table 4.1 and the supply schedule in Table 4.3, we shall be able to discover the equilibrium price in the market for palm-oil. This is shown in Table 4.4 and graphically on Figure 4.9.

Table 4.4 *Demand and Supply Schedules for Palm-Oil*

demand (bottles)	*at a price per bottle of (k)*	*supply (bottles)*
350	7	—
300	9	50
250	10	125
200	12	200
150	15	275
125	17	—
—	18	325
100	20	340

The equilibrium price is established at 12 k (point E) where the demand curve DD cuts the supply curve SS. At point E, the price of

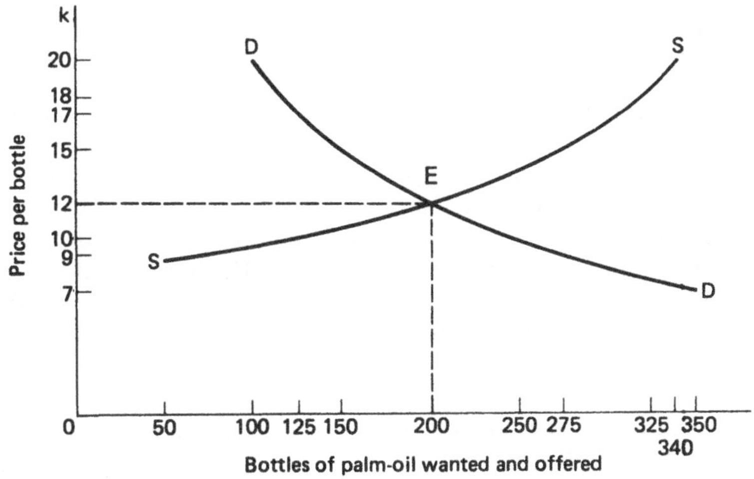

fig. 4.9

palm-oil per bottle is 12 k and the quantity which the buyers are prepared to take is 200 bottles, while the sellers are also prepared to offer for sale 200 bottles. Price is determined by the balancing of demand and supply. What this really means is that the market price is determined by striking a balance between what an article costs to produce if the sellers are the producers – marginal cost is the operative cost – on the other hand; and what the article is worth to the consumer – the marginal utility is the operative measure of worth – on the other hand.

fig. 4.10

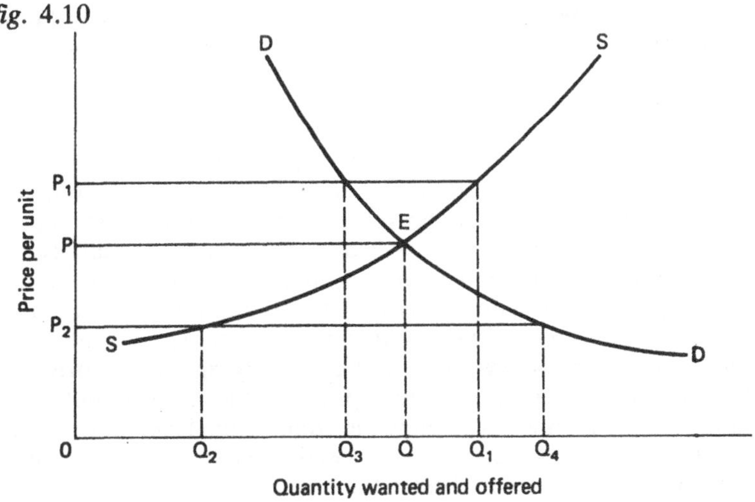

On Figure 4.10, the equilibrium price is OP, while the quantity bought at this price is OQ. At a higher price, say OP_1, demand stands at OQ_3 which falls short of the supply OQ_1 at that price. At a lower price, say OP_2, demand at OQ_4 is in excess of supply which would only be OQ_2 at that price. In attempting to satisfy the little demand that exists at price OP_1, if the price were to be as high as that competition will develop among the suppliers leading to a lowering of the price until it reached the equilibrium price of OP. On the other hand, were the price to be as low as OP_2, there would be a very large excess of demand over supply and competition among buyers to secure some of the small supply available would lead to a rising price until market equilibrium was established at price OP.

GOVERNMENT INTERVENTION IN THE DETERMINATION OF MARKET PRICE

In exceptional cases, the government may intervene in the determination of the market price, in an attempt to protect the producer or the consumer as the case may be. If it is thought that excess supply over demand may jeopardise the business interests of the producers, which in turn may affect adversely the general economic progress of the country, the government or its agency may buy at a higher price and deliberately sell the total supply at a lower price, thus incurring losses. For example, the Cocoa Marketing Boards in Ghana and in Nigeria have on occasion bought cocoa from the cocoa farmers at higher prices than the prices for which cocoa sold in the world market.

The government may also fix prices below the current equilibrium prices for certain commodities in an effort to check an excessive rise in prices. This is usuåally referred to as a 'price control' policy. The main purpose may be to protect the consumers against unnecessary exploitation by producers or the middlemen, particularly at a period of temporary shortages in the supply of the commodities concerned, or it may be an attempt to curb the effects of inflation. It must be added, however, that such a price control policy may not be effective if nothing is done to increase the supply or to reduce the spending power of consumers. Indeed, in cases where the supply has not been increased after some time, a black market, that is, illegal sales, is likely to develop, and consumers may either find themselves going without or illegally paying a higher price than the original market equilibrium price. If the government or any other agency fixes a price below the equilibrium level then, demand being in excess of supply at that price, the quantity available for sale will go to those who were first in the queue; or who by law, if any law exists, have priority claims over the others; or to those willing to buy illegally in a black market. It may eventually lead to some form of rationing per head or per unit of the family, in order to ensure that supply is fairly distributed.

It is essential to examine the time element in the price mechanism. Generally, demand adjusts itself more quickly to price changes than does supply, since consumers can very easily switch their spending from one commodity to another whereas changes in methods and in the volume of production usually take much longer.

One useful method of analysis in economics is to consider the short period and the long period. A period so short that there is no time for the total supply of an industry to alter appreciably is known as the *short period*. The *long period* is a period long enough to allow a full response of supply to a change in prices, so price will always reach its equilibrium level in the long period. We can say, therefore, that in the short-period demand (or utility) dominates the fixing of prices. This is not to say that demand alone determines price, but that the influence of demand in the determination of prices is stronger in the short period than that of supply. However, in the long period, supply (or costs) become more important in the determination of prices, as only in the long period will supply have fully reacted to changes in demand and in prices. The length of time or the fixed plant and organisation required for the production of certain commodities may be such that their supply cannot readily be increased. In such cases, therefore, the supply is relatively fixed in the short period, and price will be determined largely by the pressure of demand upon the fixed supply. But in all cases the elasticities of both supply and demand are expressed by the supply and demand curves and the price is determined by their interaction.

In the long period, there is a full response of demand and supply to changes in prices. In the long period, the reactions of buyers to changes in prices would have been completely communicated to the suppliers who would then adjust their supplies. If production is to continue price must be high enough to cover costs and allow for some profits. The longer the period, all other things being equal, the more important becomes the influence of supply (or costs) over price.

PERFECT COMPETITION

As already mentioned, the economic system of a free enterprise economy is often described as the competitive system. There are a number of assumptions made when describing a competitive system. One assumption is that any individual is free to engage in any trade or practise any profession. The system is supposed to be based on an uninhibited rivalry between buyers, sellers and factors of production. As we have already noticed in Chapter 1, the competitive system is motivated by self-interest. Above all, in a competitive system, government interference is presumed to be minimal, if any.

Competition can, however, be either perfect or imperfect. We shall start by explaining what perfect competition means in a market. Under the conditions of perfect competition it is assumed that (a) homogeneous commodities are offered for sale by competitors and that the commodity of one supplier is a perfect substitute for that of another; (b) there is perfect knowledge among the sellers and the buyers about all market conditions, including costs and prices; (c) no one supplier is able to influence price perceptibly by expanding or contracting his output, and no one buyer is able to influence the price either by buying in large or small quantities; (d) the suppliers are able to purchase the factors of production they require on equal terms in free competition; and (e) there is also the free entry and exit of producers to industries and markets: in other words, any intending producer can join the market without any impediment, and any existing producer is also free to stop production and leave the market.

It is rare to find all the assumed conditions of perfect competition to be present in any market. The products offered for sale are usually not homogeneous. This is particularly so in cases of agricultural products and locally prepared indigenous foodstuffs. It must be realised that anything at all, for instance, colour or size, which influences the consumer to prefer one type of the same commodity to another makes such commodities non-homogeneous. Also, even when there is a large number of suppliers, one or a small group may be able perceptibly to influence price. However, the concept of perfect competition is essential for any understanding of economic theory. In order to understand the significance of the deviations from perfect competition, one needs to grasp the basic conditions of perfect competition.

Under perfect competition, a supplier is faced with a given market price, which is determined for him by the interaction of supply and demand as explained above. Figure 4.11 shows the market position of a producer in a perfect market. The demand curve of a producer in a perfect market is a perfectly elastic demand curve as shown on Figure 4.12. This means that the individual supplier can sell any quantity in the market at the ruling market price. However, the quantity which an individual supplier is willing to supply to the market is governed by his marginal cost. As one can see on Figure 4.11, the marginal cost curve (MC) cuts the demand curve (PD) at

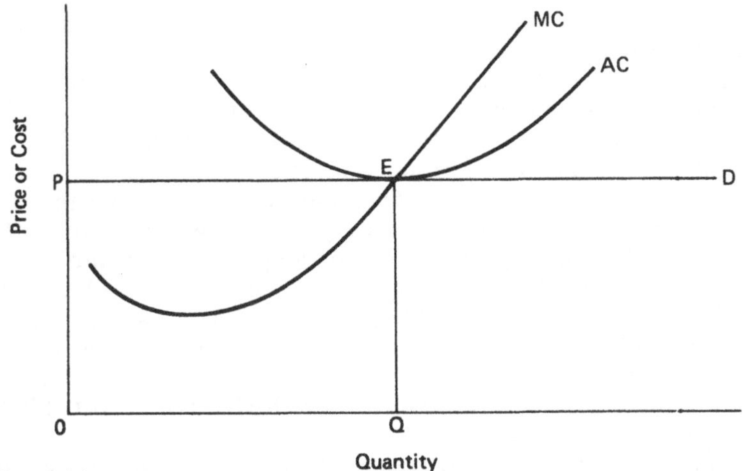

fig. 4.11

E. E also indicates output at which the marginal cost equals the average cost (MC = AC). If the supplier supplies quantity OQ at the ruling market price OP (QE) his total revenue will cover his total costs which for this analysis must be taken also to include a normal profit. If he produces any quantity less than OQ, his total receipts will be less than his total costs and he will discover that only if he expands output and sales to OQ will he cover the whole of his costs. However, if he attempts to produce more than OQ, his marginal cost will be higher than the price and thus he will make a loss on the quantities produced in excess of OQ. It follows, there-

4.12

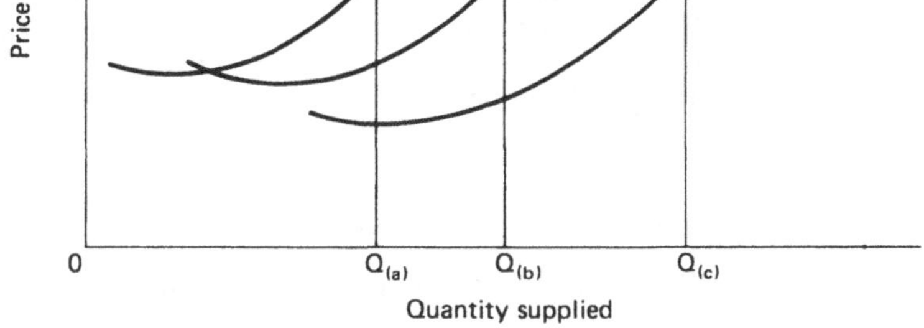

fore, that the most favourable quantity for him to produce is OQ. We have already mentioned that the costs of employing factors of production are the same to all producers. The question which one might ask is whether all the producers under perfect competition supply an equal quantity. The answer is that the quantity supplied by each producer varies according to his personal efficiency in combining his factors of production. If a producer is less efficient than his rivals his marginal cost per unit will be higher than theirs for a given output, his marginal cost curve (MC) will lie to the left of theirs and he will supply less for a smaller profit. On the other hand, if he is more efficient, his marginal cost curve (MC) will lie to the right of his rivals, and he will supply more with a larger profit. In Figure 4.12, the firm with the marginal cost curve MCa is the least efficient, producing OQa; the firm with MCb is more efficient and its production is OQb; while the firm with MCc is the most efficient firm with the output OQc.

If one goes back again to examine Figure 4.11, it will be seen that the MC curve cuts the AC curve at its lowest point E. It is at this output that the marginal cost is equal to average cost and each is equal to the price. It must be mentioned that, since the demand curve of the firm is perfectly elastic, there is no distinction between the average revenue (AR), that is, total revenue divided by the units sold, and the marginal revenue (MR), that is, the addition to total revenue generated by the sale of an additional unit; both are represented by the demand curve (PD). At the equilibrium point E, therefore, not only is the MR equal to the AR, it is also the point at which each is equal to the MC and AC.

Under perfect competition, equilibrium is at the output which provides equal profit to all the suppliers concerned it they are all equally efficient, and this profit is the minimum which will induce each firm to remain in the industry. If there is any excess profit made, more firms will be attracted to the industry, thus increasing output; and if demand remains the same, the price will fall. This will continue until the extra profit is eliminated and a position of equilibrium in the industry is established. It follows, therefore, that demand will push profit down to the minimum point which just keeps the individual producer in business. The profit made at this point is called the *normal profit.* In the long run normal profit must be made if the producers are to be persuaded to continue to function.

IMPERFECT COMPETITION AND MONOPOLY

It is reasonable to deduce that whenever any of the conditions

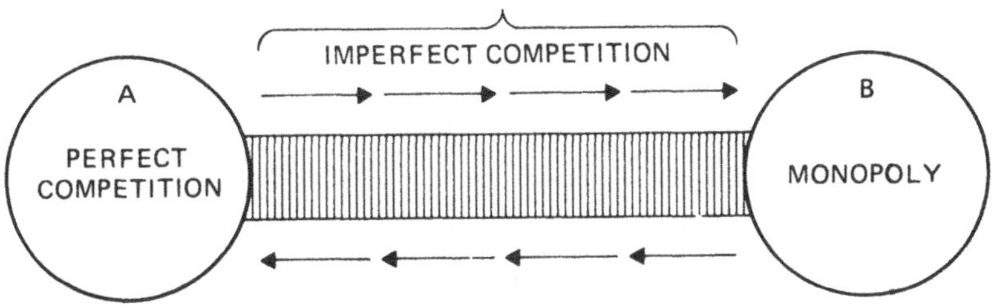

fig. 4.13

assumed under perfect competition is not fulfilled, then imperfect competition prevails. In Figure 4.13, circle A represents perfect competition, and circle B represents monopoly. The circles represent two extreme positions in market competition. Any movement from circle A to the right towards circle B creates imperfections. The degree of imperfection varies between circles A and B. The further the movement away from circle A in the direction of circle B, the greater the degree of imperfection. If a monopoly situation is broken up, either by government action, or by some changes in market conditions, such as an influx of new producers, there will be a movement from circle B towards circle A. Imperfections can be reduced, therefore, until a position of perfect competition is reached.

In order to simplify our analysis, we shall discuss the market position of a monopolist – the extreme case of imperfect competition. The main interest of the monopolist is to maximise his profit. He has the absolute control of supply. The monopolist can both decide his own price, and decide the quantity to be placed on the market, but he cannot of course make the consumers buy that quantity at the price he determines. He can only sell the amount they are willing to buy at that price. He controls supply but not demand. So he can either fix the price, then produce what can be sold at that price, or he can fix the quantity and accept the price at which consumers are willing to buy that quantity.

The long-run equilibrium position of a monopolist with an abnormal profit can be explained in terms of his revenue and costs as shown on Figure 4.14. In the case of monopoly the demand curve for the firm is the same as the demand curve for the industry. The average revenue curve AR represents the demand curve of the

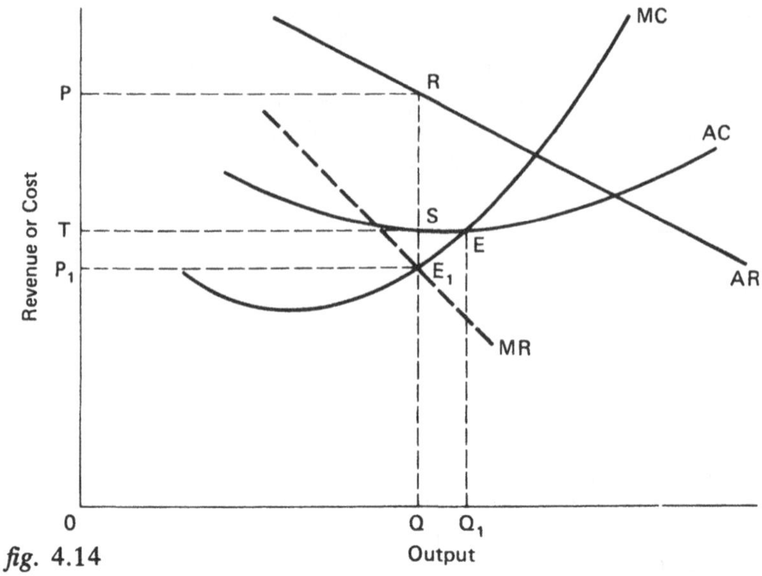

fig. 4.14

monopolist. The marginal revenue curve MR lies below the AR curve, because if he wishes to increase his sales, he has to reduce his price progressively, and this leads to marginal revenue being less than the price at which each additional unit is sold. With the objective of maximising profit, the monopolist keeps an eye on his marginal cost and his marginal revenue. If he is to maximise his profit, his marginal cost must be neither more nor less than his marginal revenue. The monopolist will produce the output at which the marginal cost curve (MC) cuts the marginal revenue curve (MR), that is at point E_1 in the diagram where MC = MR. At point E_1, the quantity supplied is OQ_1. It can be noticed that an output lower than OQ the rate at which revenue increases with increased output is higher than the rate at which costs increase with increased output; therefore the monopolist will increase his profit with increased production. Also, if the monopolist produces more than OQ, the rate at which revenue increases will be less than the rate at which costs increase; therefore, profit will decline with output in excess of OQ. It is an important conclusion, therefore, that profits will be at their maximum when MR = MC. The price which the monopolist charges is $OP(Q_1R)$. It is at this price that abnormal profit is maximised. Point R represents the amount demanded on the demand curve (AR), which also corresponds with the amount supplied (OQ).

The total revenue to the monopolist is represented by the area OQ_1RP, and his total costs are represented by the area OQ_1ST. His abnormal profit, therefore, is represented by the area TSRP. It is important to note that the monopoly output is not necessarily the optimum output. The monopoly output represented by OQ is the output which ensures maximum profit, while the output OQ_1 is at the point where the average cost curve is at the minimum. This might be regarded as more advantageous from the point of view of society, and certainly of the consumers, but it would mean that the monopolist would be making less profit than he would at the higher price and restricted output.

Perfectly monopoly is rarely found in practice. The nearest one gets to a perfect monopoly is a legal monopoly, which is granted by the government and enforced by law. For example, patent laws and copyright laws exist to safeguard inventions and published works. There is also the creation, by law, of statutory corporations for the purpose of providing some basic services to the country; for example, water and electricity. Even then, such corporations have no absolute monopoly power. If one takes the example of water, the water corporation can only control the supply of pipe-borne water, but cannot stop people from drawing water from wells or streams. Similarly, the use of various types of lamps and candles breaks the absolute monopoly of the electricity corporation. The nearest example to perfect monopoly in West Africa is, perhaps, the West African Examinations Council which controls nearly all examinations from the primary school level to external degree examinations. The only exception to its monopoly is the internal examination system of the West African universities.

THE PRICE MECHANISM IN WEST AFRICAN MARKETS: 'HIGGLING'

The practical application of the theoretical analysis of the price mechanism should be explained in the context of the West African markets. It is the usual practice of foreign wholesale and retail firms, such as Kingsway Stores and Leventis, to fix the prices of their products and to employ price-tags to indicate such prices. Customers buying in their stores are expected to pick what items they want and to pay the prices indicated on them. However, most of the sellers in local markets and a few foreign businesses, for example the Lebanese and Syrian stores, conduct market exchange transactions by higgling or bargaining. By the very nature of higgling or bargaining a great deal of market imperfection arises, thus leading to the existence of different prices at the same time and place for basically the same commodity or service. The main source of market imperfection as far as higgling is concerned is the variation in the ability to bargain. The harder one can drive a bargain, all other things being equal, the nearer one is to paying the competitive price; and the weaker one's bargaining ability, the more likely one is to pay above the competitive price. Bargaining power is also influenced by the social system – inherent and acquired. The inherent social factor arises mainly from the extended family system, and alongside this is the aspect of friendship. The acquired social factor is the differences in wealth, income and social status.

The concept of a fair price is expected to operate when a producer sells to his relations or friends. It must be emphasised, however, that each producer is always conscious of his cost of production and the need to make a profit when fixing his price. There are occasions when the minimum price for a product is fixed by a market guild, for example the market women; and no sale is to be made below this price. A seller who sells below this price is usually penalised. In most cases, there is no fixed maximum price for any commodity. In other cases where no price agreements are made, there is the cost of production to guide the seller. It is possible, therefore, for the seller to operate his price policy within a wide margin above the cost of production on the one hand and above the normal or agreed price on the other hand. Undoubtedly, the preferential treatment given to relatives and friends by sellers introduces a great deal of imperfection into the operation of the price mechanism.

Apart from relatives and friends, the seller is always prepared to operate price discrimination based on the social status of his customers. In this respect, a number of status symbols, such as the car, good and expensive dresses, high-heeled shoes and wigs for women, help the sellers to identify the rich from whom high prices may be demanded, In addition to these, the manner or attitude towards the seller also makes all the difference between being asked a higher or just the normal price. A woman who speaks English to an indigenous seller instead of the local language automatically invites the seller to exercise price discrimination against her. The use of English language is associated with affluence. Often the sex of the buyer also makes some difference to the price which the producer attempts to charge. It is thought that men have little bargaining ability, because they are less patient than women. Frequently one finds that men are asked to pay higher prices than women for the same commodities or services and often do pay them.

Chapter 5

The National Income

MEASUREMENT OF THE NATIONAL INCOME

In recent years, there has been an increasing interest in the concepts and uses of national income measurements as basic elements in the explanation of economic processes and guides for government policy. The national income is an aggregative measure of a nation's productive effort over a given period, usually a year. The total flow of national wealth produced annually by the factors of production (land, labour, capital and enterprise) is known as the national income or national dividend. The examination of its composition reveals the sources of this production and its disposition. Almost every aspect of economics is in some way closely related to national income, and the statistics on the composition of national income, and the statistics on the composition of national income are proving very useful in showing the relationship between these various fields.

It will be easier to understand the exact meaning of the national income, which is the sum of all the individual incomes in a nation, if we first examine what constitutes an individual's income.

It is customary to think of an individual's income as the money or goods which he receives. In this way, wages and salaries which labour receives for its services constitute income. Interest or dividends which a person receives on his money or securities is income to that person. Even the vegetables which a person raises on his farm or garden are income, because they are goods which he receives as a reward for his farming or gardening. It could be said, therefore, that all inflow of goods or money or increases of one's assets is income. There are two aspects of an individual's income which a student must watch carefully in estimating the total income. These are sales of assets and gifts. If a person sells some of his possessions or property the resulting inflow of money is not regarded as income. The property which was sold was merely converted into cash; and this increase in cash has been matched by a corresponding decrease in property. However, if a good is purchased at one price and sold later at a higher price by a person who is not ordinarily a dealer, the gain which has been made cannot be considered strictly as income but rather as a capital gain. The distinction between capital gains and income is not always clear-cut. If a person, in his ordinary business, continually buys and sells goods, for example, as a retailer, in order to make profit, such profit would be classified as income. On the other hand, if a man sells a plot of land for ₦1000·00 which he bought ten years ago for ₦250·00, it cannot be said that he has received an income of ₦750·00 when he sells it; instead he is regarded as having made a capital gain of ₦750·00.

Similarly, debt repayment is not regarded as income but merely as a change in the form of assets. Before the debt is actually paid, the creditor holds 'a promise to pay' by the debtor. When the debt is paid, the promise to pay is given up in exchange for money. The creditor then has no greater amount of assets than he had previously and the debtor has no less assets than he had before redeeming the promise to pay.

Gifts or charity payments, strictly speaking, are income to the recipient, as they represent a net addition to the assets of that individual. On the other hand, such payments have to be deducted from the income of the donor. Gifts or charity payments are not regarded as expenditure of income, since such payments are not made as a result of any direct benefit conferred on the donor: they represent a transfer of income from one individual or organisation or country to another. If a man receives an income of ₦2,000·00 for example, and decides to make a gift of ₦500·00 to a relative, then from the point of view of the economy it would be counting income twice if the ₦500·00 were considered income both of the relative and of the donor. For the computation of national income of a country, it is preferable to exclude gifts from the income of the recipient, and thus not have to deduct them from the income of the donor.

It follows from what has been said that if one wants to measure the national income through the income method (one of the three main methods of measuring the national income), double counting of incomes must be avoided when dealing with changes in the form of individual's assets and when considering gifts and charity payments.

In the measurement of the national income through the income method, money-incomes are by far the most important. However, incomes in a broad sense need not be in the form of money. Such incomes as wages, interests, rents and profits (dividends) are usually paid in the form of money, and are, in those forms, calculated as a part of income. But goods and services which an individual receives or produces for himself are also income. For instance, a farmer who produces a part of his own food, as well as a cash crop will have a total income which is equal to his money income from the cash crop plus the value of the food which he has produced for his own consumption. A person who built his own house and lives in it should include as a part of his income the imputed rent of the house. Imputed rent is the amount is would cost to rent the house after deducting the expenses of ownership such as taxes, upkeep and depreciation; and this is really income to the individual. If he rented the house and lived elsewhere, this house would yield him income to this amount. In addition, a careful evaluation of the income of a family would have to take into account the value of the services of the housewife, and even the value of the odd jobs done by members of the family and the domestic servants, although these elements of real income are not easily valued in money terms and so are excluded from the conventional computation of the national income.

In developing countries, particularly in West Africa, quite a large proportion of income is created daily which is excluded from the calculation of the individual's income, and thus from the national income. Nature is very kind to the people of West Africa with the result that most of the staple foodstuffs can be grown in the back garden. In most cases a deliberate planting of many of these crops is not necessary. Many crops, such as red pepper, tomatoes, vegetables, oranges, pawpaw and mangoes grow easily even if their seeds are carelessly dropped in the garden or in the bush. The value of such back-garden crops grown in spare time which do not enter into direct money exchange does not affect the calculation of the individual's income. Also, the extended family system and the social structure of West Africa make it obligatory for one to be of service to relations or friends without necessarily asking for a money reward. A man who takes his car to a mechanic, a friend, for repairs is usually not charged anything or charged only half the usual price for such repairs. But estimates are made of the output of these people who are almost entirely dependent on the subsistence economy, which also does not enter into direct money exchange, and these estimates converted to money values are included in the national income.

A multitude of such imputed incomes exists in West Africa. Indeed, if all such imputed incomes were included, any of the West

African countries would have a substantially higher value of its national income than the officially calculated value.

The orthodox economist has limited the definition of individual income and that of the national income in order to make statistical measurement in the common unit of money possible, reasonably accurate and internationally comparable. It is the force of practical necessity which has caused this limitation. It would be extremely difficult, if not impossible, to calculate the value of all the self-produced and self-consumed goods and services which are produced in small amounts by people whose major activity is production for the money economy. The student should always keep in mind, however, that there are other elements in real income in addition to those included in the statistical measurements. A definition of income which is more easily calculated and will generally be more practical in studying the economic system can be obtained by including as income only those elements which arise from economic activities for which money exchange is involved plus an estimate of the value of the output of the subsistence economy and excluding such items as work done within the home and social income, such as improved environment and better roads. Thus money payments for salaries, wages, interest and profits would all be included as income payments; and to these may be added the value of home-grown produce consumed by farmers and the output of those living almost entirely on the subsistence economy. Unfortunately, present statistics do not include such other income which is paid in goods or services rather than money, such as imputed rent and the board of domestic servants, but the principle nevertheless is that by adding up the incomes of all individuals, a total figure is obtained which, from the point of view of the economy represents total income enjoyed by the nation – the national income.

From the point of view of any individual, the calculation of income through the source is merely one aspect of his income. An individual's income can also be considered as a sum which is used either for spending, paying taxes or saving. One can calculate the sum of all the individual incomes and thus the national income by applying the expenditure and savings method. Suppose an individual has an annual income of ₦3,000 and he is asked how he got it. Logically, he might give the following tabulation:

₦2,800	salary, per annum
180	from rented house, per annum
10	interest received on savings
10	dividends received
₦3,000	Total income received for the year

On the other hand, if one asked him what he did with his income of ₦3,000, he might give the following accounting:

₦2,000	Maintenance of the family (expenditure on durable and non-durable goods)
300	children's school fees
200	financial help to relations (gifts)
200	premium on insurance (car and life)
150	payment of income tax
2,850	Total expenditure for the year
150	savings
₦3,000	Total

It can be seen, therefore, that income can be considered from either point of view and it would be quite possible to calculate the national income either from the total expenditures made by individuals plus income tax payments plus personal savings, if any, or from the total incomes received.

The payment of taxes as part of an individual's expenditure needs some explanation. Individuals pay money in the form of taxes to the government and the government pays money in the form of subsidies to individuals, such as aid to farmers, free health services, pensions to retired workers and relief to the unemployed where it exists, as it does in countries such as the United Kingdom. If all the tax revenue collected by the government is paid out to individuals in the form of subsidies, then the government would merely be an agent in the redistribution of incomes between individuals, and could not be said to be the recipient of any net payments from individuals. Likewise, from the point of view of the individuals, income would have been shifted around, but the total amount available for expenditure by individuals as a group would remain unchanged. It should be noted, therefore, that subsidies are somewhat similar to tax refunds. If one considers the individuals in a country as a group, it is clear that subsidies give back a portion of the money which was originally paid in taxes. When calculating the national income through the expenditure and savings method only net taxes are included, that is, total taxes minus all forms of subsidies given out to the citizens by the government.

The measurement of the national income which we have arrived at so far does not refer to national output. In order to understand the measurement of the national income through the output or production method, therefore, the nature of national output must first be described.

National output arises from the process of production which is carried out by individuals and enterprises in the economy. No economic goods or services can be created without a productive unit which is responsible for their creation. The term productive unit or enterprise is used broadly to cover the production of all goods and services. Manufacturers, wholesalers and retailers are easily identified as productive enterprises. Furthermore, farmers, carpenters, blacksmiths, woodcarvers and many others create goods; while doctors, lawyers, teachers and other professional people create services. Consequently they are all considered as productive units since their products and services are included in the national output. Finally, local government corporations and state, central or federal agencies provide services in such forms as law enforcement, roads and health; and in order to count all goods and services in the economy they are classified as productive enterprises. A worker who is employed in an enterprise is not considered as a separate productive unit. His effort is included in the output of the enterprise or firm for which he works, and he is merely a member of this enterprise or firm. Thus it may be seen that the definition of a productive unit or enterprise is such that each individual's work is counted along with other output in the enterprise in which he is employed, or else the individual is considered as a productive unit in his own right and his work is then counted separately. Care must be taken to ensure that no productive effort is classified in both ways so as to avoid double counting.

One of the major problems of calculating the national income through the production or output method is that of determining the value to be attached to the final products. The output of each productive unit or enterprise can be calculated at its market price; that is, the price for which it is sold in the market. In the case of government agencies where there is usually no market price for output, one method of valuation is to calculate the total costs of producing the goods and services. The total value of all outputs thus obtained would at first glance seem to be the value of the national output, but there are a number of objections to using this as a method of measurement. First, the market price is liable to fluctuations. A temporary fall in supply, other things being equal, will lead to a rise in price. Similarly, a temporary fall in demand, with supply remaining unchanged, will lead to a fall in price. If such temporary fluctuations in prices are widespread when the value of the national output is being measured, the value of some products will be inflated (those enjoying abnormally high prices) while the value of some other products (those having abnormally low prices) will be understated. The effect on the value of the national income is even worse if the general level of market prices moves to either extreme – abnormally high or low. If the value of the national output is measured through market prices, it may give a false picture of the economy by either inflating or underestimating the total value.

Secondly, past production would be included in the value of many goods which appear as products in the period when the national output is being measured. The steel which appears in a durable product may have come from iron ore which had been mined sometime in the past.

Thirdly, the gross value of all goods and services produced contains considerable double counting of products. The sales or the market price of a loaf of bread, for example, includes the cost of the materials used, although these same materials have previously appeared on the market as separate products themselves. The grain is sold by the farmer to the grain dealer, the grain dealer in turn sells it to the miller, and the miller in turn includes the cost of the grain in the price for which he sells the finished flour to the baker. Thus, it is evident that the value of the grain going into the bread would be represented at least four times. Products which pass through a number of processes, therefore, and are sold and resold many times in different forms, add up to far more than their final value when they eventually reach consumers. In order to eliminate past production and double counting from the calculation of the value of the national output, the methods of cost analysis are adopted. Thus the value of each product that makes up the national output may be represented by a complete listing of all the items of cost, plus profit; and duplication can then be eliminated and allowance made for stocks brought in from past periods or carried forward to future periods. The net output of each enterprise after duplication has been deducted is the value added by the enterprise. The total of all values added is the national output without any double counting.

CONCEPT OF VALUE ADDED

Calculation of the national income through the production method is, then, achieved by using the concept of value added. A final product which emerges from a factory or a workshop is more valuable than the semi-finished goods and raw materials which were used up in production. As we have already mentioned in Chapter 2, the process of production is the adding of value to those goods and materials which are of greater use if transformed in some way. The activities of a business unit or firm are concerned with the adding of value to the raw materials and semi-manufactured goods which have been purchased from other producers. Thus a baker by making bread has added value to flour, fuel and electricity, all of which were purchased from other producers and used up in the process of production. Value added, therefore, represents that part of the value of the commodity which is created within the enterprise by that particular unit. The value added can be obtained by subtracting the cost of the goods, materials and services purchased from other enterprises by the enterprise from the value of the product which it eventually sells itself.

Among the various business units in the economy, there is a considerable variation in the proportion of the total value of a product represented by value added. In industries such as the motor industry, where for the most part the materials purchased are components and parts, value added is relatively small. In the case of the farmer, he purchases fertiliser, spraying materials and farm tools but these are a relatively small proportion of the value of his crops. As they are bought from other enterprises they are deducted from the value of his production in order to determine his value added, just as the components and parts bought by the motor manufacturer are deducted from the value of the motor cars produced by him.

THE GROSS NATIONAL PRODUCT (GNP)

From the explanation above it will be realised that value added may be used as a measure of the production by a productive enterprise or unit over a given period of time. The value of products produced in a prior time-period are not included in value added, since only the amount by which goods have been increased in value in the relevant period due to economic activity is considered. There is no double counting in the concept of value added, because all products which have appeared as the output of other producers have been excluded. An addition of the value added in every productive enterprise or unit in the economy is equal to the total production which occurs in the economy over a period, usually one year: this is the gross domestic product (GDP). The GDP is the measure of a country's economic output for the year under consideration. In order to obtain the gross national product one has to add the net income earned abroad, i.e. GNP is value added plus income earned from abroad by the country's nationals minus the income transferred abroad by expatriates.

The term gross is used because not all of current production is available for current consumption if the economy is to continue operating at the same level. In the value added of a firm, for example, depreciation of its capital has not been considered as an item of cost. This means that there has been a decrease in the value of machines, equipment and buildings which were used in the process of production, but no account has been taken of it. Thus goods which were produced in the past (machines, equipment, buildings) have been partly worn out in the current period and so have decreased in value. Capital goods produced in another period have been consumed and have given services which have contributed to present production. If the value of capital is maintained by setting aside a portion of present production equal in value to the capital consumed – depreciation – then the remaining amount of present output will not include the contribution of capital equipment which was created in the past. In other words, to calculate the amount of goods produced in a given period the amount of depreciation of capital is one of the items which must be deducted from gross production if we want to know what the net national product is. Similarly, business taxes can be considered as sources of revenue to the government for maintaining our social and political system intact, just as depreciation expense maintains the value of capital equipment intact. Thus business taxes would represent the depreciation which has occurred on the social capital and must be deducted from the gross national product (GNP) to arrive at the net national product.

In adjusting the GNP so that it will refer to production attributed to current productive effort, it has been seen that two items are subtracted – depreciation and business taxes. After both depreciation and business taxes have been deducted from the GNP, the remainder may be considered as the net real income which has been created in the current period and is attributed solely to the efforts of the current period. In other words, the GNP less capital consumption is equal to the net national product (NNP) which is the true national income.

FACTORS AFFECTING THE NATIONAL INCOME

The volume of a country's national income is affected by a number of factors. First is the country's natural resources, such as its mineral deposits and the fertility of its soil. A country which is predominantly agricultural normally has adequate rich soil for farming and may be able to improve the available farm lands for expanding agricultural production. The use of fertilisers, the establishment of irrigation schemes and the mechanisation of agriculture all help to increase production, which in turn means an increase in the national income of a basically agricultural country. Also, the mineral deposits of a country can add to its national income. One should distinguish between mineral deposits that are known to exist and those that are known to exist and are exploited. For example, there had been some indication since the 1920s that petroleum existed in Nigeria, although the first commercial petroleum was not produced until 1956. While petroleum had not contributed to the national income of Nigeria before 1956, it has since become increasingly important in the Nigerian national accounts, but if and when the oil wells dry up, petroleum will cease to contribute to the national income. The point, therefore, is that the exploitation of known mineral deposits enlarges the national income, although minerals are eventually exhausted and so must be regarded as a wasting asset.

Secondly, the skill and energy of the working population of a country influence the national income. Whether a country is an agricultural or industrial country, its people must have the ability and willingness to work before any national income is created. Even if nature is so kind as to make it possible to grow any kind of crop on any land in a country, the productive effort of labour is still needed in order to create the national income. Similarly, if gold or diamonds could be seen everywhere on the ground, some labour is needed to pick them up and process them before they can be sold. Both liberal and technical education and training are essential to create and release the skill and energy of the people, if labour is to contribute effectively to the creation of the national income.

Thirdly, the availability of capital affects the volume of the national income. Money capital, which is one kind of capital needed, can only come from savings or borrowed capital which is someone else's savings. The savings habit of a nation, therefore, builds up capital resources for productive purposes which in turn creates the national income. In West Africa where the propensity to consume is high, due largely to the extended family system and the unusually high preference for ostentatious spending, little saving is done relative to the size and need of each country. West Africa has depended largely on borrowed capital for her economic development so far. The amount which can be borrowed by each country depends partly on the economic situation of the lending country and partly on the political friendliness which exists between the lending country and the borrowing country. If foreign capital is obtained, that part of the national income that it helped to produce will be reduced by the repayment of the capital and the interest it carries.

Fourthly, the efficiency with which the factors of production are combined will inevitably affect the national income. Abundant supplies of each factor of production, if coupled with poor combination at the production level, will not bring about maximum efficiency, and this will be reflected in the size of the national income. Better combination and co-operation of factors of production, all other things being equal, will lead to a larger national income.

Lastly, and of great interest to developing countries, political stability is essential to the growth of the national income. National production will be greater in a country with a stable government than in one which is prone to civil wars or revolutions. The political instability in most South American countries has contributed largely to their slow economic progress and low national incomes. It is pertinent to add that the military *coups d'état* which have taken place in many African countries in recent years have introduced an element of political instability. The Nigerian civil war, which was fought from July 1967 to January 1970, dislocated the machinery of normal economic growth in the country. Beside the fact that four of the nineteen Nigerian states were not fully functioning economically, most of the productive efforts of the rest of the country went to waging the war. A large number of social assets, bridges, roads, people, were destroyed. A purposeful government which is not corrupt is likely to be more stable than a purposeless and corrupt government. The more politically stable a country is, all other things being equal, the greater the chances of increasing its national income.

EVALUATION OF NATIONAL INCOME CONCEPTS AND MEASUREMENTS

Much care in evaluating the national income concepts and measurements is needed. The GNP, for example, does not necessarily represent the measurement which the analyst or economist desires. In the first place, the GNP has been inflated by the extent to which taxes are not actually a payment for currently produced government services and as such are not equivalent goods and services purchased. Secondly, it must be remembered that the GNP refers only to the measurable portion of national output and does not represent the total national output. As economic activity embraces more and more of total national output, GNP will more correctly measure total national output. For example, if a housewife decides to get a job and employs someone to do her housework, the statistics of the GNP will show an increase in national output, because housework which did not enter into the calculation previously has now been included since a money value is now attached to it, and the GNP figure will now be closer to its true value.

The defects of net national product (NNP) as an indicator of the economic state of a nation are even more serious than those of GNP. In fact, some economists refuse to make use of the statistics on NNP, on the ground that the measurement is arbitrary and not meaningful for the purpose of analysis. For example, no serious student would be willing to claim that taxes are coincidental with the depreciation that occurs in the social capital of the nation. It is true that education, health and other expenditures on children can be considered in part as an investment, and that as individuals mature and eventually die this investment is consumed. Similarly, buildings, roads and dams are all capital goods which depreciate over time. In fact, no accurate method has been devised to estimate depreciation on these items, to say nothing of the more nebulous types of social investment such as generally beneficial social services and reforms.

The statistics of depreciation on business capital are also open to criticism. When a producer buys new equipment, he estimates its useful life and charges depreciation during this period in such a way that the total cost will have been covered when the equipment has no more value. If he does not do this, he will not be counting all of the costs which are involved in his production. However, a piece of equipment may become valueless because of new techniques, inventions or changes in the demand for products, quite apart from the technical factors of wear and tear. There is considerable uncertainty as to how long equipment will be useful and thus have value since it is impossible to predict the future satisfactorily. A number of factors, including taxes and the outlook for the future, enter into the allocation of depreciation over a period of time. However, sound business practice is to be on the safe side and charge sufficient depreciation in the early years so that no matter what happens later, the cost of equipment will have been written off. Thus if a piece of equipment is depreciated at such a rate that it is written off in ten years and yet it gives continuous service for twenty years, then the actual depreciation charged in the first ten years is double the amount of true depreciation. In the last ten years, when there is no depreciation charge, there is no current recognition of the consumption of equipment which has occurred. When a national economy is growing, as is the case in most West African countries, it will possess relatively more new equipment and machinery than old, so that, during periods of growth, the NNP and the rate of net growth will be understated, if the depreciation allowances charged by business are much in excess of the actual depreciation.

In addition to the various points made above, the student should note that the method of measuring the national income in terms of money contains one more serious defect. The value of the national income in one year may be greater than in another, though the real value of the national product is no more or even less. Before any comparison between one year and another is made in respect of the national income, due allowance must be made for the changes in prices between the two periods. An estimate of the national income at current prices during a period of high prices will tend to inflate its value compared with the same real income at current prices during a period of low prices. This is corrected by comparing national income in different years at constant prices: the prices ruling in one period are used to compute the value of the real income in the second period so that the inflationary or deflationary effect of changing prices is eliminated.

Per capita income figures as a measure of economic growth or development are used to make comparisons between countries with different sizes of population or to compare one country's performance in different years when the size of the population is changing from year to year. But there are objections to its use for international comparisons. The method and efficiency of measuring the national income vary from one country to another. The more industrialised, monetised and educated a country is, the easier it is for that country to obtain a fairly accurate estimate of its national income. In developing countries, many 'economic' activities are still not being exchanged for money and not being included in the estimate of subsistence income either, hence the underestimates of national income in these countries. Also, the money economy is just developing in many of these countries, thus making it difficult, if not impossible, in some cases to attach an accurate money value to some economic activities.

The rate of growth of population, all other things being equal, has a direct effect on the per capita income of a country. If country X has a population of 100 million people, and a national income of ₦5,000 million in year *t*, the per capita income of country X in year *t* is ₦50·00. If country Y has a population of 50 million people and a national income of ₦5,000 million – the same as X – in year *t*, the per capita income of country Y in year *t* is ₦100. We can appreciate, straight away, the influence of population in the determination of the per capita income. If the population of country X increased by 3 per cent in year $t + 1$, and its national income increased by 10 per cent in year $t + 1$, its per capita income in year $t + 1$ would rise to approximately ₦53·4. However, if the population of country Y increased by 3 per cent in year $t + 1$, and its national income increased by 1 per cent in year $t + 1$, its per capita income in year $t + 1$ would fall to approximately ₦98. It can be seen, therefore, that while the overall national income may be increasing from one year to another, the per capita income may be decreasing if the rate of population growth is higher than the rate of economic growth.

Finally, it should be pointed out that none of these statistics can be regarded as an absolute measure of economic welfare or standard of living. In the first place, the measurements of the GNP and the NNP are in terms of money rather than in utility or satisfaction. Also, economic welfare and the standard of living are to a large extent dependent on the distribution of national wealth and income, and these statistics of aggregate national income throw very little light on who enjoys what is produced. The uneven distribution of wealth or income in West Africa is very marked. The money incomes range from those of the top civil servants and university professors earning ₦11,000·00 p.a. and above to that of the poor farmer with ₦80·00 p.a. or below. While the overall national income may be increasing, the entire annual increase or a large proportion of it may go to just a small section of the cummunity.

The distribution of wealth and income is considered in the next chapter.

Chapter 6

The Distribution of Wealth

THE SHARE-OUT

The distribution of wealth is concerned with the manner in which the national income is shared out among the factors which have helped to produce it and the way in which the national stock of things of value is owned. The term 'distribution' is usually reserved for the share-out of income; that is, the division of the proceeds of productive activity in the economy among the persons who provide resources used in production – persons who supply labour services, lend capital, lend the use of land and organise productive activity. In this connection, it is important to remember that one man may be able to provide different resources which may enable his income to include rent from ownership of land, interest on invested capital, wages from services performed and profit from enterprise.

As pointed out in Chapter 2, the classification of the factors of production is a matter of convenience. To the business firm or industry, all factors of production are similar, in the sense that the entrepreneur will, in order to maximise profits, substitute one factor for another if this will increase output per unit of input, measured in money, say the naira (₦1). The actual distribution of the national income among the factors of production tends to be determined mainly by the services that each factor renders to production. This is indicated partly by the marginal productivity of each factor and partly by the bargaining strength of each factor which depends on its relative elasticities of supply and demand. In a free enterprise economy, therefore, the entrepreneur dominates the distribution of income payments although he has, of course, to take account of market forces.

The distribution of the national income is one of the most controversial topics in economics. For example, it provides the foundation for most industrial or trade disputes between capital (management) and labour (trade unions), each contending that the other demands too great a share of the product of industry. Also, the distribution of income involves the question of social justice which is continually debated in modern communities.

We shall start by examining in detail the constituents of the national income: wages, interest, rent and profits.

WAGES

A wage can be defined as the price paid for labour, physical, mental or both. The term 'wages' is intended to cover wages in the ordinary sense as paid daily or weekly to the manual worker; salaries for services not of a personal nature, usually paid monthly; and fees for independent personal work, for instance, doctor's fees, lawyer's fees, and the hair-dresser's price.

Whatever happens to wage levels – an increase or a decrease – must necessarily affect the livelihood of the working population and that of those who depend on them. We should make a distinction between the money wage and the real wage.

The money wage is the amount of money received for a particular piece of work: the pay packet. The real wage constitutes the goods and services which the money wage can buy, together with any incidental advantages connected with the occupation.

A money wage is used to purchase goods and services at current market prices. During a period of low market prices, all other things being equal, the money wage will purchase more goods and services, and when market prices are high, all other things being equal, the money wage will command less goods and services. It means in effect that the real wage is the pay packet (the money wage) inflated or deflated by the price level. The comfort and prosperity of the wage-earner is governed by the extent of his real wage plus the incidental net advantages. A worker may be willing to accept a low wage in an occupation which has additional 'fringe' benefits rather than take up a job with a higher wage but without any 'fringe' benefits. These benefits are such things as free travel, the use of a company car and a servant, a house or family allowances. But there are many other advantages and disadvantages of a non-pecuniary kind which will be taken into consideration. The regularity or irregularity of employment also influences the decision to take up a job at a given wage-rate. An average worker will usually prefer a regular job at a lower wage-rate to an irregular job at a higher wage-rate. Opportunities for promotion and the prospect for higher wages in the future will also compensate for comparatively low earnings initially. In most professional jobs, wages are low in the initial stages, particularly at the final training period; but the prospects of promotion and rapid increases in income are usually good, because of the scarcity of professional workers. On the other hand, wages for most manual jobs are very much the same for almost the whole of the working life. Unpleasant or dangerous working conditions may also influence the decision of a worker by modifying his response to the money wage he is offered.

Theories of wages

A number of theories of wages have been put forward by economists. The main theories of wages in order of historical appearance are the subsistence theory, the wages fund theory and the marginal productivity theory.

Adam Smith argued that 'a man must always live by his work and his wages must at least be sufficient to maintain him'.[1] Adam Smith went further to say that wages must do more than just maintain the subsistence level of the worker alone, 'otherwise it would be impossible for him to bring up a family, and the race of such workmen could not last beyond the first generation'. In other words, wages are determined by what is necessary to maintain the worker plus an allowance to enable him to rear a family in order to maintain the supply of labour and, we might add in West Africa, to enable him to fulfil his customary obligations to the members of his 'extended family'. The subsistence theory also suggests that an increase in wages above subsistence level enables workers to marry earlier and have larger families, so that the supply of labour increases, competition appears among labour, and this ultimately brings wages back down to the subsistence level again. On the other hand, if wages fall below subsistence level, starvation will produce a fall in population, resulting in a decline in the labour force, a slackening of labour competition, and thus causing a rise in wages until they are restored to subsistence level. According to this theory, wages tend in the long run to fluctuate around the subsistence level; the level just sufficient to keep alive the supply of labour needed to meet the demand for it. This theory had in effect introduced the concept of 'the cost of living' into the question of wage determination, and undoubtedly it has led a number of economists into believing, though wrongly, that the 'cost of living' is the main determinant of wages.

The wages fund theory can be found in Adam Smith but is

[1] Adam Smith, *op. cit.*, Vol. 1, p. 60.

particularly associated with another economist, Nassau Senior. It holds that 'the demand for those who live by wages cannot increase but in proportion to the increase of the funds which are destined for the payment of wages'. The demand for labour is determined by a special fund set aside by capitalists for the payment of wages. During a given period, the special fund is assumed to be fixed; consequently any successful attempt by the workers to raise their wages can only result in less people being employed, and the only way to increase the number of people employed is for the workers to accept lower wages. Adam Smith also believed that the level and the rate of economic growth in any country must necessarily influence the general demand for labour. According to him, the demand for labour 'necessarily increases with the increase of the revenue and stock of every country, and cannot possibly increase without it'. As the national income increases and the rate of economic growth is sustained, the wages fund also increases and so more workers can be employed at the subsistence wage. One can deduce from this theory that it is not the absolute amount of national wealth but its continual increase which induces a rise in the demand for labour. But it is also possible to argue from the wages fund theory that provided the subsistence theory of wages is abandoned, the more profitable business undertakings or the more prosperous the national economy, the more wages can rise and vice versa. Of course, this is not quite so, as we shall discuss presently.

The marginal productivity theory states that a firm will hire workers up to the point at which the extra yield or revenue obtained through the last worker employed equals the value of the wage which he receives. The wage which the last worker receives will, of course, be the same for all workers of the same skill and ability, since for the same services it is impossible to pay unequal wages. For this theory to be clearly understood, it is necessary to distinguish between the terms marginal physical product and marginal revenue product. The former is the addition to the total physical production of the firm caused by the employment of an additional worker, assuming that other factors employed by the firm remain fixed. The marginal revenue product is the addition to total revenue of the firm brought about by the sale of the marginal physical product, assuming that the amount of other factors employed by the firm remains fixed. It is assumed for the purpose of our analysis that the entrepreneur buys his factors in perfect markets; the firm employs all factors of production under conditions of perfect competition. This theory recognises the important fact that labour is a factor of production just as are capital, land and enterprise. The entrepreneur is constantly faced with the problem of having to combine these factors of production in a way which achieves minimum cost possible for a given output. If, then, the amount of each factor employed is determined by its marginal productivity, the firm will maximise its profit.

This theory has a number of weaknesses. To start with, the word 'productivity' may refer to output as measured by volume; only when measured by market price can it be compared with the wage liability, and market price may fluctuate considerably from time to time as indeed may the wage paid to labour. It is also difficult to decide on how much of the value of the product can be ascribed to the factor of production being considered, in this case, labour. Further, productivity may be the result and not the determinant of wages, especially if the wages are very high. However, one important contribution which the theory made is that it emphasises that wages constitute part of the cost of production.

The modern outlook on wages

In West Africa, social and political factors have been playing the primary role in the determination of wages, while the economic forces have been of secondary importance. The question to ask is whether one can continue to set aside the basic economic forces of supply and demand in the labour market and fix wages at levels which one considers to be morally or politically 'just', 'right' or 'fair'. This can only be done in the short period, as economic factors will gather enough force in the long run to influence significantly the determination of wages. In any case, what is a 'just', 'right' or 'fair' wage? How can it be determined? In addition to justice, rightness and fairness, most money wage claims are based on one or a combination of the following: changes in the cost of living, wage differentials, profits earned by employers and the production record of the firm.

The payment of a 'living wage' is one of the most powerful of social pressures. But what is a 'living wage'? Whose standard is to be the measuring-rod? The average man may consider a living wage to be the sum of money he requires at the end of each month to enable him and his family, if he has one, to have three good meals every day of the month, and which allows him a reasonable 'surplus' for other needs. The issue is complicated if one attempts to find out what an average family should be, particularly in a West African context where the extended family system operates. The standard of living is also not clear; one man may include a glass of wine as part of his lunch, while another man may consider a glass of orange juice as a luxury. One can understand, therefore, that the notion of 'a living wage' is vague.

How strong then is the argument that wages should be increased to meet higher costs of living? One must admit that with the social conditions in West Africa, the cost of living varies almost with individuals; consequently, it is difficult to arrive at any conclusion. It is true, however, that changes in the prices of goods and services do reflect on the level of the cost of living. Higher prices mean a higher cost of living and vice versa.

The increases in government spending on development projects – particularly on social development – since the early 1950s, have increased the level of the purchasing power in the hands of the people without necessarily increasing material productivity at the same rate. In the developing countries of West Africa, a rise in the prices of agricultural export products usually leads to more purchasing power in the hands of the farmers, traders and small-scale businessmen. These are entrepreneurs who have low incomes and feel a real need to spend more on consumption. In such circumstances, the built-in brakes on the pace of inflation which exist in developed countries may even be replaced by accelerators, because the new distribution of incomes favours potential spenders rather than potential savers.

Wage differentials also influence the determination of wages. Wage differentials are the differences in the money wage rates paid to various types of labour, for example, the difference in the money wage rate of a doctor and that of a porter. Wage differentials are not only a problem between skilled, semi-skilled and unskilled workers, they apply also between industries, and between wage-earners in government and quasi-government institutions and the other sectors of the economy. Wage differentials which were originally appropriate tend to persist by inertia or custom, and if the wages in a skilled occupation remain unchanged after alterations in the work have lessened the skill formerly required, then such wages are above the economically justified level, and consequently maximum efficiency is not secured. One of the major problems of a wages policy in West Africa is that of wage differentials. It is widely held that wages should take account of the relative skill and responsibility involved in each job and these are aspects of the productivity of labour. If at any time the workers or the trade unions feel that one group of people are being paid more than their skill, experience and responsibility are worth, all other things being equal, the result will be a pressure to narrow the wage differentials through persistent demands for higher wages for the less well-paid. It is possible, also, to have wage differentials which are too narrow. In fact, there could be some economic advantages in widening them. For example, workers in key and responsible posts may need greater inducement to accept the responsibility; this may be given by widening the wage differentials.

Basing wage claims on the profitability of business is, at the moment, not of such great concern to West Africa, as it is in the developed countries of Europe and America where the bulk of the labour force is absorbed in industries. In West Africa, the government and quasi-government institutions absorb the bulk of the skilled labour, and the government's object is not to make profit as such. Even with some public corporations where one expects some surplus to be realised, the governments are only too ready to subsidise their annual losses, rather than reorganise them on a commercial basis so that, at least, they can cover their costs. Moreover, West African trade unions are not inclined to relate claims for higher wages directly to profits, because they expect the employers to reverse the claim in conditions of declining prosperity. In fact, the main difficulty which trade unions encounter in trying to secure higher wages from profits is the variation in the levels of profits from firm to firm within an industry and in various industries. The problem of the relationship between profits and wages is for the future in West Africa when one expects private enterprise to employ the bulk of the labour force.

How, then, should a wage be determined? The answer, in the strict economic sense, is that whatever ought to be, in fact wages are determined by the supply and the demand for labour.

We will consider first the supply. A man has the choice between spending the twenty-four hours of every day in leisure and facing possible starvation; and giving up part of his leisure every day to earn a living. The disutility of work or not having leisure is offset by the utility of income or wages earned by giving up part of leisure. On the worker's side, that is, on the supply side of labour, the estimate of 'worthwhileness' of giving up leisure for a particular job is complicated for it involves elements on which it is difficult to put a money-value. Given that a man is capable of doing several different jobs, if he has to make up his mind that one job is more attractive than another, he has to compare all that 'goes with' each of them. The things that 'go with' a job include prestige, regularity, chance of promotion, mental or spiritual satisfaction, leisure, access to particular social groups, cheaper houses, better conditions of living, and many others. The net advantage of a particular job takes account of these as well as of money wages. There are various markets for different types of labour and the supply in each market is influenced by a number of factors, some of which are already mentioned above. It is important to add that the activities of the trade unions could influence the supply side of labour. The main object of a trade union is to secure higher wages and better conditions of work for its members. A strong trade union such as a union of professional workers may adopt the 'restrictive practice' of admitting very few members into a profession in order to maintain or increase the money wage-rate of its members. A trade union may also resort to strike action in order to force the employer into granting concessions, either higher wages or better conditions of work or both. However, there are limitations to the power of trade unions. If the demand for labour is elastic, for example, if capital can be easily substituted for labour, the trade union will be in a weak position. During a period of severe depression and unemployment, a trade union will also be in a weak bargaining position with the employer. If a trade union is financially weak or lacks capable leadership – as is often the case in West Africa – its bargaining strength will not be great. In developed countries, for instance the United Kingdom, where unemployment benefits are paid to striking workers and where strike pay is paid by the unions, the trade unions may be able to hold out for long periods against employers in the attempt to force them into paying higher wages.

On the demand side, the entrepreneur who employs labour must be convinced that it is 'worthwhile' to employ whatever labour he engages. This he finds out, consciously or not, by the operation of the principle of equi-marginal returns of all the factors of production engaged. The last naira spent on the labour he employs (the marginal unit) must contribute to the value of total production the same amount as the last naira spent on each of the other factors of production. The contribution of a unit of labour, say, one man, at the margin, that is, the marginal productivity of labour, will then determine what the entrepreneur is prepared to pay each man employed.

In developing countries of West Africa, the pace of social and economic developments necessarily influences the demand for different types of labour. For example, more engineers and technicians are needed in the process of economic and industrial growth.

The practical problems of wages in West Africa

It is often asserted that because the various governments in West Africa fix wages, and industrial collective bargaining has become common, wages now represent much more a political and social assessment than an economic compromise. It is true that the method of settling wage-rates is different when governments fix wages for the workers or when agreements are made on behalf of organised groups instead of wage negotiations between individuals. The governments in West Africa, as the wage pace-makers, can and do fix any wage-rates they choose. The fact that the wage policy of any government has been influenced by party politics is relevant to the economist when considering the number of people employed or laid off as a result of the fixed wage-rates. As we already know, the monopolist can fix a price and allow demand to indicate the supply. So also can the government (in a free enterprise economy) fix a wage for a job and let the labour market determine how many people will apply for whatever jobs the employers are prepared to offer. Similarly, a strong trade union can compel a particular wage-rate to be fixed, just as a monopoly firm can enforce a particular price for its products, but neither can force the purchaser to buy and both must face the possibility of unsold 'stock' if the price is fixed above what the market is prepared to pay for what is on offer. The wages fixed by governments and wage-rates arrived at by collective bargaining have introduced monopolistic elements into wage determination, but they have not materially altered its economic nature.

It is also noticeable that whenever governments in West Africa revise wages, a series of industrial or trade disputes follow in the private sector of the economy. The businessman, unlike the government, is constantly faced with the problem of costs of production and the struggle to make profits. A sudden increase in the wages bill has a direct impact on costs of production and the 'worthwhileness' of employing various factors of production, consequently on whether or not to remain in business. More often, therefore, the result of increased wages is a readier disposition to examine the possibility of producing the same produce by an alternative method. Labour-saving devices may be employed, leading to the retrenchment of the labour force, and this leads to an industrial dispute.

In the short term, which may indeed extend over a decade or more depending on the rate of economic growth, the part played by non-economic factors, particularly social and political factors, is often considerable; but in the long run the tendency is for the economic factors of demand and supply to become dominant in determining wage levels.

INTEREST

Interest is the price paid for the loan of money (purchasing power) over a period of time. For the period of the loan, the lender loses control over his capital and for doing so he is rewarded. This reward, which is in addition to the repayment of the principal sum lent, is interest – the payment for the use of loan capital. Interest is the payment for the loan of purchasing power but it does not include payment for the risk taken, if any. A further payment is needed if there is any risk that the borrower may not repay the loan with interest. The nearest thing in West Africa to pure interest which is riskless and without appreciable cost of lending is the return or interest on a government treasury bill or a treasury certificate or a government bond.

In Europe, the legitimacy of interest has been much discussed for centuries. The original attitude was influenced by Christian theology, which interpreted the Bible as forbidding interest, and so looked upon 'usury' (the taking of interest) as a deadly sin. In the traditional West Africa of a century or more ago, there was no such thing as 'interest'. It was against moral principles to take interest on loans. In a society with an extended family system, loans given to one's relations are still regarded as part of the normal family obligation. Both Christian theology and the traditional African moral principle regard money as 'barren'. The lender should only expect repayment of what he had lent. This attitude arose because borrowing was rarely undertaken for any productive purposes, but for personal use to buy consumption goods and services. Being unproductive, there was no revenue out of which interest could be paid.

In Europe, a number of changes in economic conditions, particularly the advent of the commercial and industrial revolutions with their great opportunities for the productive use of capital, have made it possible for people to accept the practice of paying interest on loans. Even in West Africa, individual lending and borrowing is gradually being commercialised through the money-lenders with the growth of a free enterprise money economy and through the banks. It must be added that a growing amount of borrowing nowadays is not undertaken primarily for consumption, but for productive purposes. With the general increase in the rate and pace of economic growth, opportunities are on the increase for using borrowed capital to assist production and commerce. It has now been fully accepted that capital is a very important factor of production and its availability is dependent on its being rewarded just as with the other factors.

Interest theories

A number of theories have been propounded in the process of explaining why interest is paid. One such theory is the productivity and thrift theory of the rate of interest. This theory, which is the classical theory of the rate of interest, was put forward by the classical economists.

The central point of the classical theory is that the rate of interest is the factor which establishes equilibrium between the demand for investment and the willingness to save. The demand for loanable funds for investment derives from the productive use of capital and the supply of loanable funds is created by saving or 'thrift'. The rate of interest is the price to be paid for the use of loanable funds. The rate of interest is like the price of an ordinary commodity, the higher the rate of interest, the greater the supply of savings available for investment and the less the demand for funds to invest.

In propounding their theory, the classical economists assumed a full employment economy. They further assumed that the level of national income is constant. These two basic assumptions cannot be accepted as valid in all circumstances. In the first place, it is rare for an economy to have all factors of production fully employed. Secondly, the assumption that income is constant is inconsistent with the assumption that investment and savings are independent of one another, particularly when reacting to changes in the rate of interest. Moreover, there are two other sources of money which can be invested apart from savings. These are dishoarding, that is, the release of funds from cash balances held by individuals, and money created by the banking system.

The classical theory failed to stand up to the test of experience when unemployment was very great during the economic depression of the early 1930s. The classical theory proved unrealistic in assuming an optimistic economic world with everyone employed and incomes and investment always stable.

It is not true to say that savings always depend on the rate of interest. The automatic adjustment of savings and investment, therefore, cannot be taken for granted. Beside the rate of interest, savings depend also on the volume of income available in the community. If a community, as in West Africa, has a low income, no matter how high the rate of interest may be raised, savings will remain at a very low level. The other point mentioned earlier and which has made the classical theory subject to criticism is that it assumed that an increase in savings will be achieved out of the same income, if only the rate of interest is sufficiently raised. This is not necessarily so. Nor is it true that investment is determined solely by the rate of interest. A fall in the rate of interest will not automatically lead to an increase in the volume of investment as contended by the classical economists, because entrepreneurs will not necessarily see profitable uses for additional capital even though they can borrow more cheaply.

The second theory which we shall discuss is the abstinence theory of the rate of interest. The theory regards interest as the reward for abstaining from immediate consumption of goods and services. Because 'abstinence' implies the idea of hardship which is not always present in saving, some economists prefer to use the word 'waiting' in order to indicate that nothing more than the postponement of consumption is meant. This theory recognises the fact that capital may be accumulated without the offer of interest, but it also stresses the point that sufficient capital to meet the demand for it will only be forthcoming by the offer of interest. The main defect of such an approach to the theory of interest is that it neglects the demand argument, that is, why people demand capital and are prepared to pay interest. The theory also fails to explain the automatic savings from large incomes, and does not cover capital which appears without the inducement of interest, such as savings for old age, insurance or a national provident fund.

Keynes[1] supplied the liquidity preference theory of the rate of interest. We shall discuss only the central points of this theory. Keynes argued that interest is not a reward for saving, because people can save without investing such savings. People are rewarded only when they lend out their savings. His conclusion is that interest is the reward for parting with liquidity. Liquidity is the demand to hold money. Keynes explained that three motives control people's liquidity preference. These are the transaction motive, the precautionary motive and the speculative motive. For transaction purposes, people need money, and the amount of money needed will depend on the volume of ordinary regular transactions. The higher an individual's income, all other things being equal, the higher will be the amount of money he will wish to hold for transaction purposes. In aggregate, therefore, the higher the national income, the higher is the liquidity preference for money for transaction purposes. The amount of money needed for the precautionary motive also depends on the level of income. The normal behaviour is for an individual first to satisfy his immediate wants, and this is reflected in the transactions demand for money. If income is just adequate for immediate transactions, there will be none left for precautionary purposes, and if an unforeseen expenditure arises it may be met by borrowing. If a community is as relatively poor as in West Africa, immediate needs leave little or no reserve for possible emergencies, that is, for precautionary purposes. The demand for money for speculative purposes depends mainly on the rate of interest. The higher the rate of interest the more willing are people to buy securities for speculation in the expectation that the rate of interest will soon fall and so enable them to obtain capital gains. This means that they will not hold money but will buy securities instead if the rate of interest is high and expected to fall; their

[1]J.M. Keynes, *op. cit*.

speculative demand for money is small. The demand for money for speculative purposes is based on a number of assumptions. It is assumed that financial institutions exist for the buying and selling of securities and that people are aware of the existence of such institutions, and that they are organised to take specualtive risks.

In West Africa, there were no financial institutions permitting speculation until 1960 when the central banks of Ghana and Nigeria issued their first treasury bills. Since that date, the number of private individuals who could afford to invest in these treasury bills have grown only slowly. The unit of the treasury bills was usually of an approximate amount equal to ₦2,000 and as such they were outside the range of what most people could afford. The facilities created for speculation by the Nigerian money market are being utilised only by a few financial institutions, such as the commercial banks and the insurance companies. Prior to the creation of the Lagos money and capital markets, the funds for speculation from these financial institutions usually found their way to the London markets. In general, one can say that money and capital markets in West Africa are still to develop fully before their impact on speculation can be felt, and so the speculative motive is not yet of great importance.

Keynes also introduced the supply function to his theory, and claimed that the supply function depends on the volume of money supplied by the commerical banks controlled by the central bank. He assumed that the supply of money as determined by the banks is constant in the short term. Here again, there are a number of other important assumptions. First, it is assumed that adequate banking facilities exist; secondly, that people make use of the banks, and thirdly, that money supply does not increase or decrease through any source other than through the banks. Although commerical banking first appeared on a solid footing in West Africa in 1894, many people have not yet learnt to trust their money with the banks. The activities of the existing commercial banks are very much below full capacity in relation to the population and the level of commercial activities. Hoarding is practised extensively in West Africa, and, therefore, it remains a potential source of supply of additional money from time to time.

Keynes concluded that one role of the rate of interest in the economic system is to equalise the demand for money by the public and the supply of money by the banks. If the transaction and precautionary demands for money rise as income increases, and the money supply remains fixed, how can the demand for money equal the supply of money? The answer is that the rate of interest must rise enough to induce people to lower their liquidity preferences, that is, their demand for money for speculative purposes.

The liquidity preference theory of the rate of interest has also been criticised. The main criticism by Robertson is that the theory was based solely on a monetary approach. Robertson argued that entrepreneurs are prepared to borrow at interest because they can invest profitably and this is due to the productivity of capital. He considered the productivity of capital as the real factor which determines the rate of interest. He also criticised Keynes for denying the existence of a relationship between the rate of interest and savings. He concluded that the rate of interest is not of a purely monetary character.

Observations on the rate of interest

The modern approach to the rate of interest is that it depends on the supply and demand both for loans and for investment capital. It is important to note that there is never one price, at any given time, for the use of loan capital as such. There are a number of reasons for the existence of different rates of interest. Loans are not all wanted or offered for the same period. A loan may be required for a day, a week, a month, a year, or more, and lenders may offer loans for different periods. A loan for a week, all other things being equal, is likely to be made at a lower rate of interest than a loan for a year. Loans are for different periods and for different 'commodities' in separate markets and the rate of interest is determined by supply and demand in each.

Lending and borrowing involve some risks. With personal loans one tends to think that a loan to a friend or a relation involves less risk – even though this may not be true – than a loan to a perfect stranger. Indeed, in West Africa, a loan to a friend or relative carries far greater risks than a loan to a stranger. If a friend or relative decides not to repay the loan, which more often than not he does not repay, an action against either the friend or the relative will be considered contrary to the social convention which seeks to maintain social equilibrium at all times. In fact, the relative or friend who borrows money will be prepared to take greater investment risks than would a stranger-borrower, because the relative or friend relies on the social system to rescue him in case his investment fails and he is unable to repay the loan. Most people, therefore, are ready to give a limited amount as outright grants or gifts to friends or relatives rather than lend money to them.

The risks taken by entrepreneurs and by those who lend to them are of a different order. Production for the market is production for an uncertain future. The enterprise expects to make profits but might make losses and this is the risk which the entrepreneur as borrower and the lender who provides him with investment capital both take. For such loans the lender will expect not only the current rate of interest for long-term loans, but an additional risk premium to compensate him for the possibility that he might lose his money.

The return on loan capital varies with the nature of the business or trade for which the loan capital is required. A business or trade which is noted for its great risks will have to pay a very high risk premium in addition to the appropriate rate of interest. An established firm which has proved successfully that it is credit-worthy is likely to obtain loan capital on more favourable terms than a firm which has yet to prove its credit-worthiness. Most of the expatriate firms in West Africa are in a better position to obtain credit than indigenous business. Many of the foreign firms are old establishments backed up by reputable head offices in their respective countries of origin. Most of the indigenous firms, on the other hand, operate on a small scale, some with no business records and unable to satisfy the financial institutions as far as credit-worthiness is concerned. Loan capital to such indigenous firms, if granted at all, carries high-risk premiums in addition to interest. Loan capital for a country or district with natural risks, such as floods or earthquakes, will attract a higher-than-usual rate of interest plus risk premium.

One can summarise by saying that the rate of interest varies with fluctuations in the demand for and the supply of loan capital. In the business community, a boom or a depression tends to influence the demand for capital. A greater demand for capital is associated with a boom, while a fall in demand is associated with a depression. It should be emphasised again that businessmen tend to employ more capital when the productivity of capital is higher than the productivity of either land or labour at the margin of production. Whenever businessmen find it more profitable to substitute capital for labour or land, the demand for capital will increase.

The activities of the government can also affect the demand for capital. If a government is unable to finance its social and economic development projects solely from its revenue, it must borrow money either from its citizens or from abroad. (The finance of government development projects is discussed in Chapter 10.)

Under normal conditions, the supply of a country's loan capital depends mainly on the volume of a country's national income. (External borrowing is excluded at this stage of our study.) The greater the volume of the national income, all other things being equal, the greater will be the supply of loan capital. The factors which tend to determine the volume of the national income have already been mentioned in the last chapter. It must be added that the distribution or redistribution of income also tends to influence the supply of capital. The people with higher incomes normally save more than those with low incomes. However, this is not necessarily the case in West Africa, where the commitments imposed by the extended family system may militate against the accumulation of capital by a high-income earner. High propensity to consume leads to small savings and less supply of loan capital.

RENT

In West Africa, as in many other countries, the concept of rent originated from the use of farm land. When a piece of family land is given to a non-member of the family as farm land, he is under an obligation to give in return part of the annual harvests as rent on the farm land to the head of the family. Such rents are paid in kind, usually in agricultural food crops, the amount of which is not usually fixed. There is another kind of rent in West Africa originating from the employment of tenant-farmers. For example, if a tenant-farmer is employed to farm and crop a palm-oil estate, he is made to enter into an agreement whereby he pays the landlord a fixed volume of palm-oil annually depending on the size of the estate and the estimated yield, as mutually agreed. If the tenant-farmer is able to produce more than the agreed volume, as he normally can, the excess belongs to him, but if he is unable to produce enough to meet the agreed rent he will have to purchase palm-oil in the open market in order to make up the agreed rent. The contract 'of rent' between the landlord and the tenant-farmer is usually renewed annually. In West Africa, therefore, there are two kinds of rent; one which is obligatory, not fixed in amount and not usually recoverable by action in the customary court; the other rent is contractual and enforceable under customary law.

The theory of rent as a differential payment was first propounded by David Ricardo in England in the early part of the nineteenth century. Ricardo based his theory on a number of assumptions. He assumed that there are equal plots of land, say, A, B, C, D and E as in Figure 6.1, and that the same type of crop, say, yam, is grown on each plot. He assumed that the same quantity and quality of labour and capital are expended on each plot, and that the fertility of the plots varies, the richest being plot A, the next richest plot B, to the poorest plot E. The yield on each plot will be determined by the fertility of each plot. The most fertile plot yields most yams. The shaded areas of Figure 6.1 show the surplus revenues in yams after the costs of production (labour and capital) have been met. According to Ricardo, the economic rent of plot A would be 100 yams and of plot B nothing if the demand for yams did not amount to more

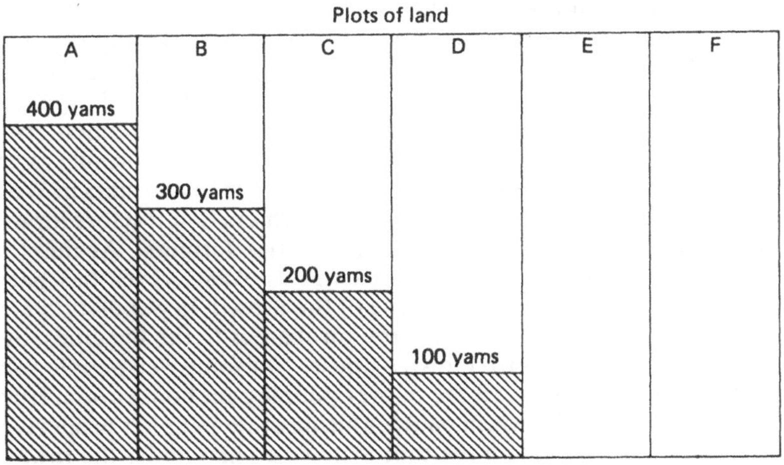

fig. 6.1

than the quantity which plots A and B could together produce. But if more yams were required, then plot C would also have to be cultivated and the rent of plot A would be 200 yams, the rent of plot B would be 100 yams but plot C would command no rent. If all five plots are cultivated, plot E has no rent, and what has been produced on it will just be adequate to meet costs of production; plot E has become the marginal plot. However, if the demand for yams becomes even greater, the price of yam increases still more thus increasing the revenue on each plot; then the rent on each plot will increase and plot E will yield some rent, and will cease to be the marginal land. Another plot, say F, will then become the marginal land.

The exposition of the Ricardian theory of rent shows that economic rent is determined by price. The higher the price of the produce, the higher the rent of the land; and the lower the price of the produce, the lower the rent. In the example given above, if the demand for yams declines so that it is not necessary to cultivate plot E then the price of yams falls, plot D will become the marginal land without any rent, and the rents on land A, B and C will fall equally, while land E will not be cultivated. The differential rent of Ricardo, therefore, does not form an element of cost, consequently it does not determine price, and Ricardo concludes that the rent of land is a price-determined surplus which does not enter into the cost of production. Economists now use the term 'economic rent' for any similar price-determined surplus which is received by any factor yet is not a necessary cost of production. It is sometimes also called quasi-rent because it is similar to, but not, the rent of land.

In practice rent is commonly conceived as a periodic payment of a price for the use of other people's property. Young people hire bicycles in order to enjoy a few minutes' ride, while older people hire a variety of items, such as houses, cars or farm equipment. Not everybody owns all the goods he requires either for his ordinary way of life or for his profession. For example, not many farmers in West African can afford to own a tractor. So farmers rent tractors for use on their farms, one tractor serving many farmers. Again, the demand for house-room in large cities in West Africa has been increasing over the years, because of the growth in population and the movements of people from the rural areas to the big cities, but not everyone can afford to own a house. Yet some rich people own more than one house. So the poorer people rent house-room from the richer people. The rent paid for hiring other people's property is a return to the owner on the capital invested in it and is the reward for the use of the factor of production he owns. If this rent is not paid there will be no tractor to hire or house to rent so it is a necessary cost if capital is to be invested in tractors and houses. It is not a surplus and so it is not economic rent. Rent as the price for hiring other people's property used as a factor of production is a cost of production to the user. But the hiring charge may cover more than the owner's costs of production, in which case he is receiving some surplus which for him is a form of economic rent. This happens, for example, when there is a temporary shortage of a commodity and the supply cannot quickly be increased. It is in effect a rent of scarcity. Any factor of production is capable of earning a rent of scarcity, sometimes called quasi-rent. Each factor of production has its reward or income: wages for labour, interest for loan capital, rent for land and profit for entrepreneurship. There are occasions when any of these factors could earn more than it is normally paid for its co-operation in the productive process, that is, more than it is worth at the margin of production. This usually arises whenever there is a disequilibrium in the supply and demand for such factors of production, if demand is higher than the supply for the factor concerned and it takes a long time to increase the supply. For example, the demand for medical doctors, accountants and engineers in West Africa is higher than the number of such professional people available and it will take four years or more to train more; consequently their wages tend to be higher than in most other jobs where shortages of people are not experienced. It means that an element of *quasi-rent* exists in the earnings of such professional people. It must be noted that the element of quasi-rent is relative rather than absolute as it depends on the relative long-term elasticities of supply and demand of the factor of production concerned. The quasi-rent of a factor of production, for as long as it exists, is an element of the supply price of that factor. In other words, before the factor can be tied down to a particular use or line of production, the supply price for it – including the *quasi-rent* – must be paid.

PROFIT

In everyday life, profit is usually conceived from the individual viewpoint as the difference between one's expenses and one's receipts or revenue in the process of running a business. A producer of any commodity or service normally incurs costs or expenses of production in anticipation of making a profit after the sale of his products. His gross revenue is the entire receipts from his sales and from this he deducts his costs of production in order to determine how much he has made as profit. Every producer of any commodity or service is constantly faced with the problem of how to make a profit.

In the broad sense, and from the viewpoint of society, profit is looked at as that part of the product of industry which goes to the entrepreneur as payment for his organising work. The entrepreneur employs labour, capital and possibly land in order to produce a particular commodity which he believes people will demand. But in organising factors of production for productive purposes he undertakes risks. The entrepreneur anticipates not only that his product will be demanded but also that the total demand will bring him adequate revenue which will enable him to cover his costs and allows an additional margin of profit; if he is wrong in this he will make a loss and that is the risk he takes.

Profit is liable to fluctuations. Such fluctuations in profit could be caused, amongst other things, by changes in the cost of production, for instance, a rise in the prices of raw materials or by a fall in the price of the commodity following an unexpected fall in demand due, perhaps, to the sudden appearance of substitutes. It follows that the concept of profit is based on 'expectations'. Profit is not a contractual income which one is sure to receive. The amount of profit which will accrue to an entrepreneur cannot be determined until final production has been achieved, and this includes the complete sale of the commodity concerned. Profit is therefore a residual income, and it can be positive, zero or negative.

A student must carefully distinguish between the gross receipts and the profit. The gross receipts are the total revenue which has accrued to the entrepreneur, while the profit is obtained after all costs have been deducted from the gross revenue. These deductions include the earnings of the various factors of production which the entrepreneur has employed, such as rent, wages and interest.

Profit is an essential element in modern production. The main purpose of organising a business is to make profit. How then can profit-making affect business decisions? In this respect, one has to distinguish between the 'prospective profit' and the 'realised profit'. Any businessman, on starting to operate, will be mainly induced by the profit which he hopes to get after production has been completed. His estimate of the 'prospective profit' is influenced by a number of factors including the general economic conditions, the current prices he has to pay for the factors of production, the current price of the commodity he hopes to produce and the price at which he intends to sell it. The entrepreneur is, therefore, influenced by the 'prospective profit' in fixing the price for his product. He will wish to sell his product for the price which will enable him to get his 'prospective profit' at least. It is 'prospective profit' which governs his decision to produce at all. In this respect, one can conclude that the 'prospective profit' is an element of cost which, in turn, determines price. However, the profit which he actually realises depends on the price at which he eventually sells his product and the quantity sold. If his estimate is absolutely correct, then his 'prospective profit' will be equal to his 'realised profit'. However, this rarely happens in practice. The entrepreneur may be lucky to obtain a realised profit which is higher than his prospective profit, and if he is unlucky, his realised profit may be lower than his prospective profit. The 'realised profit' depends on market conditions which vary from time to time. An entrepreneur will always want to compare his prospective profit with his realised profit, because it is on this that his future operation depends. If his 'realised profit' falls far below his 'prospective profit' and if there is no immediate hope for better economic and market conditions, he may decide to shift to another line of production entirely. The realisation of profit affects not only the future volume of production of each firm, it also affects the number of firms which will choose to continue to operate within the industry concerned.

Chapter 7

Money and Banking

THE ORIGIN OF MODERN MONEY

The earliest and most primitive form of exchange is by barter. Barter is a method of directly exchanging one commodity for another. A farmer would exchange his yams for another person's cloth, and a blacksmith would exchange a cutlass or hoe for the farmer's cassava or palm-oil. Exchanges of this nature were undertaken in the pre-monetary economy of West Africa. This type of exchange is cumbersome and inconvenient. In the first place, a man who wants cassava but produces a cutlass must look for a farmer who has not only produced surplus cassava but is also willing to exchange his cassava for a cutlass. In this respect, it is often difficult to achieve coincidence of wants. Secondly, the barter system does not always provide easy and satisfactory means of subdividing a commodity. For example, it is difficult to determine the number of yams that will be given in exchange for a chicken; or the proportion of a goat to be exchanged for a hoe or cutlass. Thirdly, the barter system depends on the desire to make exchanges at the same time; in practice this is often very difficult to arrange. A man who has produced more handwoven cloth than he wants for himself and who wants some yams in exchange may not be able to find a farmer who has produced surplus yams at the time he (the weaver) wants to effect the exchange.

The inconveniences of barter exchange have long been realised in West Africa, and the means of escape has been to introduce various forms of money. Broadly, it may be said that a money economy exists whenever any commodity in fairly general demand is used as a medium of exchange. Most of the early monies adopted in West Africa were items of consumption in their own right; hence they are generally referred to as commodity currencies. The adoption of a commodity currency differed from exchange by barter in that any commodity used as currency was known to be generally accepted and so came to be employed extensively for exchange rather than for pure consumption.

In Ghana gold dust derived from alluvial mining is known to have been extensively adopted as circulating money. Gold dust as a commodity currency had the advantages of almost infinite divisibility and conveniently small bulk in relation to value; but its drawbacks were the necessity of weighing in order to determine the amount to be paid in each transaction and the comparative ease with which it could be adulterated. The manilla (a metal bracelet) and the cowry (a shell) which were introduced into West Africa by the Arab traders across the Sahara desert and by the Portuguese, were extensively adopted as currencies. Iron was also used as currency in some parts of West Africa. Another popular form of currency known to have existed in the northern areas of West Africa was the strip of hand-woven cotton cloth. Other commodity currencies which existed at various times in the early economic history of West Africa included salt, brass rods, beads, cattle and slaves.

Modern money came into West Africa over a period of more than a century. It started with the Sierra Leone Company's currency in denominations of 1 dollar and 50, 20 and 10 cents in 1781. The direct importation of British silver coins into Sierra Leone began in 1808 and much later they were used in Ghana and Nigeria. A uniform currency system was introduced into the four British colonies in West Africa by the establishment of the West African Currency Board in 1912. The now-existing units of currencies are the leone in Sierra Leone, the cedi in Ghana, the naira in Nigeria and the dalasi in the Gambia. They were established after the political independence of each country.

QUALITIES OF GOOD MONEY

Good money must be generally accepted in the country or area where it is to circulate as a medium of exchange. Either by law or custom everybody in the community must be persuaded to accept it as a medium of exchange. In this respect, the old commodity currencies were generally accepted but they still lacked some other important qualities of good money. Good money is easily recognised by all citizens and all units of the same denomination are homogeneous. Also, good money is relatively scarce so that it has a high value for its weight and it has a stable value. If money is in abundant supply relative to its demand, its value will be low. On the other hand, if its supply is too small relative to its demand, the value of each unit will be too high for convenience. The supply of precious metals and stones, such as gold and diamonds, is too small relative to the demand for monetary units and consequently they are unsuitable as units of money. For any money to have a stable value, it is necessary to maintain a steady balance between its supply and demand. Good money must also be durable. It must be capable of passing from hand to hand many times without deteriorating in size or form. Perhaps one of the most important qualities of good money is its divisibility. It must be capable of being subdivided into subunits small in value which can be used for the day-to-day exchange needs of the people who deal in small quantities of many commodities. Finally, good money must be easily carried. Every citizen must be able to carry with him sufficient money for his transaction purposes and some to spare.

THE FUNCTIONS OF MONEY

The first function of money is that it serves as a medium of exchange. This is the main function of money which distinguishes exchange in a money economy from that of a barter system. The producer of cassava can now sell his product for money which he can spend on the goods and services he wants. Similarly, the weaver can exchange his cloth for money with which he can then purchase some cassava. In this way, one of the major defects of the barter system is overcome. One of the advantages of money being a medium of exchange is that it reduces transaction costs and hence facilitates the process of exchange. It also stimulates division of labour and encourages commercial transactions, which contribute immensely to the overall economic welfare of the people.

The second function of money is that it serves as a measure of wealth or a unit of account. Money helps to put a definite value on wealth. It makes it possible and easier for each individual to place a value on any unit of product and thus facilitates exchange. It solves the problem of assessing how many bananas should be exchanged for a yam or how many yams should be exchanged for a length of cloth. Each producer is, therefore, able to place a price on his product by the use of money.

Thirdly, money serves as a store of value. It means that people can keep their wealth in the form of money, and not solely in the form of cows, goats, gold, slaves or houses, as was customary in the pre-money economy era. Money as a store of value enables wealth to be stored up for a reasonably long period. The ideal is that money should not deteriorate in value, so that at any time in the future it can be changed into material wealth without any loss in its value. The value of money is affected by the general supply and demand for money; fluctuations in the value of money are referred to as inflation or deflation. The problems of inflation and deflation will be discussed presently. It will suffice to note that, with an excess of money supply, inflationary conditions prevail and the value of a unit of money falls.

THE VALUE OF MONEY

The value of money lies in its purchasing power. One can measure the value of money in terms of the goods and services one can receive in exchange for it. For example, if ₦1 can buy twenty yams, then one can say that the value of one naira is equivalent to twenty yams or that one yam is worth ₦$^1/_{20}$, that is, 5 k. Since there are many different items of consumption on which money can be spent, there is no one standard value of money. What the value of a unit of money is worth depends on the items of consumption a person chooses to buy. If a commodity is relatively cheap at one time, one may say that the value of money in respect of that commodity is high; whereas at another time if the same commodity becomes scarce and its price increases, one can say that the value of money has fallen.

The quantity of money available at a given period affects the value of money. If twenty units of a commodity are available and there is ₦20 to spend on them, one unit of the commodity will be worth ₦1. However, if the money is increased to ₦40 and the number of units of the commodity remains at twenty, then one unit will be worth ₦2 or, alternatively, ₦1 is worth half a unit; which means that the value of money will have fallen by a half. Similarly, if the quantity of money is reduced to ₦10, all other things being equal, one unit of the commodity will be worth 50 k, which indicates that the value of money has risen so that ₦1 is worth two units of the commodity.

Changes in the value of money have attracted the attention of economists for centuries, but one can start the theoretical explanation of the changes in the value of money by examining the classical quantity theory of money. The theory simply states that the value of money depends upon its quantity. In its most rigid form, the theory postulates a strict proportionality between the quantity of money and the level of prices; for example, if the quantity of money rises by 5 per cent, then the price level will rise by 5 per cent which means that the value of money will fall by 5 per cent.

It has long been realised that the rigid quantity theory does not offer a satisfactory explanation for changes in the value of money. A number of economists have indicated that some other variables apart from the quantity of money tend to affect the value of money. In the early part of this century, the main exponent of a more flexible version of the quantity theory was Professor Irving Fisher. He produced the 'equation of exchange', namely,

$$MV = PT$$

where P = the general level of prices, i.e. the inverse of the value of money,
T = the total volume of transactions conducted with the aid of money,
M = the total volume of money in circulation, and
V = the velocity of circulation of money.

In ordinary language, the 'equation of exchange' maintains that the general level of prices (i.e. the inverse of the value of money) varies directly as the total volume of money in circulation and the velocity of its circulation and inversely as the total volume of transaction: that is

$$P = \frac{MV}{T}$$

If P rises the value of money has fallen, and vice versa.

The equation is useful in showing that if the quantity of money is increased and V and T remain constant, the general level of prices must increase by exactly the same percentage of proportion and so the value of money falls correspondingly.

The trouble with this is that V and T do not normally remain constant. Although the total money in circulation at any given time can be controlled by the Central Bank, the volume of commercial transactions varies considerably through time. The rate at which money changes hands (the velocity of circulation of money) depends on social, cultural and institutional factors. The quantity theory assumes the balancing of two very indeterminate forces – the total purchasing power of money (MV) and the total quantity of goods and services being exchanged (T). It may be true to say that during a given period the quantity of money in existence is fixed, but it will be wrong to assume that the entire volume of such money will be in circulation. Experience has shown that apart from the money which one expects people to hold for precautionary, transaction and speculative purposes, a number of people in West Africa also hoard money. This affects the velocity of circulation of the money and so *MV* is affected. Similarly, not all goods that are produced at a given period are sold. There are instances when goods are held back by producers or are left on their hands unsold.

Fisher's theory also ignores some other factors which may influence the value of money, such as a loss of confidence in money which may be brought about by inflation, or balance-of-payments difficulties which may cause the currency to be devalued. A devalued currency affects a country's imports and exports and so might change the volume of transactions very considerably. The theory suggests that as the volume of money in circulation increases, the general level of price increases as well. However, experience, as in the depressions of the 1930s, has shown that during a period of slump, increases in the volume of money in circulation may fail to increase the general level of prices because the money simply circulates more slowly. Lastly, the theory fails to give adequate attention to the demand side of the problem of prices. The point to emphasise here is that, while one recognises the fact that at a given time the government fixes the volume of money in circulation, the volume which actually circulates and gets into the stream of the exchange varies. This depends on the volume of money hoarded and the liquidity preference – the demand to hold money – of the people. Although the explanation of the value of money remains largely unsatisfactory, yet one should note that the value of money depends, during any given period, on the level of the national income, on the liquidity preference of the community and on the quantity of money – including bank money – available in the economy.

PRICE INDEX NUMBERS

The inverse of the value of money is the general price level – *P* in the Quantity Theory equation. The general price level is measured by an index number. Since the measurement involves a number of commodities, the formula to adopt is:

$$\frac{\sum P_x}{\sum P_o} \times 100$$

that is, the sum of the prices in year x over the sum of the prices in the base year o, multiplied by 100.

The cost-of-living index numbers are measured by a similar method. For the cost-of-living index for a particular group of consumers, a base year, o, is also selected, and a number of commodities and services which together represent the basic and representative items of consumption by that group of consumers – usually known as the basket – are also selected. Each commodity or service selected is given a weight, *w*, which reflects its importance among the other items in the basket; for instance, a staple item of food gets the highest weight. The weights given to items in the base year, *wo*, may be used for the subsequent year, *x*. The cost-of-living index may then be measured by adopting the equation:

$$\frac{\sum W_o P_x}{\sum W_o P_o} \times 100$$

Although the cost-of-living index is often used to indicate changes in the cost of living and the changes in the purchasing power of money, yet it has a number of defects. First, it is difficult to arrive at an accurate measurement of the relative importance of the various commodities and services. The basic items of consumption vary according to the levels of income, taste, fashion and geographical location of each consumer; consequently, what is a staple food varies from one person to another. For example, cassava, yams, rice and plantain are staple foods in different parts of West Africa, as indeed in each of the West African countries. Secondly, a base year is often arbitrarily selected and this may lead to the choice of a base year with unusually low or high prices, thus leading to an unsatisfactory comparison. Thirdly, a cost of living index cannot completely elminate abnormal fluctuations in the prices of selected commodities and services. Such abnormal fluctuations in prices tend to inflate or deflate the cost of living index, as the case may be, giving it a distorted value. Fourthly, the cost-of-living index fails to take into account changes in the quality of the selected goods and services; prices may be moving up while the quality of goods and services is deteriorating. Lastly, in cases where price controls are imposed, the price mechanism will fail to register normal prices thus leading to 'unrealistic' prices being employed in the measurement of the cost-of-living index.

INFLATION

The nature of *inflation* arises directly from the consideration of the changes in the value of money. It is often thought that inflation is merely an exceptional or ill-considered expansion of currency by the government. Again, it is common for people to regard every increase in prices as inflation. Strictly speaking, inflation is a lowering of the purchasing power of money brought about by the supply of money beyond the amount required to meet exchange needs at current price levels. It must be added that an excess of money over and above exchange needs can arise without any increase in money supply by a reduction in the volume of goods and services available during a given period.

It is often said that inflation is the result of too much money chasing too few goods While this may be true in general terms, there is more to it than just that. Indeed, if inflation is just the result of too much money chasing too few goods, then the general increases in prices which will inevitably result ought to check inflation. But inflation is not checked in that manner. The fact is that inflation acts in a spiral. Increases in prices may be regarded as mere symptoms of inflation. The inflationary pressure itself occurs when the prices of goods and services continue to increase, bringing about higher costs of production at every level, thus leading to a continuous wave of price increases. When inflation becomes extreme it is called galloping inflation, or runaway inflation (as a horse gallops or runs away), or hyperinflation. Deflation is the direct opposite of inflation; it is a fall in the general level of prices. Deflation may occur if any of the various causes of inflation mentioned below is applied in the opposite direction.

Inflation can arise in a number of ways. It can, for instance, be brought about through a government policy of deficit finance. It results from a deliberate government policy to finance social and economic development projects either by foreign loan or by issuing more currency. When a foreign loan is employed to finance development projects it results in a direct increase in the volume of money in circulation. If the development projects for which the foreign loan is employed are not immediate revenue-yielding projects – hospitals and schools, for instance, are not – then the inflationary pressure is much greater. Similarly, if the government decides to finance development projects by issuing more currency, this may lead to inflation.

Inflation may occur through excess demand for goods and services. This is bound to happen if the general level of effective demand exceeds total supply of goods and services. More money will then be chasing few goods. It must be added that an excess demand inflation is more likely to occur under conditions of full employment. If all factors of production are fully employed, excess demand for particular factors can easily occur; this will lead to greater competition to secure such factors at higher prices thus leading to increased costs of production, which reappear in higher prices for consumption goods in a spiral. In developing countries, such as West Africa, excess demand inflation often arises through unemployment and underemployment. A large number of resources in these countries, for example, labour and land, remain unemployed and underemployed and fewer goods and crops are produced, thus leading to greater pressure of effective demand on the relatively few goods (including imported goods) and services which are available. In West Africa, where the main economic activity is agricultural production, it is perhaps relatively easy to cope with an excess demand inflation, by merely bring more land into cultivation and by improving the technique and system of production. In industrial countries, the cure for an excess demand inflation is more complicated as it involves both monetary and real measures. The monetary system has to be controlled so as to get as near as possible to the correct volume of purchasing power which the country needs for its economic transactions. If the supply of money cannot be quickly reduced then the level of productivity has to be raised in order to achieve a parity between goods and services on the one hand, and the volume of the purchasing power on the other. Also, inflation can occur through the manipulation of the credit system of the commerical banks. If the government, through the Central Bank, decides to increase the volume of money in circulation, it can encourage commercial banks to increase their levels of loans and advances to the public. This can be done by a reduction in the official bank rate, thus making it cheaper to borrow at all levels. Similarly, through open market operations, which have already been mentioned, the commercial banks can be put in a position to create more bank money on the strength of increased cash deposits by the public. If increases in bank credits do not match any increase in goods and services produced or available, then deflation may occur.

Again, inflation may arise through the activities of the trade unions. In any economy where the trade unions are well organised and strong they tend to have great influence on the determination of wages. It is important to be reminded that there are two broad methods by which trade unions may influence the level of wages. The trade union, by adopting restrictive practices, may limit the supply of labour. This may be achieved by limiting the number of new entrants to particular types of jobs. The direct influence of such a policy is to create an artificial scarcity of labour relative to demand, thus forcing up the price for labour, that is, wages. Further, through strike action, the trade unions can put pressure on employers to pay higher wages in certain cases. A labour-induced inflation is more likely to occur in a free enterprise, full employment economy, than in the developing countries of West Africa. Increases in wages will inevitably increase the wages bills of industrialists thus leading to higher costs of production and ultimately to higher prices. A labour-induced inflation may be avoided if increases in the level of wages are directly related to increases in productivity. In Britain, for example, the government has at times introduced a prices and incomes policy in order to tackle the labour-induced inflation facing the country. The basic principle of the policy is to relate wage increases to increases in productivity. An additional objective involved in this policy is to relate the overall wage increases to the national rate of growth. Under this policy, the government will only support a wage increase in any sector of the economy if such a wage increase is matched by an increase in the productivity of that sector which is, of course, part of the overall growth of the national economy. A labour-induced inflation in West Africa takes a slightly different form. It usually starts with increases in wages, but ends with an excess demand inflation as already explained above. The demand for wage increases in West Africa is often based on increases in the cost of living. For example, in Nigeria, wage revisions have occurred at more or less regular intervals of five years since 1946. The standard adopted in assessing the changes in the cost of living is that of the minority of the population living in the big cities. The position of the peasant farmers who constitute the bulk of the working population is often ignored. The ultimate result has been for prices to go up, because the farmers who were ignored in the wage negotiations take care of themselves by increasing the prices of their farm products – foodstuffs.

Lastly, inflation occurs under the abnormal conditions of war. The normal process of production is interrupted during the war. In addition to this, the major problem is how to finance the war. It usually means that a large proportion of the government revenue has to be devoted to purchasing arms and to maintaining the armed forces. A case in point is the Nigerian civil war (1967–70). The Nigerian government purchased arms from a number of foreign countries and paid for them from its foreign exchange reserves, which are used under normal circumstances to purchase goods and services from abroad. This resulted in shortages of imported consumption goods which in turn led to increases in prices. The worst impact of wartime inflation on the public is often checked by rationing and price control so that the level of demand does not exceed the general level of supply.

Inflation tends to favour debtors, profit-seekers and speculators; but it tends to harm creditors, fixed-income earners and hesitant investors. Debtors are able to repay their debts in lower value money which is to their advantage, whereas creditors receive lower value money which is to their disadvantage. The rising prices which are associated with inflation tend to encourage investors as the prospect of making a financial profit is improved. Indeed, it is accepted by some people that a certain degree of inflation is desirable in a free enterprise economy, but perhaps one is also justified in saying that inflation is an incurable disease in any free enterprise economy. However, the main problem which has been confronting economists over the years is to find the means of ascertaining the correct dose of inflation which should be allowed in any economy from time to time in order to achieve sustained growth.

COMMERCIAL BANKING

There are three categories of commercial banks in West Africa: foreign or expatriate, indigenous and government-owned. The foreign and indigenous banks are all private enterprise undertakings. These banks are joint-stock companies operating with the object of making profit. The government-owned commercial banks were established for two major reasons. First, in countries where there were no indigenous commercial banks, the government felt the need to break the monopoly of banking business held by foreign banks; hence the establishment of government-owned commercial banks, such as the Ghana Commercial Bank. Secondly, the governments believed that the ordinary commercial banks failed to cater for some groups of people in the economy, particularly the farmers, and consequently, some special banks were created. For example, the Nigerian co-operative banks, and the Nigerian Agricultural Bank were established to provide credit for the farmers and co-operative societies.

It must be emphasised that all commercial banks operate for profit. In pursuing profitability, the commercial banks must ensure that public confidence in commercial banking is maintained. Public confidence can only be achieved if the commercial banks perform their functions effectively and satisfactorily. This they do by striking a balance between liquidity, that is, being able to meet the cash demands of customers, and profitability, investing to some extent in assets of short-term maturity which, in the face of excessive cash withdrawals, can be sold to the Central Bank without loss or held to maturity when they receive cash for them.

The functions of a commercial bank are basically embodied in what is usually referred to as 'ordinary banking business'. Ordinary banking business includes the safe keeping of the customers' money and the transfer of money from one person or institution to another which is primarily the payment of debts. The first function is to ensure that money kept with the bank is safe. The second and more important function is the transfer of money with the aid of the cheque. The commercial bank provides facilities whereby an individual or institution can transfer large sums of money without actually handling any physical cash. Not only can one transfer money within a country, but it is also possible to transfer money to different parts of the world through the medium of commerical banks. Commercial banks also undertake to keep for their customers important documents, such as wills, certificates and deeds, and valuables such as jewelry and rare paintings. Lastly, commercial banks act as trustees to execute wills and administer trust funds.

THE CREATION OF CREDIT

The commercial banks have come to realise that not all the money kept with them is withdrawn at the same time by their customers. It is, therefore, unprofitable for the banks to keep all the cash in the strongroom waiting for the customers to come along to claim money. So commercial banks use the money deposited with them to support a credit system. The credit system is operated within the legal framework of the banking laws, which usually stipulate the extent to which credit must be backed by cash in reserve. For example, if a new cash deposit of ₦2,000 is made in a commercial bank, that bank is liable to the customer to the full amount of ₦2,000, but to keep 100 per cent cash-reserve is both unprofitable and unnecessary. The bank, therefore, holds the ₦2,000 as cash reserve to support total deposits of perhaps as much as ₦10,000. The additional deposits of ₦8,000 are created by the bank lending this amount to other customers who of course pay interest to the bank. If the cash reserve ratio stipulated by law is 20 per cent of total deposits, it means that ₦400 has to be kept in the bank, while the rest, ₦1,600, can be used to support deposits of ₦8,000, of which 20 per cent is ₦1,600. It is important to note that the commercial bank has deliberately created more money than it has, but the money created is bank money and not new coins or currency. In other words, the commercial banks are able to create bank money, lending to people or businesses who urgently need money and who are prepared and able to pay for the use of such money, provided the banks have sufficient cash in hand to meet the legal reserve obligations and to pay out cash to any customer who wishes to withdraw all or part of his deposit. Strictly speaking, in the short period, every bank is insolvent. This means that, if all the customers of a bank rushed into it at the same time demanding to withdraw their deposits, the bank would be unable to satisfy them all, because customers' deposits greatly exceed the cash in hand. The bank will only be solvent if and when it can sell all its investments and securities and recover the loans it has made to its customers.

A number of factors tend to control the limit to which the commercial banks can create money. First, the Central Bank can control the credit system of the commercial banks in three ways: it can manipulate the official bank rate which affects all rates of interest; or through open market operations in which it buys or sells securities, so affecting the commercial banks' cash reserve; or through changes in the legal cash ratio it can force the banks to hold more cash or reduce their deposits.

If the Central Bank raises the official bank rate, all the other rates of interest will also go up; consequently it will be dearer to borrow money from the commercial banks and so some customers will reduce their loans. On the other hand, if the official bank rate is lowered, it will be cheaper to borrow money from the commercial banks and this may lead to an expansion of bank credit to its customers. The Central Bank can also increase or reduce the volume of bank money by its open market operations. If the Central Bank buys securities, for example, government bonds, from the public, the holders of such securities will receive money which they deposit in their banks. This will increase the volume of cash deposits with the commercial banks, and all other things being equal, it will give the banks greater opportunities to create more credit. On the other hand, if the Central Bank sells securities to the public, those buying them will pay out of their bank deposits, thus reducing the volume of deposits with the commercial banks. This will reduce the amount of credit which the commercial banks can create.

The Central Bank may directly control the volume of bank money, that is, credit, by changing the statutory cash reserve ratio of the commercial banks. A higher cash reserve ratio reduces the volume of credit that may be created with a given amount of cash held by the banks; while a lower cash reserve ratio increases the volume of credit that may potentially be created.

Even though the commercial banks can create bank money (credit), they do this with great caution. The loans and advances granted by the commercial banks are such that the borrowers can pay interest on them and can repay the loan at the date agreed; or alternatively such loans and advances must be backed by adequate and marketable securities which could be realised, that is, turned into liquid assets – cash – if there is any default in the repayment. All commercial banks demand adequate security to back up loans and advances to their customers. Indeed, one of the main criticisms of the commercial banks in West Africa has been that they operate too cautiously in granting loans and advances to their customers. However, it must be realised that the commercial banks must pursue the principle of adequate security if they are to remain in business. Land and buildings, which are the obvious items on which to secure loans in West Africa, are often tied up by customary law which makes them inalienable and thus bad securities as far as borrowing from the commercial banks is concerned.

Another factor which influences the credit system of the commercial banks is the economic climate of a country. In a period of boom, more money is likely to be deposited in the commercial banks, which, in turn, gives more room for creating credit. On the other hand, in a period of depression, less money is deposited with the commercial banks, thus leading to less credit creation by the commercial banks. It follows, therefore, that whatever happens to the official bank rate and the cash ratio, the economic climate of a country determines, to a great extent, the volume of credit that may readily be created by the commercial banks.

ASSETS OF COMMERCIAL BANKS

One part of a commercial bank's assets is the money deposited with the Central Bank. This amount is fixed by law and it must be deposited with the Central Bank before a commercial bank can obtain a licence to operate. This asset does not give any direct revenue to the commercial bank. In fact, it is that part of the commercial bank's assets which is kept by the Central Bank as a guarantee to safeguard the interest of the public in case of liquidation.

The second asset is 'cash in bank', which is kept in order to meet the day-to-day requirements of the customers. A commercial bank must at all times keep cash adequate to satisfy the demands of its customers. The confidence of the public will be shaken if a commercial bank is unable to provide money when asked to do so by any of its customers. Indeed, a bank which fails at any time to do this is unlikely to survive. The 'cash in bank' is a proportion called the cash ratio of the commercial bank's total liabilities to its customers. In England, for example, the cash ratio normally maintained by the commercial banks is between 6 to 8 per cent of total bank deposits. However, in West Africa, the Central Banks stipulate the cash ratios. The 'cash in bank' does not yield any direct revenue to the commercial bank.

The third type of asset is 'money at call'. This asset is not readily available to commercial banks in West Africa, because of the absence of a strong money market which makes use of this kind of money. However, it is the practice of most banks in West Africa to invest in this asset in overseas countries where such facilities exist, particularly on the London money market. 'Money at call' takes the form of very short-term loans to the money market for periods ranging from twenty-four hours to seventy-two days. The interest rates charged on money at call are relatively low. The main point to remember is that the nearer money is to liquid cash, the less the rate of interest on such money.

The next type of asset held by the commercial banks is 'bills of exchange'. Bills of exchange are extensively used to finance international trade. A bill of exchange can be regarded as a 'loan' which is usually due for payment after three months. For example, if X buys goods from Y and gives Y a bill of exchange for the value of the goods, this is a promise to pay the holder of the bill the agreed sum of money on a given date, usually three months ahead. However, if Y needs the money urgently he can discount the bill at his, Y's, bank. Instead of waiting for three months Y sells the bill to his bank for a little less than its face value and when the bill matures in three months the bank collects the full value from X. Y's bank has, in effect, charged a discount on the bill for providing him with money before he is actually due to receive it from X. For example, if Y is due to receive ₦100 from X in three months' time, Y can discount the bill and obtain ₦98 now instead of waiting for three months to receive the full amount of ₦100. The ₦2 he loses represents the discount charged by the commercial bank. After three months, on the date the bill actually matures, the commercial bank will claim to the full amount of ₦100 from X. In this way, the commercial bank is able to make some revenue from buying bills at a discount.

Government treasury bonds constitute another important type of asset held by commercial banks. A treasury bond is government indebtedness for the amount shown on the bond to the person holding it. The first-ever treasury bonds issued in West Africa were by the Nigerian and Ghana governments in 1959 and 1960. Such bonds are repayable after a specified period, usually of several years, and pay a higher rate of interest the longer the period they take to mature. One important point to bear in mind is that investment in treasury bonds is safe, because these bonds have the backing of the government which has an unlimited power to raise money from the public if necessary to repay the bonds. Treasury bonds are called gilt-edged securities to indicate their superiority over ordinary securities. A recent innovation in the assets available to commercial banks in Nigeria is *treasury certificates* which were first issued during the Nigerian civil war, 1967–70. A treasury certificate is in every respect like a treasury bond except that it matures quicker – in under twenty-four months – than a treasury bond. The issue of treasury certificates was introduced in Nigeria as a wartime measure to enable the government to borrow more money and at the same time to provide commercial banks with an added avenue for investments.

The last item of the assets of a commercial bank are advances and loans to the bank's customers. Advances and loans are 'bank money', the creation of which we have already discussed. They increase the liabilities of the banks in the form of deposits by the same amount as the assets created. Interest rates on advances and loans are the highest and provide the largest single source of income for the banks.

In addition to the interest which a commercial bank receives on its assets, it also charges some fees for performing services to its customers. A customer is charged a periodic fee for keeping the accounts of a current or demand deposit with the commercial bank. The commercial banks also charge fees for transferring money from one person or institution to another. Commercial banks are also paid for their services as trustees, executors of wills, and for the safe keeping of customers' documents and articles.

THE CENTRAL BANK

Central banks in West Africa owed their origin to political developments. The colonial monetary system which had its foundation in the West African Currency Board began to disintegrate with the attainment of political independence in Ghana in 1957. Before 1957, however, Ghana and Nigeria had each separately considered the creation of a Central Bank in anticipation of future economic and political developments. Ghana felt the need for a separate currency identity; consequently she abandoned the Currency Board system and established the Bank of Ghana and her own currency in 1957. Under similar circumstances Nigeria established the Central Bank of Nigeria in 1959. Also, in 1963, the Bank of Sierra Leone was established. The Gambia remained on the old West African Currency Board system until August 1964 when the Gambia Currency Board was established. The Central Bank of the Gambia was established in 1971.

All the West African central banks perform similar functions. We shall discuss, therefore, the main functions of a Central Bank. The Central Bank is the sole bank of issue. In other words, the Central Bank is responsible for the supply of the currency notes and the coins in circulation. For many years, the Royal Mint in England supplied the West African countries with the amounts of currency notes and coins they needed, but Nigeria, Ghana and Sierra Leone have each established a company responsible for printing currency notes and for minting coins. For example, the Nigerian Security Printing and Minting Company (NSPMC) was established in 1963. Apart from supplying currency notes and coins to the Central Bank, the company is also responsible for the printing of postal orders, stamps, wireless and vehicle licences, stock certificates, treasury bills and other government security documents.

Secondly, the Central Bank acts as the government's banker. It means that all government banking transactions are handled by the Central Bank.

Thirdly, the Central Bank is the financial adviser to the government. It advises the government on monetary and financial matters, including the supply of money, the stability of the national currency and exchange control, and on fiscal measures, which may affect the international value of the national currency.

Fourthly, the Central Bank acts as the banker to the commercial banks. The commercial banks maintain accounts with the Central Bank and, through regular consultations, matters of mutual interest are discussed. The commercial banks can fall back on the Central Bank for financial help in case of any difficulty. In this respect, the Central Bank can be referred to as the lender of last resort.

Fifthly, the Central Bank handles all the banking and foreign exchange transactions of the country. It must be added that in order to discharge this function effectively, it usually appoints a number of the commercial banks as agents to handle foreign exchange transactions on its behalf.

Sixthly, the Central Bank exercises general control over the activities of the commercial banks. As we have already mentioned in Chapter 6, the Central Bank fixes the official bank rate which affects all the other interest rates being operated by the commercial banks. Also, it fixes from time to time the cash reserve ratio of the commercial banks, thus controlling credit creation activities. Through open market operations, the Central Bank can exercise control over the volume of credit created by the commercial banks. Beside the general statutory requirement that each commercial bank must furnish the Central Bank with monthly accounts, it also has the statutory power to appoint examiners to look into the business of any commercial bank.

In addition to these basic functions, the central banks in West Africa have some other peculiar functions which those of the most developed countries do not perform. For example, they are given the function of promoting the general economic development and stability of the country. This embraces a wide range of actions and it has included so far the granting of credit to the marketing boards in

Nigeria and the development of money and capital markets.

OTHER BANKS

Mention must be made of two other banks because of their special nature. These are the Nigerian Industrial Development Bank and the African Development Bank.

The Nigerian Industrial Development Bank Ltd (NIDB) was established in January 1964. The main object of the bank is to provide medium- and long-term loans to private enterprises in Nigeria. The bank helps to finance enterprises which by reason of their size will make significant contributions to the economic development of the country. However, the operation of the bank does not cover cottage and small-scale industries. The bank also encourages indigenous and overseas investors to join with it in its investment and lending operations. The financial assistance that can be obtained from the bank is flexible and may take the form of stock or debentures, medium- or long-term loans, long-term debt instruments with convertibility features; and any combination of these types of assistance. Loans from the bank may be granted for periods up to fifteen years, but a longer amortisation period can be considered in exceptional cases. The bank does not participate in the management of any enterprise it helps to finance. However, the bank supervises its investments by enforcing follow-up and reporting procedure; and it tries to maintain adequate reserves out of its earnings to offset any possible losses. In all cases, the bank's investment decisions are made entirely on business criteria.

The idea of establishing an African development bank was first suggested at the All African People's Conference in Tunis in 1960. Many of the newly independent countries decided to take control over their own development projects and provide funds amongst themselves. After the preliminary arrangements which included the drawing up of the articles of association and the signatures of the initial thirty participant countries, the African Development Bank was established in September 1964. In November 1964 the bank's council of governors held its first meeting and decided that Abidjan, the capital of the Ivory Coast, should be the headquarters of the bank. The authorised capital of the bank, which is subscribed by member states, was set at 250 million US dollars. According to the bank's charter, its main objective is to promote the economic development and social progress of its member states. The bank gives priority to multinational projects and finances development programmes designed to make the economies of member states more complementary to each other. By 1970, the bank had financed a number of projects including road development in Kenya, water supply in Uganda, irrigation in Tunisia and a fertiliser factory in the Invory Coast.

THE MONEY MARKET

The money market consists of institutions engaged in the borrowing and lending of short-term funds. The main transactions on the money market cover short-term credits, bills of exchange and treasury bills. As we have already mentioned above, these items represent most of the liquid assets of the commercial banks. The main financial institutions responsible for the operation of the money market are the Central Bank and the commercial banks. In West Africa, most of the commercial banks also perform the functions of accepting houses or merchant bankers. They 'accept' bills for their clients. The process of acceptance merely consists of the accepting house placing its signature upon the trader's bill of exchange and thereby guaranteeing the bill and making itself responsible for the bill's payment. Basically, such acceptances do not involve the accepting house in any financial outlay because clients have undertaken to provide the accepting house with funds to meet the face values of the bills when they mature. The accepting house or the commercial bank, as the case may be, earns commission for performing the function of accepting bills. In fact, the commission is the discount charge which we have already mentioned above. The accepting houses in effect transform bills drawn on reliable but unknown traders into first-class securities by adding their signatures to such bills and thus making them internationally transferable and acceptable.

A large number of insurance companies invest on the money market. They are continually in receipt of large sums of money – premiums from clients – for which they seek investment. The liabilities of insurance companies are usually spread over periods of years. They can also calculate such liabilities with great accuracy. They are, therefore, prepared to lend money out in short-term securities which will earn them additional revenue. These securities are selected to mature at a date convenient for meeting their future liabilities.

In West Africa, money markets are still in the process of developing. Since 1960, both the Bank of Ghana and the Central Bank of Nigeria have been issuing government treasury bills and bonds. The main object is to provide bills which will form the nucleus of short-term first-class securities suitable for commercial banks' portfolios or investments. The issue of treasury bills in these two countries has increased considerably since 1960 and the investments of commercial banks in treasury bills and on other government securities is very substantial.

THE STOCK EXCHANGE

A stock exchange is an organised market for the purchase and sale of stocks, bonds and shares. From our discussion of joint-stock companies we know that most limited liability companies obtain their long-term capital by issuing shares to prospective investors. Those who eventually buy shares become shareholders. The purchase of new shares is the conversion of saving into investment. The stock exchange, in fact, provides facilities for mobilising savings and investments. If any shareholder decides to disinvest, that is, to discontinue as a shareholder, he will be able to sell his shares on the stock exchange. It must be added, however, that the stock exchange only deals in stocks and shares registered with it.

The only existing stock exchange in West Africa is the Lagos Stock Exchange which was established in 1961. By 1976, the Lagos Stock Exchange had handled a number of the Nigerian government development loan stocks and the shares of companies registered in Nigeria.

Chapter 8

International Economics

THE SCOPE OF INTERNATIONAL ECONOMICS

For every country the first initiation into international economics is through foreign trade. West Africa first had the experience of international exchange through the trans-Saharan trade between West and North Africa. It began with simple exchanges of West African products for Arab products and later for the manufactures of Europe which found their way into North Africa. By the fifteenth century, the development of the sailing ship had made possible direct maritime contact between Europe and West Africa; and about the same period, the Atlantic slave trade was started by the Portuguese. In many respects it is regrettable that the first major contact which West Africa had with the rest of the world, particularly with Europe and America, was in connection with the slave trade. However, with the abolition of the slave trade early in the nineteenth century, West Africa began to exchange its agricultural products and natural resources for European manufactures. Despite the fundamental evils of the slave trade, it must be added that it created the basic international exchange mechanism on which the 'legitimate' trade which followed had its foundation.

Most of the early foreign trade exchanges, until about the middle of the nineteenth century, were in the nature of barter; goods were exchanged for goods. As we already know, a few commodity currencies and a number of foreign coins were adopted as media of exchange in West Africa. It must also be mentioned that no one of the West African countries had any clear national identity as we know it today. Following the Berlin Conference of 1885, which led to the partition of Africa, the British government established its influence in West Africa and through time gave separate colonial identities to the Gambia, Sierra Leone, the Gold Coast (now Ghana) and Nigeria. Even at that stage each of the countries remained under the full control of Britain and, as such, none was directly exposed to the full impact of international economics. By 1912, Britain had established a currency system for West Africa but continued to regulate trade through colonial legislation. Britain, therefore, stood between West Africa and the rest of the world as far as international trade was concerned.

The direct experience and influence of international economics in West Africa is very recent. It was after the West African countries attained political independence that they had to face the full implications of international economics. Each country had to grapple with its own peculiar economic and social problems in the light of the modern economic conditions in which it suddenly found itself on attaining political independence. Since independence, the government policy throughout West Africa has been based essentially on achieving rapid economic growth. Each country has had to create its national currency and the monetary mechanism involved in international trade. In this chapter, we shall examine briefly the major complexities of international trade; the characteristics of international trade; international trade theories; the balance of international payments; and customs duties and foreign exchange.

CHARACTERISTICS OF FOREIGN TRADE

In an earlier chapter we saw how specialisation increases productivity. If we turn to international specialisation we discover that it has its foundation on the same principles as specialisation among people. Foreign trade arises because the resources of each country are limited in some way, and because these resources differ from the resources of other countries. In the first place, the geographical location of each country affects its agricultural potential and, secondly, nature has not been generous enough to endow each country with abundant or equal resources. The West African countries, for example, have been selling their abundance of tropical agricultural produce – palm products, groundnuts, cocoa and cotton – and their minerals – tin, gold, diamonds and petroleum – to other countries which cannot or do not produce them for themselves. At the same time, the West African countries purchase most of their manufactured goods, which they are unable to produce, from other countries. It means, therefore, that one reason why foreign trade appears is because each country exchanges its relatively abundant produce, and supplements its relatively poor resources from the abundance of other countries.

Under normal conditions, a country will be willing to enter into international trade for three basic reasons. First, a country will want to purchase those commodities which it cannot produce at home because of climatic and/or geological conditions. For example, the temperate European countries purchase the West African produce mentioned above. Secondly, a country will buy from abroad those commodities it produces only in insufficient quantities. For example, the West African countries buy cotton goods from Europe and Japan; while England purchases dairy products from Australia and New Zealand. Thirdly, a country may purchase from abroad commodities which it can produce only at greater expense than the commodities it exports to pay for them. It must be added that the various stages of economic growth in different countries tend to affect the motive for, and the composition and volume of, international trade. The fact that the soil and the climatic conditions in a given country favour the growing of, for instance, cocoa will not bring about any international trade of itself. The country concerned must actually grow cocoa and be willing to sell it to those countries which want to purchase cocoa. Similarly, it is not enough to have the knowledge that a mineral deposit exists in a country; such a mineral must be exploited before it can be used for international exchange. The knowledge of the existence of natural resources all over the world and the degree to which they are utilised determine the extent and direction of international exchange. For example, cocoa did not become the major export of Ghana and Nigeria until it was introduced into these countries in the second half of the nineteenth century and was being grown extensively by peasant farmers. Similarly, petroleum did not enter into Nigeria's foreign trade until 1957 after exploration revealed that it could be produced in a commercial quantity.

Fundamentally, foreign trade is not different in nature from the domestic trade between different districts of the same country. What differences do exist between internal trade and foreign trade arise from international, social, economic and political friction hindering the free operation of demand and supply at the international level. Two such instances result from natural barriers and from national boundaries. Many countries remain separated by natural barriers such as the sea, deserts and mountains. These natural barriers prove very formidable at the early stages of world commerce.

Modern developments in transport and communications have bridged the gaps created by these natural barriers. It must be added that some natural barriers also exist in any country, but these are usually overcome much more quickly. Modern ocean shipping, jet aircraft and powerful and fast motor vehicles have contributed substantially to the growth of modern international trade.

The existence of national boundaries, however, has created many problems for international commerce. Indeed, the friction of national boundaries presents the major difference between domestic trade and international trade. Closely associated with national boundaries are a number of symbols of national identity. In the first place, differences in political doctrines tend to influence international contacts. For very many years, when the West African countries were under colonial rule, the British did not allow them to trade freely with the countries of Eastern Europe which are communist countries. However, now that all the West African countries have attained political independence, they have established trading relationships with most of the other countries in the world.

The refusal of America to give political recognition to Communist China until 1972 is an example of a purely political issue which put a strong barrier across the channel of normal international trade between the two countries.

Apart from basic political differences, each major country of the world has its own national monetary system based on a separate currency. The managements of national currencies, therefore, bring with them other regulations and controls, such as exchange control, which limit the normal flow of international trade.

THEORIES OF INTERNATIONAL TRADE

The best-known theory of international trade is the theory of comparative cost advantage. This theory was first clearly stated by Adam Smith, but later developed by David Ricardo and John Stuart Mill. It has come to be known as the classical theory of international trade. Adam Smith stated simply:

> It is the maxim of every prudent master of a family never to attempt to make at home what it will cost him more to make than to buy . . . What is prudence in the conduct of every private family can scarce be folly in that of a great kingdom. If a foreign country can supply us with a commodity cheaper than we ourselves can make it, better buy it of them with some part of the produce of our own industry employed in a way in which we have some advantage.

Ricardo took over Adam Smith's theory, developed it and made it more precise in its application to the trade between two countries. Suppose there are two countries A and B each possessing two units of labour which they can employ to produce commodities x and y. Suppose also that if country A employs one unit each in producing x and y, its total production will be $1x + 5y$ commodities, and that if country B employs one unit each in producing x and y, its total production will be $5x + 1y$ commodities. The total production of the two countries A and B will be then $6x + 6y$ commodities. In this illustration country A can produce commodity y more efficiently than can country B, while country B can produce commodity x more efficiently than country A. The argument of the comparative cost theory, therefore, is that both countries will benefit if each of them concentrates on producing the commodity it can produce more efficiently and exchanges that commodity with that which it can only produce less efficiently. If country A employs its two units of labour on producing commodity y, all other things being equal, country A will have a total production of $10y$, and if country B does a similar thing, it will have a total production of $10x$. This means that the total production of both countries will be $10x + 10y$ commodities; that is, an increase of $4x + 4y$ commodities over and above what they could produce were there no specialisation.

In this simple example, country A has an absolute cost advantage over country B since one factor unit in A can produce $5y$ whereas one factor unit in country B can produce only $1y$. In contrast country B has an absolute cost advantage over country A in the production of x. But the theory of comparative cost advantage can also demonstrate that even if the factors of production in one country are more efficient than those of another country in the production of both commodities, nevertheless there will be gains from trade for both countries provided there are comparative cost differences. For instance, if in country A one factor unit can produce either two units of x or five units of y and in country B one factor unit can produce either one unit of x or four units of y, there will be advantage from trade to both countries if A specialises in x and B in y.

The comparative cost advantage theory is based on a number of assumptions. For instance, it is assumed that there is free mobility of all factors of production: in other words, land, labour, capital and enterprise are free to be employed where they can make the most contribution to production. In addition to the factors being mobile, the classical model also assumes that factors of production are equally efficient in all lines of production. The theory also assumes a certain level of technical knowledge in relation to production. Another assumption is that the volume of production per unit of a factor cannot be increased by raising the productivity of the factors employed. Finally, the theory assumes negligible transport costs and free trade conditions.

The other theory which we shall discuss – the vent-for-surplus theory of international trade – also has its origin with the classical economists. The theory was first stated by Adam Smith.

> Between whatever places foreign trade is carried on, they all of them derive two distinct benefits from it. It carries out that surplus part of the produce of their land and labour for which there is no demand among them, and brings back in return for it something else for which there is demand. It gives a value to their superfluities by exchanging them for something else, which may satisfy a part of their wants, and increase their enjoyments . . .

The essential aspects of the vent-for-surplus theory are as follows. First, international trade does not necessarily reallocate factors of production but enables the output of the surplus resources to be used to meet foreign demand. Secondly, the population density of a country largely determines its export capacity. It helps to determine the total volume of production, the level of internal consumption and the volume of surplus production that may be exported. Lastly, in relation to West Africa, the surplus productive capacity of resources enables the farmers to produce export crops without necessarily reducing the production of food crops which enter into domestic trade.

The vent-for-surplus theory of international trade can be explained in the context of West African trade. The rapid expansion of the exports of West Africa, particularly in the first half of the twentieth century, was not due to any great changes in the techniques of production which could have secured higher productivity. Farmers clung to the traditional methods of production, and the production for export was achieved merely by bringing into use factors hitherto unused and by employing fully those factors that were already being used. It must be noted that surplus productive capacity exists if a factor of production is employed below its full productive capacity. The development of transport and communications, the establishment of a proper monetary system and the introduction of new export crops helped to utilise the hitherto unused resources of West Africa.

This theory can also be applied specifically to the major export crops of West Africa. Until very recently, there was no local demand for cocoa and the local demand that existed for palm-kernels was not of such substantial volume as to affect the quantity exported, consequently, total production of these crops constituted direct surpluses for export. Some of the other crops, such as cotton, groundnuts and palm-oil, had very high local demand, and it was in regard to these crops that the surplus argument became applicable. In order to provide more cotton and groundnuts more land had to be brought under cultivation, and in order to increase the volume of palm-oil production more attention had to be paid to the wild palm which had been left untended for many decades. The farmers continued to adopt their old techniques of production, so that there was no question of increasing physical productivity through technical innovations. With the exception of gold and, in recent years, petroleum, for which there was some local demand, almost the entire mineral output of West Africa was surpluses only produced for export. The surplus nature of the export trade of West Africa was further proved by the fact that for a long period West Africa maintained self-sufficiency in basic food crops. International trade did not divert the efforts of the farmers from meeting local needs to producing export crops. There were occasional shortages of local crops, brought about mainly by climatic conditions, but these were quickly corrected.

The agricultural labour force which previously concentrated on subsistence production and was underemployed was used to meet the demand for agricultural export production.

Although a number of economists have used either the theory of comparative cost advantage or the vent-for-surplus theory to explain why international exchange takes place, yet it must be realised that neither of them gives a satisfactory explanation of international trade. It must also be understood that neither theory destroys the basic, arguments of the other theory. In fact, one can say that the knowledge of both theories is relevant to the study of international trade. While the theory of comparative cost advantage explains the principles of international division of labour, the vent-for-surplus theory, on the other hand, seeks to explain the principles of international trade in terms of both domestic and foreign demands. It is fully recognised that absolute or comparative cost advantages bring about international exchanges of goods and services. However, under normal conditions, the point at which the comparative cost advantage begins to operate depends very much on the availability of a surplus of production over and above domestic needs.

It means that under normal circumstances, a country will not export its produce merely on the comparative cost advantage principle, if the volume produced is inadequate to meet its domestic demand. The point at which the product of a country enters into international trade is determined at the time when it can produce a surplus. If a country is unable to produce a surplus over its domestic demand, it can 'create' a surplus by adopting a number of policies which reduce the local demand for the product concerned. For example, a country which produces motor-cars can impose a heavy purchase tax on domestic buyers of cars in order to reduce the internal demand and thus make more cars available for export; this has been the practice in some industrial countries of Europe for some years. Surpluses can be created by restricting internal demand. It follows, therefore, that the creation of a surplus depends on the nature of the product concerned. If the product is one for which there is no close substitute, such as palm-oil in West Africa, it may be difficult to reduce the internal demand, since palm-oil is the main source of vegetable oil in West Africa. But if the commodity constitutes a luxury, such as a car (although cars can be necessities in some circumstances), then it may be possible to induce people to postpone or abandon their demands and thus create a surplus. The relative elasticities of internal demand determine the volume of surpluses that may be produced or created.

Just as surpluses can be created, so also can scarcity be deliberately created. A country which deliberately prohibits the export of its product, for which it has a comparative cost advantage, to another country will automatically create a scarcity for its product. The fact that its surplus produce is not allowed to be exported to a country where it is needed defeats the principle of comparative cost advantage. It is sufficiently clear, therefore, that the production or 'creation' of surpluses is a prerequisite of international trade. The appropriate theory of international trade which tends to satisfy the theoretical as well as the practical aspects of international trade is a combination of comparative cost advantage and vent-for-surplus theories. The basic principles are that there must clearly be comparative cost advantages before international division of labour can arise, and each country must be able to produce or create a surplus which it is willing to allow into international trade.

For a number of reasons, it is perhaps not necessary to spend much time and space debating the microeconomic theory of international trade. The comparative cost theory which has prescribed the ideal conditions of international exchange remains virtually the exclusive luxury of the academics. That a country can concentrate on producing goods and services which it can produce at a comparative cost advantage and exchange these for those it could only produce at higher comparative cost is well accepted. Similarly, the vent-for-surplus theory which emphasises the correlation between internal production and consumption on the one hand and surpluses for export on the other is also accepted as the foundation on which the former theory could be firmly based.

However, two basic factors have dominated contemporary international exchange. First, it is no longer practical to continue to view the nation's international trade within the realm of microeconomics alone. The international trade performance of a country is a function of global international economics. International trade agreements, be they bilateral or multilateral, international monetary systems, and the world political climate all influence the pattern and structure of international trade.

Secondly, and probably more important, is the consciousness that international exchange for its own sake is no longer compatible with contemporary attitudes to economic growth and development. The era of indiscriminate imports and exports has virtually disappeared. Each country now deliberately calculates which items to import from time to time in the light of its development policy. It means in effect that the imports of the country reflect the immediate growth needs of the country. Also, exporting just for the sake of obtaining foreign exchange is no longer the important issue for the nation. Its international trade has to reflect the need to earn foreign exchange on the one hand and on the other provide the necessary raw materials for home industries. In addition, the country has to consider the judicious distribution of its trade so as to achieve maximum utility from its international trade. The utility need not be in purely money form; it includes good neighbourliness on a world scale, and the maintenance of the country's international credit-worthiness.

There is no doubt that in recent years the macroeconomic aspect of international trade has been receiving increasing attention. Each nation is being made to be aware of the effects of its trading activities on the growth and distribution of wealth in other countries. It is being realised more than ever before that strict adherence to the pure theory of international trade based on comparative cost tends to make the rich countries richer and the poor ones poorer. So governments are interfering with foreign trade for reasons other than economic advantage; for instance, foreign trade imports are being controlled to ensure that essential commodities are made available to the bulk of the population, while restrictions are placed on luxury items in an attempt to reduce the impact of the inequality of incomes.

As we have already indicated, international trade is the exchange of goods and services among the countries of the world. The exchange of goods and services between one country and another is strictly called bilateral trade; while exchange between one country and several other countries is known as multilateral trade. It is also important to distinguish between visible and invisible exports and imports. The visible exports of a particular country are its exports of physical goods. Visible exports of West African countries include cocoa, palm-oil, palm-kernels, groundnuts, cotton, coffee, gold, diamonds, tin and petroleum. The invisible exports are the services performed for foreign nationals and institutions. Such services include banking, insurance, shipping and tourist services. Visible imports, on the other hand, are the goods and services which a particular country purchases from other countries. One can distinguish between visible and invisible imports just as we have done in the case of exports.

We need to explain briefly how invisible exports and imports arise. The simplest example may be taken from international travel. Suppose X from Ghana travelled by Nigerian Airways to Nigeria on holiday. First, he paid his fare to the Nigerian airline. On reaching Nigeria, he deposited his Ghanaian money (cedis) with a Nigerian commercial bank which converted his cedis into Nigerian naira. He later issued a cheque to pay for a car he hired and in which he toured Nigeria. He also paid an insurance premium on the car to a Nigerian insurance company and bought petrol. Then he paid his bills for hotel accommodation. He thus made use of the following services: transport, banking, insurance and a hotel room. When he paid for these services with the money he brought from Ghana, it meant that he had consumed services provided by Nigeria. If his total holiday expenses in Nigeria cost him ₦2,000, this amount would represent an invisible export from Nigeria to a Ghanaian national and an invisible import to Ghana by a Ghanaian national.

We should also explain what is meant by a 're-export'. A re-export arises when a country imports some semi-finished or fully finished commodities and then exports such commodities again either in the same condition as when imported or after further processing. For example, country A may import semi-finished goods from country B and, after processing them, exports the goods to country C. There may also be a case where country D acts as an international intermediary for other countries. For example, country D may import finished goods from country E, and re-export them to countries F and G. The most significant thing about re-exports is that the production of the commodities involved in the re-export does not originate in the country which re-exports. The commodities must have been partially or totally produced in another country before they were imported and later re-exported. In the example given above, the re-export by country D is the completion of the export by country E.

THE BALANCE OF PAYMENTS

The balance-of-payments account of a country summarises all the international monetary transactions of that country. It is the balance sheet of a country. In addition to the exchange of goods and services it covers also such other items as gifts and foreign aid which involve international monetary transactions. The balance-of-payments account is divided into three main sections: the current account, the capital account and gold movements (Table 8.1).

The current account includes all payments for both the visible and invisible exports and imports. It is important to point out that early economists, many centuries ago, paid greater attention to visible exports and imports. It was common, therefore, to find arguments on the pattern of trade based on what is known as the balance of trade. The balance of trade is the difference in the money values of total visible exports and total visible imports of a country. The balance of trade may be related either to the trade between one country and another, or between one country and the rest of the world. A country is said to have a favourable or active balance of trade when the money value of its total exports exceeds the money value of its total imports; and there is an unfavourable or passive balance of trade if the reverse is the case.

Table 8.1 *Balance-of-Payments Account*

	Receipts	*Payments*
Current Account	1 Visible Exports	1 Visible Imports
	2 Invisible Exports	2 Invisible Imports
Capital Account	3 Loans Received	3 Loans Repaid
	4 Gifts Received	4 Gifts Given
Gold movements	5 Gold Received	5 Gold Paid
Total	*Total receipts*	*Total payments*

Both the visible and the invisible items of trade are considered together in order to obtain the balance of payments on current account. If the money-value of the visible and the invisible exports taken together exceeds the money-value of the visible and the invisible imports together there is a favourable balance of payments on current account, and there is an unfavourable balance of payments on the current account if the total amount being paid out for visible and invisible items exceeds the amount being received.

It is probably appropriate to introduce at this juncture another concept, that of the 'terms of trade'. The terms of trade measure the relationship between the price of imports and the price of exports, so enabling one to make comparisons of exchange in real terms. For example, if in 1970 a ton of cocoa in country X fetched ₦1,000, and it cost that country ₦1,000 to import a car, then one can conclude that in that year, a car was equal to a ton of cocoa. If in 1975, the price of cocoa stood at ₦800 per ton and the price of the same type of car rose to ₦1,200, then country X would have to give up 1·5 tons of cocoa in order to obtain a car. During the five years there would have been an adverse movement in the terms of trade against country X. Or, if in 1975, the price of cocoa stood at ₦2,000 per ton and the price of the car was ₦1,000, then country X could obtain one car for 0·5 tons of cocoa, so the terms of trade would have moved in country X's favour. It is usual to measure movements in the terms of trade by comparing the relative changes in an index of import prices with an index of export prices. If the index of import prices is divided by the index of export prices and multiplied by 100 then we have an index of the terms of trade. If this index rises from year to year, then there is an adverse movement of the terms of trade for that country: if it falls, the terms of trade are moving favourably.

Most of the developing countries in Africa are primary producers of some agricultural products. These countries rely mainly on the exports of their agricultural products for the bulk of their earnings of foreign exchange. For many years, particularly during the colonial era, export earnings of the developing countries determined the amount of their imports. It was the visible trade that was important to these countries as far as their foreign earnings were concerned. Until very recently, and only in a few developing countries, such as Nigeria and Ghana, the invisible exports of these countries were very small, while they incurred heavy charges for invisible imports, since they had to rely almost completely on foreign services, mainly British, for insurance, banking and shipping. These countries did earn large sums from the sales of their export products but a large proportion of such earnings had to go into paying for invisible imports. Some developing countries, however, are now able to provide for themselves at least a part of the banking, insurance and shipping services they require and this reduces their invisible imports. For example, Nigeria now has a number of indigenous banking and insurance companies and its expenditure on shipping has been reduced, if only slightly, by the establishment of the Nigerian National Shipping Lines. In contrast to the developing countries, some of the developed countries earn large amounts from both visible and invisible trade. In the Western world, America and Britain are good examples. Britain frequently has an unfavourable balance of visible trade, but when her earnings from invisible exports are taken into consideration she manages, on occasion, to show favourable balances on the current account.

Every item on the balance-of-payments account has two entries: on one side is a 'payment' and on the other side is a 'receipt'. When the whole account is totalled, current account, capital account and gold movements, the balance of payments must always balance if there are no errors, smuggling or inadvertent omissions. This is because any excess of payments due to foreign countries which are not covered by receipts results in debts to the foreign countries and these debts will be an item on the capital account where a debt is equivalent to a receipt. So too a favourable balance on current account will be offset in the capital account.

The capital account is made up mainly of long-term and short-term loans and investments which private citizens make or receive from foreign private citizens; and long-term and short-term government loans and credits through various channels. One should be very careful in interpreting the items on the capital account. For example, if a Sierra Leonean buys Nigerian treasury bills, he has 'exported' money in return for the treasury bills he now holds. This will represent a 'payment' on the Sierra Leone balance-of-payments account and a 'receipt' on the Nigerian balance-of-payments account. Similarly, when a country lends abroad it gives rise to a 'payment' and when it borrows from abroad it gives rise to a 'receipt'. For better clarification one can say that whenever payments exceed receipts in respect of one country, that country is making its national currency available abroad. In other words, capital is flowing out of the country concerned. On the other hand, whenever receipts exceed payments, there is a capital inflow.

Both the current account and the capital account are finally balanced by gold movements. If the final position on the current account shows that there is a net balance of payments over receipts, and the capital account does not show adequate net receipts, it will lead to the movement of gold on the receipts side of the account in order to ensure an overall balance. Similarly, a net balance of receipts over payments, if not compensated for on the capital account, will lead to the movement of gold on the payments side in order to achieve equilibrium. If a country has no gold reserves and so in consequence no gold can move out, then the account has inevitably to be balanced by foreign loans, possibly made involuntarily by the creditor countries.

As we have already mentioned, the balance-of-payments account must always balance. However, not all countries can achieve equilibrium. Countries often experience disequilibrium either in the form of deficits or surpluses.

A nation's balance of payments is in equilibrium when its normal demand for foreign exchange is equal to its normal supply of foreign exchange. Surpluses and gold inflows of some years help to offset deficits and gold outflows of other years. A persistent disequilibrium is a serious problem for a nation. Continuous surpluses on the current account mean that a country is accumulating unwanted stocks of gold and credits or foreign bank deposits; and a nation experiencing a persistent deficit loses gold and foreign bank deposits. Countries experiencing persistent surpluses are exporting more goods and services than they purchase abroad; and therefore they must grant credit to finance the import deficits of foreign countries. This they do by making grants and long-term investments in deficit countries and receiving gold from them. But the gold reserves of the deficit countries will eventually become exhausted. The deficit countries are forced, therefore, to reduce imports, which in turn may affect the composition and structure of the national income and foreign exchange rates.

West African countries have had mixed fortunes regarding their balance of payments. For example, from the end of the Second World War up to and including 1954, Nigeria had consistent favourable balances of trade which made possible the accumulation of sterling balances. The main contributory factor to this economic phenomenon was the high prices of agricultural export produce, particularly cocoa, during the period. From 1955 onwards, this trend was reversed and adverse balances of trade were experienced for a number of years until 1966, partly as a result of increases in public expenditure and of the expansion of foreign private capital development. A high level of capital development in each of the West African countries has continued. In the case of Ghana, it depends largely on the export earnings from cocoa; and when the world price of cocoa fluctuates about a low average, it finds it difficult to pay for the foreign capital goods needed for economic development. The balance-of-payments position of Ghana had consistently worsened since 1964. This had been attributed to high payments for freights, insurance, finance of embassies, expenditure by Ghana Airways, repayments of loans and other items on invisible accounts, but especially to the very large increase in the price it has had to pay for its imports of petroleum since 1973. By 1965, Ghana's estimated balance-of-payments deficit was £G52·5 million (in 1965 £G1 = 100 old pence sterling). In the case of Nigeria the value of her total imports increased by about 50 per cent while that of exports rose by only 5 per cent. Imports, particularly of capital goods, continued to rise as more development projects were undertaken. By 1965, the balance-of-payments account of Nigeria showed a deficit of £₦63·7 million (in 1965 £₦1 = £1 sterling).

Table 8.2 shows an example of a balance-of-payments account. The Nigerian balance-of-payments position worsened during the civil war 1967–70, but after the end of the civil war the position improved because of the increased revenue from exports, particularly from petroleum, and reduced importation of arms, ammunition and some luxury items. Many developing countries are not as lucky as Nigeria in their endowment of natural resources which can earn foreign exchange. Such countries incur balance-of-payments deficits on current account because the value of domestic output often falls short of the level required to provide the exports needed to pay for increased imports.

Table 8.2 *Balance of Payments by Type of Transactions, Nigeria, 1974*

		₦ m.	
	Item	*Receipts Credit*	*Payments Debit*
A	*Current transactions*		
	1 Merchandise (exports, f.o.b., imports c.i.f.)	6,105·7	1,666·4
	2 Non-monetary gold	—	—
	3 Freight and insurance on international shipments	30·4	20·0
	4 Other transportation	43·4	69·6
	5 Travel	8·0	78·3
	6 Investment income	97·6	473·4
	7 Government transactions	24·8	296·9
	8 Other services	31·4	612·1
B	*Transfer payments (unrequited transfers)*		
	9 Private	4·0	61·3
	10 Official	2·2	7·0
C	*Capital and monetary gold*		
	Non-monetary sectors	1,148·9	1,154·8
	Allocation of special deposit receipts	—	—
	Monetary sector	270·4	3,372·6
	Errors and omissions	45·6	—
	TOTAL	7,812·4	7,812·4

There are two main measures that could be taken to correct a disequilibrium in the balance-of-payments accounts. First, an increase in foreign earnings can help to correct an imbalance. An increase in the volume of exports or an increase in the price of the exported products or both can increase foreign earnings. Secondly, a nation may correct its imbalance by adjusting its foreign exchange rate by devaluation or revaluation. But before we examine foreign exchange adjustments, it is important to understand what is meant by foreign exchange.

FOREIGN EXCHANGE

Foreign exchange is concerned with the exchange of national currencies. An exchange rate is the price of one national currency in terms of another. Thus the exchange rate for the Nigerian naira in January 1978 was approximately US $1·56. Foreign exchange rates developed out of the increasing volume of international transactions for trade, investments and currency speculation. There is a reciprocal relationship between currencies and this explains why any change in the price of one currency causes an inverse change in the prices of other currencies. For example, before the USA devalued its currency early in 1972, the then Nigerian pound (£₦) was equal to US $2·8. However, the devaluation of the dollar automatically led to the revaluation of the £₦.

Like any other price, the price of a currency, that is, its rate of exchange, is determined by supply and demand. If the Nigerian naira price of American goods falls, all other things being equal, there will be a greater demand for American goods. This means that Nigeria will require more dollars to purchase such goods; the quantity of dollars demanded by Nigeria increases. If more naira are offered to buy the extra dollars required, dollars will rise in value in terms of naira. On the other hand, if the dollar price of Nigerian goods falls, all other things being equal, America will want to buy more from Nigeria. America will, therefore, need more Nigerian naira. If Americans offer more dollars to buy the extra naira they want then the value of the naira in terms of dollars will rise; then the dollar falls. The supply and demand for the US dollar and for the Nigerian naira determine the exchange rate between the two countries' currencies.

The rate of exchange can be used to adjust balance-of-payments disequilibrium. For example, if the rate of exchange of country A is reduced; i.e. if the currency of A is devalued in relation to other currencies, it will being about a fall in imports of country A by making foreign goods dearer; and there will be a rise in the country's exports as goods produced in that country become cheaper. This approach can be adopted by a country whose balance-of-payments problems have been caused mainly by an adverse balance of trade. Similarly, a country with continuous surpluses in its balance of payments may revalue its exchange rate upwards in order to increase imports and check exports. This action is rarely adopted by any country, but West Germany has on occasion done this and Japan in 1971 revalued its currency upwards in order to help to correct the American balance of payments. It must be added that the policy of devaluation could be inadvisable, especially for a country which depends largely upon importation of food for its population, and on the importation of raw materials to supply its industries. Similarly, it is economically inadvisable for a developing country to adopt this policy if its major industrial materials are being imported in the process of rapid economic growth.

EXCHANGE CONTROL

An important aspect of the management of a national currency is the operation of exchange control. A country which has or anticipates balance-of-payments problems may adopt an exchange control policy. One purpose of control might be to reduce or eliminate fluctuations in the rate of exchange of a national currency. It has been explained in the last chapter that the Central Bank has the statutory power to operate foreign exchange control. By this power the Central Bank is given a monopoly over all foreign exchange transactions. All foreign exchange earned by exporters has to be sold to the Central Bank, and importers can only obtain exchange from the Central Bank to pay for imported goods. In addition to the direct control of foreign exchange transactions, the government can also impose other restrictions on exchange transactions. Import licences may be introduced in order to check the total volume of imports. In addition, or as an alternative policy, import quotas may be fixed by governments. Other measures include controls over transfers of money by emigrants and students studying abroad and limited allowances of foreign exchange for tourists.

Recent examples of foreign exchange controls in West Africa relate to Nigeria and Ghana. At the outbreak of the Nigerian civil war in 1967, the federal government imposed foreign exchange restrictions. Certain items of imports were totally banned, and import licences were introduced to cover a number of other items. In Ghana, the balance-of-payments problems forced the government to adopt strict exchange control at the end of 1971.

Although foreign exchange control may achieve the desired

effect of maintaining an equilibrium rate of exchange, at least in the short period, yet it is subject to some limitations. The operation of the policy calls for a high degree of administrative competence. An exchange control policy which fails to recognise the essential need of a developing nation may check the process of economic growth. An adequate volume of foreign exchange must be made available if the capital goods essential to development are to be imported. Exchange control unfortunately encourages black markets in foreign exchange. Similarly, restrictions on imports tend to encourage smuggling. Above all, a foreign exchange control policy should be operated in such a way as not to undermine the confidence of foreigners in the currency concerned.

TRADE RESTRICTIONS

If the principle of comparative costs advantage were allowed to operate freely, it would undoubtedly be in the long-term interests of all countries to concentrate on the products they were best fitted to produce. If free trade existed between different countries, under conditions of perfect competition and full employment of resources, as assumed by the comparative cost advantage theory, an automatic international price mechanism would facilitate international trade. The classical case for free trade is difficult to accommodate to the dynamics of the contemporary world economic systems. Indeed, the first scientific criticism of the free trade doctrines of David Ricardo was by Fredrick List, who said:

> We do not want, by exporting wheat in return for British manufactures, to make the most of our existing skill and equipment. Our standard of living is below that of the British; let us accumulate or borrow capital, educate our people, until our productivity and our standard of living is higher.

In practice, modern international trade is bedevilled by restrictions. Perfect competition is not allowed to determine international trade. National and international monopoly groups control many industries and products and an increasing proportion of world trade is being handled either by agents of the state or by international cartels and transnational corporations.

International trade restrictions arise because a country regards national frontiers as economic frontiers and regulates trade solely for its own national interest and with the object of attaining national security, or aims at being as self-sufficient and economically independent as possible.

A number of arguments have been put forward in favour of protection by a country of its own markets and industries from foreign competition. First, protection encourages a diversity of industries, which may possibly provide security of supplies in time of emergency or war. Secondly, it may contribute to the prosperity of the country by the creation of an assured home market for its products. Thirdly, it can possibly create employment if goods in substitution for imports can be produced at home. Fourthly, it allows 'infant' industries to grow until they are able to withstand competition. 'Infant' industries are those which may have relatively high costs when first established and whilst operating on a small scale but which, if protected for a time by import tariffs, are capable, with growth, of securing the economies of large scale. Protective duties can also be imposed to offset lower foreign costs of production, so as to ensure fair and better competitive conditions for home producers, but we should note that this is in effect reflecting the potential gains from international trade. Fifthly, the government may be able to increase its revenue through import duties. Sixthly, protection can prevent 'dumping' of foreign goods. If goods are 'dumped', that is, sold at a price below the cost of production in the exporting country, it could damage the economy of the receiving country. In some West African countries legislation exists against the 'dumping' of goods.

THE COMMON MARKET AND WEST AFRICA

Attempts have been made on many occasions in different parts of the world to liberalise international trade. In the British Commonwealth of Nations, imperial preferences were introduced in the early 1930s to give special trade concessions to members of the Commonwealth. Also, after the Second World War, the General Agreement on Tariffs and Trade (GATT) was concluded in 1948 between most nations of the world. Under this agreement, Britain undertook not to impose or increase customs duties on certain goods or to lower preferences granted to British goods by Commonwealth countries. These agreements applied to West Africa under colonial rule. However, on attaining political independence each country has since reviewed its position in relation to these agreements.

One significant trade association in recent years is the European Common Market which grew out of the Customs Union formed in 1947 by Belgium, the Netherlands and Luxembourg. The European Economic Community or European Common Market was formed in March 1957. The original members of the community were Belgium, the Netherlands, Luxembourg, France, Italy and West Germany. After operating for a few years, and in 1972, the membership was extended to include the United Kingdom, Ireland and Denmark, and the Belgian-Luxembourg Economic Union was recognised. Other Western European countries are negotiating to join the community in the future. The Treaty of Rome, which is the basis of the Community, provides, amongst other things, for the progressive reduction and ultimate abolition of customs duties between the member countries, and for the separate external tariffs of the member countries to be consolidated into a single tariff system for the entire community. The abolition of duties is spread over a period of between twelve and fifteen years, and a market of about 270 million people will eventually exchange goods free of any customs duties.

Apart from the enlarged market which is being created, a number of other economic factors were covered in the agreement establishing the Common Market. It was agreed that the Community should provide conditions which would make it possible for free mobility of factors of production, particularly of labour and capital, within the Community. In fact, the Community expects each country to surrender a large part of its national sovereignty in the economic field.

France, on joining the Common Market, brought the former French-speaking African countries, except Guinea, into the organisation as associate members. Nigeria also negotiated to join the Common Market but did not succeed in joining because France refused to ratify the agreements which needed the signature of all member countries. In fact, the whole affair was overtaken by the events of the Nigerian civil war, 1967–70.

In West Africa, political leaders and some economists have expressed a wish for the creation of a West African Common Market. It is generally agreed that such a market has some economic advantages. For example, it would eliminate the curious situation whereby a country like Benin imports beer and cement from Europe, instead of purchasing them from Nigeria which is its neighbouring country. With the establishment of a West African Common Market, resources, particularly manpower, could be more fully utilised.

It is important to note, however, that initially, there are some impediments in the way of creating a West African Common Market. In the first place, the colonial backgrounds of the West African countries differ significantly. The French-speaking countries had closer economic ties with France than the English-speaking countries had with Britain. Political and economic policies of the French-speaking countries were partly dependent on the reaction of France. It was difficult for these countries, therefore, to negotiate freely any long-term economic agreements with the English-speaking countries. Apart from the vestiges of colonial rule, each of the West African countries has been going through a period of political instability characterised by military coups. The internal political problems of these countries make it difficult at first for any of them to agree to a wider economic association which might have political implications. Unstable domestic politics militate against wider political and economic association. Another factor which has to be considered is the lack of complementarity in agricultural and industrial production among West African countries. The fact that these countries are mainly agricultural with almost identical products necessarily limits the advantages that can be derived from international exchange. As far as industrial production is concerned, Nigeria is the only country with a rapidly expanding industrial sector. With these in mind, and with the aspiration of the countries to industrialise, the negotiations to liberalise trade among the West African countries are a difficult affair.

However, on 27 May 1975, fifteen West African states formally established the Economic Community of West African States (ECOWAS). The fifteen countries are Mauritania, Senegal, the Gambia, Guinea-Bissau, Guinea, Sierra Leone, Liberia, Ivory Coast, Mali, Upper Volta, Ghana, Togo, Benin, Niger and Nigeria.

The treaty of ECOWAS covers a number of important international matters. The objectives are the elimination of customs and similar duties between the member states, abolition of other restrictions on trade among the states, the establishment of a common customs tariff and commercial policy towards other countries. On signing the agreement member countries agreed immediately to 'freeze' duties or taxes on trade between them for an initial period of two years after which negotiations for total elimination of trade restrictions would start. A transitional period of fifteen years was set within which to achieve total economic union. However, all duties on trade were to be completely eliminated eight years after the signing of the treaty.

The treaty contained an elaborate provision about the 'rules of origin' of goods which were to be subject to common tariff treatment by member states. For example, the goods had to be wholly produced by enterprises whose headquarters were located within the community and of whose equity at least 51 per cent was held locally and of whose directors at least half represented member states. It was also agreed that all duties designed to protect domestic goods would be abolished within ten years. Also, member states could continue to impose restrictions, in the interests of security, on the control of weapons, the protection of health and morality, the transfer of gold, silver or precious stones or the protection of national treasures.

The ECOWAS treaty established 'a fund for co-operation, compensation and development'. A formula was agreed upon for subscribing to the fund. The formula reflected the population and the volume of international transactions of each member state.

Other provisions of the treaty covered the free movement of labour and locally owned capital among member states, and the commitment to exchange industrial feasibility studies and information about industrial experience. It also provided for the exchange of reports on technical partners in their territories, as well as on research and minerals.

The community set up a tribunal to ensure 'the observance of law and justice' and to interpret the provisions of the treaty and settle disputes referred to it.

INTERNATIONAL FINANCIAL INSTITUTIONS

As we have already discussed in the last chapter, an individual or a business firm which needs financial help can approach the commercial banks for assistance. Similarly, international financial institutions exist to provide basically the same kind of service to the nations of the world. Undoubtedly, one of the major problems of most developing countries since the end of the Second World War has been that of inadequate capital for the finance of development projects. However, a number of international public and private financial institutions now provide financial help to many countries. Two of these institutions deserve mention.

The World Bank

The International Bank for Reconstruction and Development (IBRD), commonly referred to as the 'World Bank', was created in 1946 as a result of the Bretton Woods monetary and financial conference of July 1944. The main purpose of the Bank is 'to assist in the reconstruction and development of its member countries by facilitating the investment of capital for productive purposes, and thereby to promote the long-range growth of international trade and the improvement of standards of living'. In order to achieve this purpose, the Bank has power to grant loans out of its own resources. It is also empowered to promote private and public investment by guarantees of, and participation in, their loans and investments.

The Bank has three main sources of funds: the paid-in contributions of member countries; sales by the Bank of its own bonds; and sales by the Bank of securities it has obtained from borrowing countries in return for earlier loans wholly financed by itself. Subscriptions by members are assessed on the basis of their estimated economic strength, and only 20 per cent of such subscriptions is required to be paid up. Two per cent of this is payable in gold or dollars and 18 per cent is subject to call if and when required by the Bank to meet its obligations. The Bank's bonds are held by pension and trust funds, insurance companies, savings and commercial banks and other private institutional and individual investors as well as central banks and government agencies.

Two main conditions govern the Bank's lending policy. One concerns the security of the loan, the other the type of project for which aid is sought. The Bank can make loans only with the guarantee of the borrowing government. This guarantee is required whether the loan is made to the member government, to a government authority or agency or to a private enterprise. The Bank also satisfies itself that the country concerned is solvent and likely to be able to repay the loan. It will not lend to countries which are in default on their public foreign debts. The project for which the loan is required must be a specific one of reconstruction or development, and of sufficient importance to the borrowing country to warrant the incurring of a foreign exchange liability to finance it. Before making a loan, the Bank generally sends a mission composed of appropriate experts to confirm that the project concerned is sound and likely to fulfil expectations. The Bank reserves the right to supervise the spending of its loan. Borrowers are free to use the money to make purchases in any way they wish, provided that economy and efficiency are observed. Primarily, the Bank is to promote private investment rather than to compete with it. Usually, a loan will be refused if the Bank considers that such a loan could be obtained from private sources. The Bank is able to offer low interest rates on its loans, because it is under no obligation to pay interest on members' subscriptions and because of the virtually gilt-edged status accorded to its bonds. In addition to granting loans, the Bank gives advice to its members and their dependencies concerning the preparation and execution of economic development programmes.

The International Monetary Fund (IMF)

The International Monetary Fund, like the World Bank, was a product of the Bretton Woods conference. Its contribution to the finance of development is an indirect one, in that drawings on the Fund are made to supplement foreign exchange reserves rather than to finance any specific development project.

The IMF provides the machinery for consultation and collaboration between member countries on international monetary problems. It aims to provide exchange stability and to avoid competitive exchange depreciation, that is, devaluation, and also to assist in the elimination of foreign exchange restrictions which may hamper the growth of world trade. Member countries which are experiencing temporary balance-of-payments difficulties may draw on the Fund to supplement their foreign exchange holdings.

The IMF also obtains its financial resources from its members, partly in the form of gold and the remainder in their national currencies. Generally, member countries pay 25 per cent of their quota to the Fund in gold and the balance in their own currencies.

When first set up, each member of the Fund was required to establish in co-operation with the Fund the par value for its currency expressed in terms of gold or the US dollar. Any subsequent changes in par values could be made only after consultation with the Fund and they generally required its concurrence. But this system has collapsed and most countries now allow their exchange rate to float; that is to say, they allow the supply and demand for their currencies to determine their exchange rates from day to day, subject to the interference by each country's Central Bank when it is thought advisable.

As already mentioned, each member has a quota which represents the dollar equivalent of its subscription to the Fund in gold and in its own currency. A member is entitled to purchase, against its own currency, the currencies of other members to the value of 25 per cent of its own quota during any one year. Its aggregate purchases should not exceed 100 per cent of its quota. The Fund is known to have waived the 25 per cent limitations on a number of occasions. As a general rule, members are expected to re-purchase their own currency, i.e. to repay their earlier drawings, within three to five years. Such re-purchases have to be effected in gold or in convertible currencies. Members of the Fund are expected to make use of their drawing rights only to overcome temporary financial difficulties. Balance-of-payments deficits which can be attributed to fundamental disequilibrium in the economy are intended to be dealt with by other means such as stricter internal monetary policies or, if need be, devaluation.

In spite of all these facilities, international liquidity has been inadequate to meet the requirements of a growing volume of world trade. In consequence a new device to increase the quantity of international means of exchange became an urgent necessity. To meet this the IMF invented Special Drawing Rights which are allocated to member states and supplement the drawing rights of the original Bretton Woods agreement.

Like the World Bank, the IMF gives advice to member countries. It acts as a centre for the collection and exchange of information on monetary and financial problems and it prepares studies designed to assist members in formulating their monetary policies.

Chapter 9

Public Finance

INTRODUCTION

Public finance lies on the borderline between economics and politics. It is concerned with the income and expenditure of governments, federal, state, regional or local; with the adjustment of one to the other, and with the control of the national economy. It is not possible to discuss public finance outside the existence of an organised community. It follows, therefore, that political organisations' developments and changes affect the system of public finance that may be adopted in any country.

Before the advent of colonial rule in West Africa, the numerous indigenous administrations which existed levied taxes and collected revenues. Revenues were collected in kind, mainly in foodstuffs, and by performing services, for example, providing labour and serving as warriors. The structure and organisation of the indigenous tax systems varied. However, the indigenous fiscal systems were most advanced in kingdoms where the Islamic faith had been embraced. In most other states only a rudimentary indigenous tax system existed. Indeed, some greedy rulers occasionally enhanced their revenues by confiscating goods owned by their subjects. With the gradual assumption of political power by the British, the fiscal system in British colonial territories in West Africa began to change, but not without some problems.

The introduction of a modern tax system by the British led to a number of riots. The imposition of the hut tax on three of the five districts of the Protectorate of Sierra Leone in 1898 met with opposition and eventually led to the hut tax war. Also, in Nigeria there were tax riots in various parts of the country when an income tax system was introduced in the late 1920s and early 1930s. Similar conditions were experienced in Ghana in 1932.

It has been said that 'the first need of a modern government is a revenue, which is indeed the breath of its nostrils'. Public revenue comes mainly from taxation, direct and indirect, and many people view taxation with great disfavour. We shall, therefore, proceed to examine the basic principles of taxation and government expenditure.

SOURCES OF GOVERNMENT REVENUE

The day-to-day running of a modern government entails great expense. The government must be able to lay its hands on adequate funds for the efficient running of its ordinary business. The government, unlike a company, has no shareholders and thus no subscribed capital. It relies on the society for its revenue. A government may obtain revenue from a number of sources. It can obtain revenue through the ownership of property. For example, revenue can be derived from the sale of government land.

Secondly, revenue can be obtained from commercial and industrial undertakings established by the government, for instance, revenue is obtained from postal services, railways and electricity if these services are nationalised.

Thirdly, some government revenue comes from fees, fines and licences; in the course of administering justice, fines are imposed and these constitute income to the government; and certain business and social activities are often regulated by the payment of fees, such as licences for the sale of tobacco and liquor, and for keeping a dog.

Fourthly, the government can finance its business by obtaining loans, both domestic or internal loans and external or foreign loans. When a government borrows from its own citizens either by issuing bonds or by selling securities, or by borrowing from public institutions such as the marketing boards, we can regard these as internal or domestic loans. Whenever a government seeks financial assistance from outside the country and borrows from foreign governments, institutions and individuals, these are rightly referred to as external or foreign loans. Any loan raised by the government internally or externally forms part of the national debt.

Fifthly, governments may obtain money by printing more currency notes for circulation. This is not a normal way to raise government revenue. However, when a government resorts to this method, it has far-reaching consequences both inside the country concerned and outside it. Revenue raised in this way is likely to cause inflation and is a form of concealed taxation. Prices of ordinary consumption goods will rise, thus limiting the purchasing power of the citizen, particularly of those on fixed incomes. Such increased prices may reduce the level of savings and investments and, in the long run, production and consumption. Higher internal prices may increase the cost of production to firms, and this could have serious economic consequences for a country which relies heavily and almost exclusively on the export of industrial products. Foreign demand for the country's products may fall off and thus lead to or increase balance-of-payments difficulties.

Lastly, governments raise revenue by taxation which is by far the most important source. Taxation consists of levies or deductions made directly or indirectly by the government from individual and company incomes, property or estates, charges on the sale of goods and services, and import and export duties. Table 9.1. shows an example of a government revenue structure.

Table 9.1 *An Example of a Government Revenue Structure: Current Revenue of the Federal Government of Nigeria, 1975*

Type and Source	*₦ m.*	
Direct taxes		4,839·8
Company tax (including supertax)	476·9	
Personal income tax	3·3	
Petroleum profits tax	4,330·8	
Other tax revenues	28·8	
Indirect taxes		1,145·6
Import duties	964·2	
Export duties	4·2	
Excise duties	177·2	
Interest and repayments		266·1
Mining (royalties, rents, fees, etc.)		1,749·8
Miscellaneous		41·1
		8,042·4

Sources: Board of Customs and Excise returns and Federal. Republic of Nigeria *Official Gazettes.*

DEFINITION OF A TAX

A tax can be defined as a compulsory contribution imposed by the government without reference to the exact amount of service rendered to the taxpayer. It may be argued that this definition applies readily to an income tax and not to an indirect tax, for example, a tax on beer or cigarettes. However, it is obvious that anybody who wishes to purchase a product on which there is a tax must compulsorily pay such an indirect tax. It is also important to note that a tax is not a fine or penalty as a court fine is.

Three main conclusions can be drawn from this definition. First, a tax is a compulsory payment; every taxable citizen is expected to pay tax. Non-payment amounts to tax evasion, which is punishable under the law. Secondly, a tax is paid without reference to the benefit which the taxpayer derives from the government.

CLASSIFICATION OF TAXES

It is difficult to arrive at any satisfactory classification of taxes. Taxes may be classified in different ways for different purposes. We shall examine a few classifications of taxes.

One classification distinguishes personal taxes and real taxes. Personal taxes are levied on individuals, for instance, personal income tax; while real taxes are levied on the property owned by citizens.

Next, we have a classification which is determined by the system of government; federal taxes, state taxes and local taxes. In a federal system of government as exists in Nigeria, these three types of taxes are found. There are certain taxes which are exclusively in the domain of the federal government, for instance, customs duties and purchase taxes. State taxes include personal income tax within the state. Local taxes are levied by a local authority.

One widely used classification is as direct or indirect taxes. The basic idea underlying this distinction is that the impact and the incidence of a direct tax fall upon the person on whom it is legally imposed; while an indirect tax is legally imposed on a commodity or service and may be partly or wholly shifted from the person who first pays it to another person. The three main types of direct taxes are income tax, supertax and estate duties. Indirect taxes are usually placed upon commodities and are paid as part of the price of such commodities; for example, the tax on cigarettes. This is paid initially by the importer or manufacturer, and then passed on to the consumer in the price he pays. Generally, there are two kinds of indirect taxes; customs duties, chargeable upon goods imported from abroad, and excise duties, levied on goods produced at home, such as the excise duty on beer and cigarettes. When considering indirect taxes, it is important to distinguish between a specific tax and an *ad valorem* tax. A specific tax is based upon a physical measurement, such as a unit of weight or volume; for example a tax of 2 kobo on each kilogramme of tea sold or 1 naira on a litre of beer. An *ad valoren* tax is based upon a unit of value; for example, a tax of 20 per cent on the value of an imported commodity.

Another classification is threefold; taxes on income, taxes on capital and taxes on outlay. It keeps capital taxes separate from income tax, but one may note that capital taxes include some local rates on real property such as land, which, in practice, are closer to income taxes, and that since capital gives rights to receive income in the future, taxes on capital can be regarded as taxes on the income it generates.

PURPOSES OF TAXATION

The primary purpose of taxation is to raise revenue for financing the necessary functions of government. Traditionally, these functions include administration, defence and, in the case of monarchs or rulers, it includes the personal expenditure of the ruler. However, in a modern community, some other purposes of taxation have emerged. Taxation may be imposed for protective purposes. This applies mainly to indirect taxation. Customs duties may be imposed on foreign goods in order to protect home industry from foreign competition. Also, tariff arrangements may be concluded among countries to induce traders to purchase or sell in certain markets. Examples are; British Empire imperial preference, European Common Market trade agreements and the ECOWAS treaty. Indirect taxation is sometimes imposed for moral purposes. Taxes on alcoholic drinks, and on certain patent medicines, are often levied to restrict excessive consumption. Perhaps the most important aspect of taxation in recent years relates to the social purposes of taxation.

Inequalities of wealth and income exist in most modern societies. Such inequalities often create friction among the various classes of the community. It is often the practice, therefore, to tax the better-off classes in the community in order to provide for the less fortunate groups. In this connection, it is important to add that the very existence of an organised community often confers some economic benefits on certain individuals in that community. For example, the value of land appreciates as the community develops economically and with it the potential wealth of a landowner increases. Such capital gain, as it is called, may be taxed in order to compensate the community for contributing to the increase in wealth. Lastly, taxation may be employed as an anti-inflationary measure. Purchase taxes or an increase in income tax may be imposed in order to reduce the purchasing power of the community and thus prevent a rise in prices.

PRINCIPLES OF TAXATION

Adam Smith suggested four maxims of taxation, namely, equality, certainty, convenience and economy. First, he said that every citizen 'ought to contribute towards the support of the government, as nearly as possible in proportion to their respective abilities . . .'. Secondly, 'the tax which each individual is bound to pay ought to be certain, and not arbitrary. The time of payment, the manner of payment, the quantity to be paid ought all to be clear and plain to the contributor and to every other person.' Thirdly, 'there should be convenience of payment and collection'. Lastly, 'every tax ought to be contrived so as both to take out and keep out of the pockets of the people as little as possible, over and above what it brings into the public treasury of the state'; in other words, taxes should be the kind that can be collected with least cost. These basic maxims have some relevance to modern taxation as we shall see presently.

A tax system can be looked at from three viewpoints; the state, the individual and the national economy. An efficient tax system should be productive of revenue to the state and economical in its collection, be fair to every citizen and interfere as little as possible with the economic life of the country. In order to fulfil these requirements certain basic principles must be observed. From the government viewpoint, a tax should be amenable to accurate forecasting of revenue to be derived from it. The tax system should be elastic so as to accommodate possible changes in the financial needs of the government. As far as the national economy is concerned, a good tax system should ensure maximum productive incentive or minimum disincentive to all sectors of the economy.

Perhaps the most debated aspect of taxation is the effect of a tax system on the citizens. Generally, from the individual's standpoint, every tax is an evil, because it reduces the purchasing power in the hands of the citizens. However, one cannot condemn a tax system without considering the benefits which each citizen derives from government expenditure. As we have already mentioned, taxes should be levied at times and by methods as little disturbing as possible to the taxpayer. This explains why income tax which at one time was assessed and levied once a year is now, so far as possible, deducted before the income reaches the pockets of the income-receivers. It should be added that an indirect tax provides a convenient way of raising revenue from the bulk of the population; and apart from the period immediately after the imposition of such a tax, it is scarcely felt in the long run because the taxpayer is not conscious of paying it.

In examining the equitable distribution of the direct money burden of a tax, certain principles have been suggested. One view is that taxpayers should contribute equally. This means that each citizen, irrespective of variations in income, will contribute the same amount to government revenue. This basis offends against every principle of equity or fairness. Secondly, it has been suggested that a tax system should be based on the principle of service. In some cases this principle can be applied, for example, when paying for postal services, electricity and similar services where the consumer pays for what he gets. It is difficult, however, to estimate the cost of providing for the individual taxpayer police protection or the services of the judiciary. Thirdly, there is the proportional principle. Under this principle, taxation would be levied at a uniform percentage rate on all incomes. Proportional taxation of this kind does not demonstrate fairness because larger incomes can endure greater reductions by taxation than can smaller incomes, and no attention is paid to the size of the extended family and other social family commitments which constitute the responsibilities of the taxpayer. Taxation should take account of the fact that the law of diminishing marginal utility also applies to income. Under normal conditions, the greater the income the less significant is the additional unit of income. An extra naira is worth more to a man earning ₦500 per annum than it is worth to another man earning ₦5,000 per annum. However, this law can only be applied if we assume that individuals have the same utility for any unit of income. If this is so then the theory is in accord with the principle of minimum sacrifice. The proportional principle, therefore, will not secure fairness or equity.

Lastly, we have the principle of progressive taxation. By this principle, increased incomes pay not merely a greater amount but also a higher proportional or percentage rate. The amount of tax to be paid increases more than proportionately with income. However, it is important to point out that the progressive principle would be best adopted under a single tax system, i.e. where the only tax was based upon income. This is impracticable in a modern community. A multiple tax system from which revenue is raised partly by taxes on incomes and partly by taxes on commodities tends to distribute the burden of taxation more widely. However, a tax on staple foodstuffs results in a heavier real burden on the poor family or the large one than on the small or rich one.

Taxation of necessary items of consumption tends to be regressive in that a low-income earner pays a higher proportion of his income through such taxation than a high-income earner. Nowadays, the question of ability to pay is usually decided in favour of the imposition of progression in taxation. The income tax system in West Africa is now steeply progressive. This is achieved partly by granting some allowances to taxpayers. Such allowances are often dictated by social conditions. There is an allowance for a married man, and there are allowances also for children and dependent relatives. After these allowances have been deducted, the remainder of income is subject to progressive taxation.

As we have already noticed, the principles of taxation often conflict with each other. However, the best tax system must aim at a compromise between the principles. It must find the least objectionable as well as the most effective arrangement of taxes. It must also cause as little inconvenience and as few hardships as possible; and it must distribute the tax burden as fairly as possible between the different sectors of the economy.

INCIDENCE OF TAXATION

The incidence of taxation touches on the problem of who pays the tax. Strictly speaking, we may say that the incidence of a tax is upon the person who bears its direct money burden. One should distinguish between the direct and indirect burden of a tax, and also between the money burden and the real burden. The total direct money burden of a tax is the total revenue which the tax yields. However, the real burden of, say, 10 kobo paid in tax is tied up with the marginal significance of the 10 kobo to the taxpayer in terms of sacrificed satisfaction. The real burden is the economic welfare lost by paying a part of one's income in tax.

It is difficult to explain the difference in incidence of direct and indirect taxes. In order to determine who bears the money burden of a tax, one should know the person who actually pays the tax. As for the income tax, the incidence falls directly on the taxpayer. Under the pay-as-you-earn (PAYE) system, whereby taxes are deducted before the worker receives his salary, there is no problem in determining who bears the direct money burden of the tax. The extent to which a taxpayer can shift the incidence of an income tax is negligible. However, in exceptional circumstances, an income tax, say, on rent accruing to the landlord, may be shifted to the tenants in the form of higher rents.

The incidence of an indirect tax raises some problems. A tax imposed on a commodity may be intended by the government to be paid by the producers. Although producers may pay the tax in the first place yet it may be possible to pass on the burden to the consumers. The extent to which the producers can pass on the burden of an indirect tax on a commodity depends on the elasticity of demand for the commodity taxed. The more elastic the demand for a commodity, all other things being equal, the more will the incidence of a tax on the commodity fall upon the seller or producer. Similarly, the more elastic the supply of a commodity, all other things being equal, the more will the incidence of a tax on the commodity fall upon the buyer. It follows, therefore, that all other things being equal, the commodities most suitable for taxation to raise revenue will be those the demand for which is inelastic. On the supply side, there are cases of inelastic supply. For example, the supply of land in a populated area, say on Lagos Island, may be regarded as absolutely inelastic. In such a case, a tax on land will be paid by the owner, and it may not be possible to pass on the tax at all for a very long period. We may conclude by saying that the direct money burden of a tax imposed of any commodity, object or service is divided between the buyers and the sellers in the proportion of the elasticity of supply of the commodity taxed to the elasticity of demand for it. It is also important to add that the incidence of a tax imposed upon the buyers of a commodity may fall, not upon such buyers, but upon the buyers of some other commodities, the production of which depends on the former commodity.

SOME ECONOMIC EFFECTS OF TAXATION

Apart from the direct incidence of taxation which has been discussed above, there are some economic effects of taxation which should be mentioned. Taxation can affect production. Any tax which reduced the taxpayer's efficiency will affect his productive capacity. It is always difficult to determine at what level of income to draw the line below which taxation is likely to reduce efficiency.

Since production depends partly on investment, any taxation which reduces the level of savings tends to affect production adversely. By the very nature of taxation, all taxes, particularly on those who can afford to save, reduce the ability to save.

The effect of taxation on the desire to work depends partly on the individual's reaction to taxation. Generally, a taxpayer's reaction is governed by the elasticity of his demand for income. A man who needs a certain fixed amount of income to meet his personal and extended family obligations is likely to work harder to obtain that income in the face of increased taxation. It is also important that people are often reluctant to change the pattern of their expenditure; consequently an increase in taxation is met with the desire and willingness to work harder.

A tax system should not distort the optimum distribution of resources. In other words, taxes should not be imposed so as to dislodge factors of production from their most efficient uses. For example, where property tax is high, the establishment of new industries may be discouraged, and new businesses will be established in areas with lower tax.

Taxation has some effects on the redistribution of income. One tax system is preferable to another if it has a stronger tendency to check inequality of income. In this respect, a progressive tax system helps to reduce inequality, while a regressive tax system tends to increase the inequality of income. However, although a progressive tax system may be preferable on the grounds of its effect on income distribution, yet it may produce an adverse effect on an individual's marginal valuation of leisure as against work after a certain level of income. If by working harder, so giving up some leisure, the additional income earned attracts a higher rate of tax, the worker may prefer to keep his leisure rather than exchange it for additional income. If, for example, the tax is 60 k in the ₦1 on the first ₦6,000 a year of income and 70 k in the ₦1 on the next ₦1,000 per annum, the additional tax attracted by the additional ₦1,000 per annum is ₦700, that is 70 per cent although the average tax on ₦7,000 is only 61·5 per cent. The marginal rate of tax increases faster than the average rate, and it is the marginal rate which influences the actions of a taxpayer who cares to make such calculations.

GOVERNMENT EXPENDITURE

The basic functions of the government necessarily involve some expenditure. Traditionally, it is the function of the government to protect the country against external aggression. The government also maintains internal law and order. Over the years, however, the functions of government have increased. As a result, the pattern of government expenditure has changed from that of a colonial period to that of the modern period of political independence. Under colonial rule, the bulk of government expenditure went on the civil establishment, but political changes in West Africa, particularly since the end of the Second World War, have changed the pattern of government expenditure considerably. Table 9.2 shows an example of a government expenditure structure.

Table 9.2 *An Example of a Government Expenditure Structure: Expenditure of the Federal Government of Nigeria, 1977*

Type and Source	₦ m.	
Administration		1,040·4
General administration	275·9	
Defence and internal security	764·5	
Economic services		191·7
Agriculture	42·0	
Construction	73·0	
Transport and communications	27·1	
Other economic services	49·6	
Social and community services		368·5
Education	248·4	
Health	85·1	
Other social and community services	35·0	
Transfers		4,652·5
Public debt servicing:	191·6	
Internal	(155·3)	
External	(36·3)	
Statutory appropriations to states	1,572·5	
Non-statutory appropriations to states	424·4	
Pensions and gratuities	30·1	
To development fund	2,433·9	
TOTAL		6,253·1

Source: Federal Republic of Nigeria *Official Gazettes.*

In West Africa, government expenditure in modern times is normally upon the following:

1 *The cost of maintaining security.* Internal security is maintained by means of the judicial system, the police force, prison and other law enforcing agencies; and external security by means of the armed forces. The position of the armed forces has changed since 1966 following the advent of military government in many West African countries. The armed forces, and in the case of Nigeria the finance of the civil war between 1967 and 1970, have contributed to increased government expenditure.

2 *Government expenditure on day-to-day administration.* The cost

of administration includes expenses in maintaining ministers and other legislators, the civil service, the judiciary and diplomatic and consular services abroad.

3 *Government expenditure on social services.* Although West African governments have not embarked on any elaborate welfare schemes, yet expenditure on such items as education and health services has increased partly as a result of increases in population, and partly as a result of providing better conditions of life for the people.

4 *Government-maintained basic public works and services.* For example, the maintenance and management of the national currency, public roads, the postal system and electricity supply.

5 *Economic development.* This is discussed in the next chapter.

BUDGETING

A budget is an annual account showing how a government intends to adjust expenditure to income. The budget is usually presented at the beginning of the financial year of twelve months, which starts on 1 April, except for Ghana where it has started on 1 January since 1965. Every budget deals almost entirely with technical financial accountability. In recent years, it has been realised that the most important issue is not the strict accounting records presented in the budget, but the basic orientation to development problems which such accounts reflect. Whether a government budgets for ₦500 million or for only ₦20 million is immaterial, but any amount budgeted should reflect the true economic position of the government *vis-à-vis* economic needs and priorities and scarce resources.

The presentation of the budget, however, has proved to be a convenient occasion on which to embark on a wide-ranging review of the general economic conditions of the country concerned. It offers an opportunity for the government to justify its past policies and to persuade or convince the people of the appropriateness of measures that may be proposed for the future. It also affords the public an opportuntiy of appraising government policies. Under a civilian administration, it would be necessary to persuade the electorate that government social and economic policies on which public funds are to be expended are popularly acceptable. However, the nature of military administration does not impose such a responsibility on the rulers.

A budget has widespread ramifications throughout the economy. In West Africa, there is great reliance on the economic functions of the public sector and, as such, the size of the budget in relation to the rest of the economy has grown enormously in recent years. The result has been that the power of the budget to affect the rest of the economy has been greatly enhanced.

Briefly, the following are some of the ways by which a government can use the budget as an instrument of economic policy. First the budget can be used to stimulate or reduce the level of economic activity. Except during an emergency period, such as a time of war, the budget is expected to be balanced. Total expenditure is planned to equal total revenue; and there is no intentional surplus or deficit. However, if the government intends to reduce the level of economic activity usually as a measure to curb inflation, it will prepare a budget which will show a net surplus, that is, an excess of income (revenue) over expenditure. In this way the government reduces the purchasing power in the hands of the public. On the other hand, if the government wants to stimulate economic activity, it will present an unbalanced budget with a net deficit. It means that more purchasing power will pass into public hands than will be taken out by taxation.

Secondly, an important feature of a budget is the pattern of taxation that goes with it. The government, through the budget, can reduce the inequality of incomes by manipulating the tax system. Thirdly, the budget can be made to express the international political and economic policies of a government. The importation of goods from an unfriendly country may be prohibited or restricted. Similarly, customs duties on the import of particular items may be imposed in order to improve the balance of payments.

PUBLIC DEBTS

Apart from obtaining revenue from taxation, another source of government fund is by borrowing. A government usually borrows money to finance major development projects and/or to prosecute a war which normal revenue could not cover. Loans made to the government constitute the national or public debt. Since 1946, West African governments have been borrowing large sums in order to finance major economic and social development projects. The Nigerian government also borrowed a huge sum to finance the 1967–70 civil war.

Apart from the fact that government borrowing may be either internal or external, as already mentioned earlier in this chapter, some distinctions are also made between the purposes for which external debts are incurred. When a public debt is incurred in order to finance a major development project this constitutes capital formation, and is regarded as a reproductive debt. An external debt incurred in the development and extension of railway services or electricity will fall within this category. On the other hand, if public debt is incurred to finance a war, such as happened in the case of the Nigerian civil war, it is regarded as a deadweight debt, because it does not strictly contribute to capital formation and no assets are acquired in return for the expenditure. Public debt is also classified as floating or funded. The floating debt is short-term loans, particularly treasury bills and certificates; while funded debt is the long-term debt due to be repaid in not less than two years. Development bonds and war bonds are examples of funded debt.

Generally, the burden of the public debt falls on every citizen in the present and future generations. Since the public debt is never liquidated it is passed on to oncoming generations. We shall not concern ourselves with the ethics involved in one generation incurring a debt for future generations to pay. However, we shall discuss briefly the burden of internal borrowings owed by the government to its own citizens or financial institutions. Interest on such loans is paid out of normal revenue from taxation. Such payments, therefore, are said to be merely transfer payments, because they transfer money paid by the citizens who are taxpayers to the citizens, usually small in number and rich, who lend to the government. The long-run effect of an internal loan, therefore, may be to create greater inequality of income.

External borrowing is reflected in the balance-of-payments position of a country. Apart from paying interest on the loan, in the long run the borrowing country will also have to repay the principal amount. The payment of interest on an external loan and the refund of the loan itself are a liability which the nation has to meet but the burden is not usually felt if the loan has been utilised productively so as to increase the national income at a rate higher than the rate of interest plus repayment of the loan. However, if the external loan is used unproductively, for example, to prosecute a war, part of the national wealth which would have remained in the country will have to be sent abroad.

LOCAL TAXATION

In a democratic society local government by the local authority, known as a native authority during the colonial period, is an indispensable instrument of national or state government for the performance of certain basic economic and social services. Usually, a local authority provides and maintains local roads, market stalls, schools, maternity homes, dispensaries, post offices and town halls. In addition, a few rich local authorities engage in some commercial activities such as the provision of public transport.

A local authority needs money to enable it to perform these functions effectively. The revenue of a local authority comes mainly from the following sources.

1 Grants from the central or state government can be subdivided into general grants and specific grants. A general grant is provided without any directive from the central or state government as to how the money should be spent; while a specific grant is to be administered for a specific purpose or project.
2 Revenue is obtained from the profits of trading or commercial services undertaken by the local authority. In West Africa, these include revenue from the renting of market stalls, municipal transport services and water supply.
3 The administration of justice at the local level through the customary courts provides another source of revenue in the form of fines and court fees.
4 Revenue is received from licence and registration fees. The local authority obtains fees for granting licences to some people, such as goldsmiths and timber merchants, and for registration of births, deaths and marriages.
5 On occasion, local authorities levy special rates for specific development projects, such as for the building of a maternity home, post offices and water and electricity supplies.
6 The most regular and major source of revenue for the local authority is taxation. Local taxation is usually in the form of a flat rate payable by every able-bodied adult male.
7 In recent years, a tenement rate has been introduced as a source of revenue. The rate is levied on buildings according to the structure and location of such buildings. For example, a house built of concrete blocks and situated in the heart of a busy city, say, Lagos, Accra or Freetown, will carry a greater levy than a mud house in a rural area.

Some basic characteristics of a good local tax should be explained. First, the revenue from the local tax must not be subject to wide fluctuations; revenue must be stable through both good and bad times. The need for a stable revenue can be appreciated if one realises that local authorities have only limited power to make internal borrowings and no power at all to raise foreign loans. Secondly, a local tax can be levied only on property or incomes within the jurisdiction of the local authority. Only people and property within the area of jurisdiction can be successfully taxed. Thirdly, the base of the local tax should be as wide as possible so that many people are required to contribute to it. Fourthly, local taxes should if possible find bases of taxes which are not used by central or state tax structures.

The incidence of local taxation can be discussed, first in respect of a flat-rate tax and secondly in respect of property tax. A flat-rate tax levied on all male adults irrespective of their incomes is regressive. Indeed, the fact that every male adult must pay, whether employed or unemployed, except for those undergoing some form of formal training, makes such a tax inequitable. It also increases the inequality of income within the community. For those taxpayers who are unemployed, their relations have to pay for them in order to avoid legal action against those who have not paid. This adds to the regressiveness of the local tax.

Local taxes used to vary from district to district within a country, particularly during the colonial period. The result was that many people migrated to districts where local taxes were lower. Since all that was needed to avoid prosecution was a tax receipt, many other people paid taxes and obtained receipts in districts with lower taxes. In the end, areas of higher taxes invariably lost revenue.

Property tax is relatively new in West Africa and it is only adopted as a source of revenue in a few big cities. The property tax is usually a tax or rate on houses. It is legally imposed on the owner or the landlord, but it can be shifted on to the tenants. Where the tenant is a shopkeeper he, in turn, can shift it to the consumers. In a country where there is no enforceable rent control, the landlord can shift the incidence of a property tax completely to the tenants. However, if rent control is enforced, the incidence may be shared between the landlord and the tenant. It should be noted that the structure of property taxes should be such that the burdens are almost identical in all districts. This is expedient in order to avoid lower rates in rich districts and high rates in poor districts, as this could lead to an undesirable movement of factors of production.

Chapter 10

Economic Development and the State

COLONIAL DEVELOPMENT PLANS

The *laissez-faire* view to which the British colonial administration in West Africa was committed in the nineteenth century necessarily involved it in a restrictive view of its economic functions towards its overseas territories. The result was that it undertook very little by way of direct economic development. *Laissez-faire* is a French phrase meaning 'free to act' and is used to describe an economic system in which trade and industry are left to free enterprise without any regulation by the state. Apart from the traditional functions of government, which we have discussed in the last chapter, the colonial government did not contribute significantly to financing social and economic development projects before 1890. By the close of the nineteenth century, the only major development project with which the colonial governments were involved was the construction of the railway systems in the Gold Coast, Nigeria and Sierra Leone. The policy of 'constructive imperialism' adopted by the British at the close of the nineteenth century did not make any significant impact on economic development.

The first recorded deliberate attempt at planning for economic development in West Africa was made in Ghana. At the 1919 budget session of the then legislative council of the Gold Coast, a ten-year development programme for the period 1920–30 was put forward by one of the Gold Coast's (Ghana's) most imaginative and progressive colonial governors, His Excellency Brigadier-General Sir Frederick Gordon Guggisberg. The development programme was concentrated on the development of the transportation infrastructure. It included the development of a harbour, railways and roads. The governor saw in the improvement of transport – harbour, railways and roads, in that order – the key to all economic development. In fact, Guggisberg anticipated many other development projects that were undertaken years later, including the possibility of harnessing the Volta River which his government considered as long ago as 1924. The plan was only partly implemented because the Gold Coast government could not raise sufficient funds to execute all the projects and there was not an adequate supply of the skilled manpower necessary for the plan's fulfilment.

The British government policy towards economic development in the colonies was modified through time. In 1929, British financial assistance to the colonies, which used to be in the form of grants-in-aid, was extended by the Colonial Development Act, which established an annual fund for schemes of economic development. The main object of the Act was to help the colonies to be of more economic use to Britain. The 1929 Act was superseded in 1940 by the Colonial Development and Welfare Act. The funds provided under this Act were for any project likely to promote the economic development of any colony or the welfare of its people.

The West African countries needed to make progress in the provision of primary economic and social services, such as the transportation infrastructure, banking and financial facilities and better health conditions on which to lay the foundation of a strong economy. The Colonial Development and Welfare Act encouraged the colonies to plan their economic and social development with the technical and financial assistance of Britain to augment their own resources. The few plans that emerged in the colonies were based on certain broad lines of policy suggested by the British government. A few projects were undertaken including the development of roads, public health improvements, tse-tse fly and rinderpest investigations, irrigation, geological surveys and general research on the production of primary products. A few institutions such as the West African Cocoa Research Institute and the West African Institute of Oil Palm Research were financed partly from the fund.

In 1945, a new Colonial Development and Welfare Act was passed and it provided more funds for colonial development for the ten-year period 1946–56. The Act enabled long-term plans to be made by abolishing the earlier requirement to surrender unspent annual balances and provided that the money could be drawn on at any time within the ten years, subject to an upper limit fixed for a year.

With the Colonial Development and Welfare Act, more attention was paid to the development of the colonies, but none of the West African countries had any specific national economic and social development plan. In each country, the various departments of government implemented the few isolated development projects that were formulated. For example, the Public Works Department was responsible for the development of roads; the Marine Department for the harbours; and the Health Department for improvements in medical services. Deliberate economic planning for the entire economy did not exist.

DEVELOPMENT PLANNING

It was explained in Chapter 1 that there are two basic economic systems: a free enterprise economy and a controlled economy. In every country, whichever system is adopted, economic and social development involves some form of deliberate planning to speed up the process of economic growth. In a free enterprise economy such as that in West Africa, economic planning involves the introduction and implementation of policies within which all economic and other action takes place and which provide the needed impetus for economic growth. Economic planning cannot be achieved in a vacuum. It involves the various sectors of the economy acting together to motivate and accelerate the process of growth. It involves the careful allocation of resources and their optimum utilisation. The private sector must co-operate with the public sector, and vice versa.

The basic objective of planning is influenced by the political background of a nation. In West Africa, where for many years the British colonial administration was responsible for major economic decisions and activity, each country had to learn how to employ its resources for economic growth. The interests of the colonial power had to be replaced by national interests. It follows, therefore, that in West Africa economic planning does not only involve accelerating the rate of growth and the rate at which the standard of living can be raised; it also involves an increasing measure of 'indigenous' control over the country's economy.

At the initial stage of planning, the primary aim is to reach the 'take-off' stage. This can be achieved by diversifying the economy so that it can generate sufficient income and savings to finance a steady rate of economic growth, thus eliminating an unduly large dependence on external sources for capital and skilled manpower. It means also that it must be possible to have established at optimum efficiency the basic institutions, procedures, infrastructure and basic industries which will make such growth possible.

Apart from the inherent problems of underdevelopment, a general factor which must be taken into consideration is that a development plan is much more than a series of unrelated projects. For development projects to make sense at all under a global plan, they must be taken and considered together rather than in isolation. The project must constitute a programme. This distinction between a project and a programme is more than a formal one and lies at the root of development planning. In projecting a housing development, for example, provision must also be made for roads, water supplies, electricity, schools, shopping and recreation centres and other concomitant services, all of which must be integrated into the programme. It may be difficult to decide on priorities among this group of interrelated projects. One project involves a derived demand for other projects which are closely related to it. It is for this same reason that it may be difficult also to attempt to select single isolated areas of development effort on a long-term basis. Indeed, such an approach could lead to grave problems which could frustrate the very object of development planning. The best that can be done is to identify groups or areas of activity that must be tackled together as part of an interrelated programme.

THE NEED FOR PLANNING

The ultimate goal of planning is to achieve a high degree of economic independence and an adequate standard of living for the whole nation. For West Africa, this can only be achieved by eliminating some basic defects in the economies concerned. First, the economy of each country must be transformed from one dependent on primary production to one which is more diversified and industrialised. Diversification is also necessary by virtue of the fact that the introduction of efficient techniques into primary production – agriculture and mining – must inevitably lead to labour displacement and its redeployment.

Secondly, and connected with the foregoing, is the need to support this economic evolution with good transportation and communication, water supplies and power, education and skills, medical and health facilities, housing and social welfare facilities, and basic information and research.

Thirdly, West Africa's dependence on external capital imports necessitates not only more and varied domestic production for export in order to obtain adequate foreign exchange to purchase capital goods, including foreign skills, but also the conservation of foreign exchange by reducing imports through the substitution of domestic production where practicable.

Fourthly, there is the need to pursue measures designed to expand foreign trade with all countries. The restrictions placed on trade with particular countries during the colonial period, for example, the USSR, Eastern European countries and Japan, had to be lifted in order to derive maximum advantage from international economic transactions.

Fifthly, fiscal and monetary reforms have to be implemented to reflect the economic needs of the country, and finally, in order to carry the burden of administration which will be generated by the process of development, the civil service must be fortified by proper training and recruitment programmes and the administration of law and order must be strengthened.

PRE-INDEPENDENCE PLANNING

After the Second World War, the British government continued to finance a few social and economic development projects under the Colonial Development and Welfare Act. In the meantime, political awareness in West Africa had increased and a number of constitutional changes took place which brought increasing African participation in the affairs of government. Political leaders began to see economic development as a prerequisite to political independence. Although no national development plan ever emerged in any of the countries, yet a few development projects were undertaken. In Ghana, for example, a development plan was approved by the country's legislative council in 1951. The plan made provision for capital expenditure which covered the following items: economic and productive services, communications, social services, common services and general administration. These projects did not include the Volta River project. The introduction of the federal system of government into Nigeria in 1954 complicated the planning machinery. The federal government and each of the then regional governments formulated separate development plans for the period 1955–60.

One important feature of development planning after the Second World War was the establishment of development institutions which were responsible for executing projects. These institutions, where they were established, took over the function of development from the various government departments which had hitherto handled this function. In Nigeria the following institutions were established: the Federal Loans Board, regional production development boards (later known as development corporations), electricity corporations, the Ports Authority and the Coal Corporation. Similar institutions were established in Ghana and Sierra Leone. In addition the marketing boards continued to undertake some development projects.

POST-INDEPENDENCE PLANNING

Ghana was the first of the British West African countries to attain political independence, in February 1957, followed by Nigeria in October 1960, Sierra Leone in April 1961 and the Gambia in February 1965. Political independence brought with it many economic problems. Each country had to plan its economy so as to achieve a better standard of living for its people and to become an economically viable political unit. It was generally agreed among the African leaders that economic planning was necessary for rapid economic growth. It was thought that the great economic resources of these countries should be deliberately channelled into certain productive 'pipes' if economic growth and the general economic welfare of the people were to be increased within a reasonable length of time.

In Ghana, a seven-year development plan was introduced covering the period 1963/4 to 1969/70. The main object of the plan was to create a socialist society in Ghana, in which every individual would be able to enjoy a modern standard of living in his home supplemented by an advanced level of public services. The long-term projection towards a socialist state was to cover a period of twenty years. The plan admitted that during this period the economy of Ghana would be a mixed one – a mixture of capitalism with socialism.

In order to finance the public sector of the plan, the Ghana government expected to raise funds from surpluses of revenue over recurrent expenditure during the plan period, from external sources and from domestic loans.

With an annual population growth of about 2·6 per cent, a gross economic growth of 5·6 per cent was needed if Ghana was to achieve an overall real annual growth rate of 3 per cent per head. The seven-year development plan was to achieve this and to bring a significant degree of modernisation and offer direct new employment to some 200,000 people.

A number of development institutions were established to help the government in executing the plan. These included the Industrial Development Corporation and the Agricultural Development Corporation. The government also introduced legislation to encourage industrial development. Pioneer industries and companies were granted some concessions for operating in Ghana. Midway through the plan period, the country experienced the *coup d'état* of 1966 and the plan was abandoned.

In 1962 Sierra Leone introduced a ten-year plan of economic and social development. The plan was to cover the period 1962/3 to 1971/2 and was made to cover the basic economic infrastructure without which the plan could not succeed. An important feature of the plan was the attempt made for the first time in Sierra Leone to include private sector plans, and to extend it as far as possible over the entire economy. The private sector did not present adequate information on future projects but in spite of this, investment in the private sector for the plan period was high. The bulk of this was to be invested in an aluminium plant for processing bauxite from the Mokanji Hills mine. Other development projects under the plan included water supplies, the Guma Valley Dam, the Lungi Airport, an oil refinery, a plastic shoe factory, a palm-kernel processing factory and a diamond-cutting industry. The plan had been in operation for about five years when there was a military takeover in Sierra Leone. The political problems which the country has faced since 1967 have disrupted the execution of the plan.

When the Gambia attained political independence, it formulated a development policy. The main objectives of the policy were: to develop the agricultural sector and thereby strengthen the economy; to diversify the economy by encouraging the growth of new industries; to increase employment opportunities; to ensure fair distribution of income; and to stabilise the Gambian currency. The first of the post-independence development plans in the Gambia covered the period January 1964 to June 1967. The size of the country and its limited financial resources restricted the amount that could be committed to development projects. The main emphasis of the plan was on transportation infrastructure which took about a quarter of the total cost. The overall aim of the plan was to increase the annual economic growth rate from 2·5 per cent to 5 per cent.

Nigeria has had the most elaborate development plans in West Africa. The first national development plan covered the period 1962–8. The plan estimated that a 4 per cent annual average rate of growth of gross domestic product (GDP) should be maintained, while the population growth rate was estimated as between 2 and 2·5 per cent per annum. Within a month of launching the plan, Nigeria was plunged into a prolonged period of serious political and social disturbance which finally culminated in the civil war which began in July 1967 and lasted until January 1970. The overall performance of the Nigerian economy during the first national plan period, as reflected in changes in the GDP, was one of unsteady expansion. The growth rate of the GDP was 6·7 per cent in 1963–4, but fell to 3·8 per cent in 1964–5. There was a temporary revival in 1965–6 when it rose to 5·7 per cent, only to fall again to 4·2 per cent in 1966–7. The major economic projects successfully completed during the plan period included an oil refinery, the Niger Dam, the Nigerian smelting and minting plant, a paper mill and a sugar mill; and in the field of communications, the Niger bridge, port extensions and the construction of some major roads.

The second national development plan, 1970–4, for Nigeria was launched in November 1970. The plan had a set of objectives, namely, a united strong and self-reliant nation; a great and dynamic economy; a just and egalitarian society; a land of bright and full opportunities for all citizens; and a free and democratic society. The third national development plan, 1975–80, went further to elaborate on the basic objectives enumerated above. The third plan emphasised the following: an increase in per capita income; a reduction in the level of unemployment; an increase in the supply of high-level manpower; diversification of the economy; balanced development; and indigenisation of economic activity. The major items of expenditure in order of importance were the transportation infrastructure, education, agriculture, defence and security, industry, health, fuel and power, and communications.

FINANCING THE COST OF DEVELOPMENT

Each country normally strives to finance development from its annual revenue. However, experience has shown that in order to speed up the rate of economic growth a country would need more than its usual annual revenue. In fact, one of the important issues which has been continually debated is the availability of capital funds for economic development in the countries of the Third World. This depends largely on the level of savings, which in turn depends on both the general level of income and the propensity to consume. It follows, therefore, that in any developing country where the income per capita is low, with a relatively high propensity to consume, one can hardly expect any high level of savings. The low levels of private saving and investment in West Africa necessarily limit the economic contribution of indigenous private enterprise. There are also limits to what the government can do by way of direct investment through the activities of various government development corporations. Annual government revenue, which is liable to fluctuate because of its large dependence on customs duties, is so small as to limit the amount which can be devoted to investment.

The governments of West Africa have relied partly on foreign aid to finance their various development plans. The volume of aid, financial and technical, from Europe and America to West Africa has increased greatly since the end of the Second World War. Apart from intergovernmental loans, financial and technical aid came from a number of financial institutions such as the World Bank and the Colonial Development and Welfare Fund. As for intergovernmental loans, or loans and grants made by international agencies,

West African countries have come to realise that the international political strings attached infringe their political as well as their economic sovereignty. The result has been that these countries are becoming increasingly cautious of accepting foreign loans. In fact, in its second national development plan, Nigeria planned to raise about 80 per cent of the funds needed internally. This might be achieved in the case of Nigeria, but it is important to realise that the economic potential and prosperity of Nigeria cannot be compared with the other West African countries which have to rely more on foreign aid.

One ought to appreciate the main reason behind the very cautious, almost reluctant, attitude of the governments towards foreign aid. The bulk of the aid comes mainly from former colonial powers. The West African countries, which were ex-colonies, are afraid of falling under foreign economic domination, having just escaped from political domination. Whatever might be the economic benefits of foreign aid, the genuine fear of economic domination must be taken seriously. As far as possible, the lending countries would be well advised to demonstrate, through their policies, that none is intended. However, the West African countries must strike a balance between protecting themselves from unfair economic exploitation and obtaining adequate foreign assistance in order to achieve rapid economic growth. It is evident that in many cases government-financed projects alone cannot quickly bring the moment of economic 'take-off' and of self-sustaining growth. Foreign aid given and accepted with due regard to the feelings and aspirations of the governments and people concerned might achieve it within an acceptable time.

CONCLUSIONS

The success or failure of any plan, however brilliantly conceived, however expertly designed, depends largely on how it is finally put into operation. One of the major problems facing any development plan is the gulf between those who formulate the plan and those who will execute it. The execution of any plan needs a great deal of courage and determination on the part of the people and the government. In addition, the government must be able to retain the confidence of the entire people in its leadership. It is essential that political stability be maintained. Any development planning must necessarily touch on the lives of the ordinary people. The government must be able to educate the people on the social and economic changes which are inevitable in the process of development. The government should be conscious of the cost-benefit effects of its social, economic and political measures. The manner in which social and economic changes are brought about under state economic planning will determine the destiny of the West African countries.

Appendix: Questions and Essay Topics

CHAPTER 1

Multiple Choice Questions

1 Which of these would not be included among the fundamental principles of a free enterprise economy?
 (a) Private ownership of the factors of production.
 (b) The right to organise factors for productive purposes.
 (c) The right to make private profit.
 (d) The government's control of mobility of factors of production.
 (e) The government's financial assistance to small-scale businesses.

2 Which of these would determine, in a planned economy, how the factors of production are to be allocated among different productive activities?
 (a) Fairness.
 (b) The distribution of income and wealth.
 (c) Private needs determined by the market.
 (d) Public need, which is determined by the government.
 (e) The ability of a business to make a profit.

3 Which of these is not strictly included in the study of economics?
 (a) The study of wants.
 (b) The study of choice.
 (c) Whether there is plenty or scarcity.
 (d) Whether one commodity or service can be substituted for another.
 (e) Whether a particular want satisfies a good or bad purpose.

4 Which of these is the real cost of satisfying any want in the sense of the alternative that has to be forgone?
   (a) Variable cost.
   (b) Capital cost.
   (c) Prime cost.
   (d) Opportunity cost.
   (e) Total cost.

Essay Questions

1 How would you describe an African economic system?
2 What are the main differences between a planned economy and a free enterprise economy?
3 'Economic laws, unlike decrees and Acts of Parliament, can be infringed with inpunity.' Discuss.
4 How would you define 'economics'?

CHAPTER 2

Multiple Choice Questions

1 Which of these would not increase the population of a country?
   (a) An increase in the birth-rate.
   (b) A decrease in the death-rate.
   (c) Emigration.
   (d) Immigration.
   (e) Better medical facilities.

2 The working population of a country is:
   (a) the total population.
   (b) the number of male workers.
   (c) the number of workers in the public service.
   (d) able-bodied men and women above the age of 15.
   (e) all citizens contributing to the productive efforts of the nation.

3 The optimum population of a country is reached when:
   (a) all factors of production have been fully employed.
   (b) the productive effort per man is at its highest with a given volume of resources.
   (c) the total population increases.
   (d) the national resources increase.
   (e) the working population increases.

4 The marginal physical product of labour is:
   (a) the output which a firm could produce unaided by machinery.
   (b) the extra revenue which a firm will get by selling the output of one additional worker.

(c) the amount of extra output that is produced when one additional worker is employed and other factors of production are increased proportionately.
(d) the difference in the total outputs of two firms.
(e) the amount of extra output that is produced when one worker is added to a fixed amount of other factors.

Essay Questions

1 What are the factors of production? Which of them is most needed in West Africa today?
2 Is Ghana or Nigeria overpopulated?
3 What do you understand by the law of diminishing returns? How does it operate?

CHAPTER 3

Multiple Choice Questions

1 In Economics, production is complete when:
  (a) goods are produced in the factories.
  (b) goods are sold to the wholesalers.
  (c) goods and services are produced by the government.
  (d) prices are fixed for goods and services produced.
  (e) goods and services finally reach the consumers.

2 Small-scale production is most suitable when:
  (a) the product is standardised.
  (b) there are many joint-stock companies.
  (c) there are many consumers.
  (d) production caters for special tastes.
  (e) there is no government control of business.

3 Under normal conditions, economies of large-scale production are least likely to be found in:
  (a) co-operative organisations.
  (b) partnerships.
  (c) public corporations.
  (d) joint-stock companies.
  (e) international corporations.

Essay Questions

1 Can division of labour be extended indefinitely?
2 Explain the importance of joint-stock companies in modern economic society.
3 What are public corporations? Explain their increasing importance in modern West Africa.

4 How can economies of large scale be achieved?
5 Explain what factors influence the size of a business unit in any of the West African countries.
6 To what extent do you consider it desirable that any West African government should influence the geographical distribution of industry?

CHAPTER 4

Multiple Choice Questions

1 In Economics, a market is only said to exist when:
   (a) people meet in a certain place to buy and sell a particular commodity.
   (b) market women meet to discuss sales.
   (c) buyers and sellers are in touch with one another.
   (d) goods are offered for sale for money.
   (e) production is not centrally planned.

2 A rational consumer will adjust his spending pattern so that:
   (a) he buys only the one item that gives him the most total satisfaction.
   (b) the marginal utility he gets from the last unit of each item is the same.
   (c) the total utility he gets from each item is the same.
   (d) the marginal utility he gets from the last naira spent on each item is the same.
   (e) he buys the same number of each item.

3 In the context of supply and demand analysis what the economist means by the 'supply schedule' is:
   (a) the quantity of a good sold each year.
   (b) the quantity of a good that would be offered for sale at different prices during some time-period.
   (c) the quantity of a good that sellers have on hand at a particular time.
   (d) the quantity of a good that consumers have bought.
   (e) the total quantity of a good offered for sale.

4 If product X is complementary to product Y a rise in the price of X will probably:
   (a) increase the price of Y.
   (b) decrease demand for Y.
   (c) leave demand for Y unchanged.
   (d) increase demand for X.
   (e) none of the above.

5 The derived demand for a factor is more elastic:
   (a) the more inelastic the demand for the product using the factor.

(b) the smaller the technical possibilities of substituting another factor for this factor.
(c) the more inelastic the supply of jointly used factors.
(d) the larger the portion of the cost of this factor in the total cost of the product.
(e) the greater the tendency of the industry using the factor to hold the product price constant when faced with an increase in factor cost.

6 When the price of a good is held above equilibrium for some reason the result will be:
(a) a shortage of this good.
(b) a surplus of this good.
(c) an increase in demand.
(d) no change in the quantity demanded.
(e) no change in the quantity supplied.

7 The numerical measure of elasticity is:
(a) $\frac{\%\text{ change in } P}{\%\text{ change in } Q}$
(b) $\frac{\%\text{ change in } Q}{\%\text{ change in } P}$
(c) % change in P multiplied by % change in Q.
(d) $\frac{\text{change in } Q}{\text{change in } P}$
(e) % change in Q plus % change in P.

8 A producer will maximise his profit by employing any factor up to the output at which:
(a) its marginal cost is equal to the marginal cost of other factors.
(b) its marginal cost relative to the marginal cost of the other factors becomes a constant.
(c) its marginal cost is below its marginal revenue product.
(d) its marginal cost equals its marginal physical product.
(e) its marginal cost equals its marginal revenue product.

9 When economists refer to the working of the price mechanism, they mean:
(a) the system by which government controls prices in the economy.
(b) the fact that prices do not normally move up or down by themselves.
(c) the way in which the general level of prices rises.
(d) the fact that some goods tend to be scarce in relation to demand.
(e) the way in which resources are rationed amongst consumers.

10 A perfect competitor maximises his profit at the output at which:
(a) the marginal cost equals total revenue.
(b) the average cost equals total revenue.
(c) the marginal cost is zero.
(d) the marginal cost equals the average revenue.
(e) the average cost is zero.

11 A monopolist will produce the output at which:
(a) the average cost is equal to the marginal cost.
(b) the average revenue is equal to the marginal revenue.
(c) the marginal cost equals the marginal revenue.
(d) the average revenue is equal to the marginal cost.
(e) the average cost is equal to the marginal revenue.

Essay Questions

1 What is meant by the price mechanism and what functions does it perform?
2 'Overhead costs do not influence the price in the short period.' Examine the validity of this assertion.
3 What is meant by elasticity of demand?
4 How is price determined under perfect competition?
5 Explain how a monopolist will fix the price of his product.
6 What do you understand by 'market higgling'?

CHAPTER 5

Multiple Choice Questions

1 Which of the following is not a component of national income?
(a) Wages.
(b) Indirect taxes.
(c) Rent.
(d) Undistributed corporate profits.
(e) Interest.

2 The difference between net and gross national product is:
(a) net changes in stock.
(b) depreciation.
(c) indirect taxes.
(d) net property income from overseas.
(e) personal income.

3 For a given company, 'valued added' is:
(a) the total revenue from sales.
(b) the profit it makes on sales.
(c) the increase in value of its capital stock.
(d) the difference between its sales and the cost of its purchases of raw materials and other items from other firms.

(e) the increase in the value of its inventories.

4 Other things being equal, if a corporation increases its dividend payments to stock holders:
(a) national income goes up.
(b) net national product goes up.
(c) undistributed profits go up.
(d) the business debt of the corporation goes up.
(e) none of the above.

5 If a man were to stop going to a barber regularly and cut his own hair instead, all other things being equal:
(a) measured GNP would go down.
(b) measured GNP would not change.
(c) measured GNP would go up.
(d) real GNP would not change, but naira GNP would go down.
(e) none of the above.

Essay Questions

1 Per capita GNP estimates are frequently used to indicate changes in economic welfare over time. Are these estimates adequate for this purpose?
2 How would you measure the national income?
3 Examine the factors which tend to affect the size of a country's national income.

CHAPTER 6

Multiple Choice Questions

1 Profit is the reward for:
(a) fixing a high price.
(b) selling at a price higher than that of a competitor.
(c) taking business risks.
(d) producing at reasonable costs.
(e) buying raw materials at low prices.

2 Interest is paid on loanable funds because:
(a) some people have saved part of their incomes.
(b) some people are prepared to invest in business.
(c) some people prefer greater income in the future to consumption now.
(d) the demand for loanable funds is greater than the supply if no interest is paid.
(e) money has value.

3 Rent in the Ricardian sense is:
(a) the price paid for the purchase of land.

(b) the profit from the sale of land.
(c) the price for the hire of any factor.
(d) determined by price.
(e) none of the above.

4 A wage is normally determined by:
(a) the physical strain of the job.
(b) the number of trade union members.
(c) the number of available workers relative to demand.
(d) the amount a worker spends on smoking.
(e) none of the above.

5 The precautionary demand for money is:
(a) related to the interest rate in somewhat the same way as the speculative demand for money.
(b) related to income in somewhat the same way as the transactions demand for money.
(c) probably unrelated to either income or the interest rate.
(d) likely to increase as the interest rate increases.
(e) the same thing as the supply of money.

Essay Questions

1 Analyse the notion of 'profit'.
2 What is meant by 'economic rent'?
3 Explain the factors which tend to make rates of interest rise or fall.
4 Why is the wage of a farm labourer different from that of a doctor?

CHAPTER 7

Multiple Choice Questions

1 Which of the following is not a function of money?
(a) To serve as a unit of account.
(b) To bring about the double coincidence of wants.
(c) To assist exchange and specialisation.
(d) To act as a standard for deferred payments.
(e) To be used as a store of value.

2 Which of the following characteristics is it essential that money have and not merely desirable?
(a) Acceptability.
(b) Durability.
(c) Divisibility.
(d) Intrinsic value.
(e) Portability.

3 Which of the following items would *not* be listed as an asset of a normal commercial bank?
(a) Loans outstanding.
(b) Demand deposits.
(c) Cash on hand.
(d) Building and fixtures.
(e) Treasury bills.

4 When the public withdraws currency from the banking system, assuming that the banks are 'fully loaned up':
(a) new loans can be extended, because the withdrawals reduce deposits.
(b) loans will stay the same, because the withdrawals reduce both reserves and deposits by the same amount.
(c) loans must be reduced, because withdrawals will reduce bank reserves below the legal reserve requirement.
(d) nothing happens to loans, because currency withdrawals do not affect either deposits or reserves.
(e) none of the above.

5 Which is the most liquid of the following financial assets held by an individual?
(a) A credit balance on a savings account.
(b) Credit standing in a current account in a bank.
(c) A loan made to a brother for six weeks.
(d) An insurance policy.
(e) Unused current postage stamps.

Essay Questions

1 'The value of money depends upon its quantity.' Do you agree?
2 'Money can best be defined in terms of the functions which it is required to perform.' Discuss this statement.
3 What do you understand by the 'ordinary business' of a commercial bank?
4 What normally are considered to be the functions of a central bank?
5 Examine the functions of either (a) the African Development Bank or (b) the International Monetary Fund.
6 'Banks can only lend what is lent to them.' 'Banks lend by creating deposits.' Explain these statements.
7 What do you understand by the term 'inflation'?

CHAPTER 8

Multiple Choice Questions

1 The balance of trade is:
  (a) the difference between agricultural exports and industrial exports.
  (b) the total value of exports and imports.
  (c) the difference between the total volume of exports and imports.
  (d) the difference between the total value of exports and the total value of imports.
  (e) the total volume of exports and imports.

2 The terms of trade are:
  (a) the trade agreement between two countries.
  (b) the differences in the volumes of exports of two countries.
  (c) the proportion of the total value of exports to the value of total trade.
  (d) the value of a unit of exports in relation to the value of a unit of imports.
  (e) None of the above.

3 The balance of payments represents:
  (a) the payments of all capital goods imported into the country.
  (b) all the monetary transactions of one country with other countries.
  (c) the total amount a country receives from exports.
  (d) the balance between the volume of exports and the volume of imports.
  (e) payments for imported raw materials.

4 The foreign exchange rate is
  (a) the interest rate fixed by the central government.
  (b) the rate at which the Central Bank issues money.
  (c) the price of one national currency in terms of another.
  (d) the rate of interest on government bonds.
  (e) none of the above.

5 One main object of exchange control is to:
  (a) eliminate fluctuations in the rate of exchange of a national currency.
  (b) reduce the amount of money being hoarded.
  (c) increase the volume of loans and advances of the commercial banks.
  (d) help the government borrow money from its citizens.
  (e) enlarge the annual government budget.

Essay Questions

1 Outline the vent-for-surplus theory of international trade.
2 Explain the economic circumstances in which a policy of protection would be justified in international trade.
3 What is meant by a nation's 'balance of trade'? How does this differ from its 'balance of payments'?
4 What are the main economic reasons for the creation of the Economic Community of West African States?
5 What are the essential differences (if any) between domestic trade and international trade?

CHAPTER 9

Multiple Choice Questions

1 Public finance is concerned with:
(a) how public corporations borrow money.
(b) the income and expenditure of joint-stock companies.
(c) the income and expenditure of government and the adjustment of one to the other.
(d) how individuals spend money on public utilities.
(e) the open market operations of the Central Bank.

2 Which of these is not a source of government revenue?
(a) Fines, fees and licences.
(b) Loans.
(c) Taxation.
(d) Government property.
(e) A subsidy to farmers.

3 An *ad valorem* tax is:
(a) the total amount of an income tax.
(b) a tax of a certain percentage on the value of an imported commodity.
(c) a tax on an export item.
(d) a tax on land.
(e) a profits tax.

4 Which of these is not included in Adam Smith's maxims of taxation?
(a) Tax evasion.
(b) Ability to pay.
(c) Certainty of the amount of tax.
(d) Collection with least cost.
(e) Convenience of payment and collection.

5 The total direct money burden of a tax is:
(a) the total revenue which the tax yields.

(b) the cost of collecting the tax.
(c) the expenditure of a government on defence.
(d) the amount of grants to local authorities.
(e) the total amount of money paid as pensions.

6 A government budget is:
(a) the revenue from custom duties.
(b) annual financial returns from joint-stock companies.
(c) an annual account of government expenditure.
(d) an annual account showing how a government intends to adjust expenditure to revenue.
(e) none of the above.

7 Which of these is not a source of local government revenue?
(a) Customs and excise.
(b) Grants from the central or federal government.
(c) Licences.
(d) Tenement rate.
(e) Special levy for specific social and development projects.

8 A progressive tax system exists when taxpayers:
(a) contribute equally.
(b) contribute according to the services they each receive from the government.
(c) contribute in proportion to their incomes.
(d) contribute on the principle of equality of sacrifice.
(e) Pay As You Earn.

Essay Questions

1 Discuss the view that 'every tax is a necessary evil'.
2 What are the main objects of public expenditure in recent years in any one of the West African countries?
3 What do you understand by 'a progressive tax system'?
4 Consider the effects of different forms of taxation on the incentive to work and to save.
5 What is a public debt?

CHAPTER 10

Multiple Choice Questions

1 Using economic analysis to decide on government policy questions:
  (a) requires a clear statement of the objectives the policy is to achieve.
  (b) is helpful in choosing among alternative sources of action.
  (c) can identify the ways of achieving desired goals.
  (d) can assist in eliminating economic waste.
  (e) all of the above.

2 The main object of a national development plan in West Africa is to:
  (a) eliminate private profits.
  (b) increase government expenditure.
  (c) produce only those goods and services approved by the government.
  (d) increase the growth rate and the economic welfare of the nation.
  (e) increase the growth rate of the agricultural sector.

Essay Questions

1 Is there any justification for the increasing participation of the government in economic activities in West Africa?
2 What is a development plan? Is one really necessary for a West African country?

ANSWERS TO MULTIPLE CHOICE QUESTIONS

Chapter 1	1(d), 2(d), 3(e), 4(d).
Chapter 2	1(c), 2(e), 3(b), 4(e).
Chapter 3	1(e), 2(d), 3(b).
Chapter 4	1(c), 2(d), 3(b), 4(b), 5(d), 6(b), 7(b), 8(e), 9(e), 10(d), 11(c).
Chapter 5	1(b), 2(b), 3(d), 4(e), 5(d).
Chapter 6	1(c), 2(d), 3(d), 4(c), 5(b).
Chapter 7	1(b), 2(a), 3(b), 4(c), 5(b).
Chapter 8	1(d), 2(d), 3(b), 4(c), 5(a).
Chapter 9	1(c), 2(e), 3(b), 4(a), 5(a), 6(d), 7(a), 8(d).
Chapter 10	1(e), 2(d).

Index

For Product Safety Concerns and Information please contact our EU representative GPSR@taylorandfrancis.com Taylor & Francis Verlag GmbH, Kaufingerstraße 24, 80331 München, Germany